How to Do *Everything* with

Photoshop®

How to Do *Everything* with

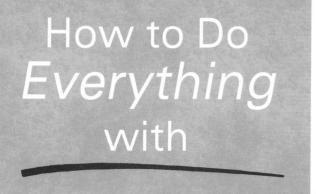

Photoshop® CS

Colin Smith

McGraw-Hill/Osborne

New York   Chicago   San Francisco   Lisbon
London   Madrid   Mexico City   Milan   New Delhi
San Juan   Seoul   Singapore   Sydney   Toronto

The McGraw·Hill Companies

McGraw-Hill/Osborne
2100 Powell Street, 10th Floor
Emeryville, California 94608
U.S.A.

To arrange bulk purchase discounts for sales promotions, premiums, or fund-raisers, please contact **McGraw-Hill**/Osborne at the above address. For information on translations or book distributors outside the U.S.A., please see the International Contact Information page immediately following the index of this book.

How to Do Everything with Photoshop®CS

1234567890 DOC DOC 019876543

ISBN 0-07-223143-2

Publisher	Brandon A. Nordin
Vice President &	
Associate Publisher	Scott Rogers
Executive Editor	Jane Brownlow
Acquisitions Editor	Katie Conley
Project Editor	Elizabeth Seymour
Acquisitions Coordinator	Athena Honore
Technical Editor	Al Ward
Copy Editor	Lisa Theobald
Proofreader	Susie Elkind
Indexer	Valerie Perry
Composition	Lucie Ericksen, Kelly Stanton-Scott, Tabitha M. Cagan
Illustrators	Kathleen Fay Edwards, Melinda Moore Lytle
Series Design	Lucie Ericksen
Cover Series Design	Dodie Shoemaker
Cover Illustration	Colin Smith

This book was composed with Corel VENTURA™ Publisher.

About the Author

Colin Smith is a Photoshop author and trainer, and an award-winning graphic designer who has caused a stir in the design community with his stunning photorealistic illustrations composed entirely in Photoshop. He is also founder of the popular web resource PhotoshopCAFE.com for Photoshop users and web designers. Colin has authored or co-authored more than seven books on Photoshop. He has also authored training videos at PhotoshopCD.com. When he is not running his design studio, he lectures at conferences and schools throughout the United States.

Colin writes weekly columns for Planet Photoshop and the NAPP member site. He has also been a contributing writer for *Photoshop User* and *MacDesign* magazines.

Contents at a Glance

Contents

Acknowledgments

A big thank you goes out to Katie Conley for contacting me and managing this project. In spite of looming product releases and deadlines, we did it! Thanks to Elizabeth Seymour and Lisa Theobold for taking care of all of the editing and making me look good. Thanks to the hard working people in production who have made this book look good. Thanks to my good friend and technical editor, Al Ward, for your help. Thanks to Malachi Maloney for your collaboration on the cover illustration. Also thanks to Pattie Lee for your vision and art direction on the cover. Thanks to Mauriahh for modeling for me once again. Thanks to Jens Karlsson, Bert Monroy, Oliver Ottner, and Phil Williams for contributing art to the gallery. You guys rock!

Thank you to the members at PhotshopCAFE and especially the moderators who have done such an awesome job of running things while I have been otherwise occupied writing this book. Frank (c-fire), Mike, Phil, Sue (Tech chick), Realist, Chris, Christian, DO2, and Al—you have made the Café the friendly place that it is.

To the entire crew at NAPP, especially Scott Kelby, Jeff Kelby, Chris Main, Felix Nelson, Dave Cross, and Stacy Behan: I love your spirit of sharing. You are all great to work with.

Thanks to the people that count the most, my family and friends. To my parents who brought me into the world and raised me to think for myself and be all that I could be. To my pastors, George and Hazel Hill, thank you for helping me to dream big and do it! To the special woman in my life, Susannah: thanks for your support and encouragement.

Finally and most important, thanks to God for the gifts he has given me and the opportunity to use them.

Introduction

I am so happy that you have picked up this book. You have made an excellent decision and I will tell you why.

Photoshop is the industry standard in image editing and the most powerful image-editing software available. Photoshop reminds me of a tiger disguised as a domestic pet. What I mean by this is that even though Photoshop is a complicated and rich program, it is a very accessible program—a complete beginner can jump into the software and produce something right away. The interface is so user friendly, that sometimes you don't realize just how powerful the software really is. You will find that as you grow and learn, you will not outgrow Photoshop; rather, you will discover new and better ways of doing things.

You will learn many ways to accomplish the same task. As you learn and grow, you can forge your own workflow and choose the methods that work best for you. This book is not written in such a way as to force you to embrace a particular workflow. It is written to teach you how the tools in Photoshop work and to show you how to perform the most common tasks that you will face in your career so that you become a "thinking" Photoshop user.

This book can either be read from cover to cover in a linear fashion or used as a reference. If you are brand new to Photoshop, I urge you to start at the beginning of the book and read all the way through to the end. The extra time invested now will bring many rewards in the future.

You do not need to have any previous experience with Photoshop or image editing to read this book; however I do assume that you are somewhat familiar with your computer. I will cover a lot of ground, but basic operating system knowledge is assumed and outside the scope of this book.

This book is broken into four parts with an inspirational gallery at the end.

Get to Know Photoshop CS   In this section, you will learn all the Photoshop basics, such as the tools and workspace. Like an orientation on your first day on the job, I cover the basic elements of the Photoshop program—tools, documents, colors, file types, and resolution.

Beyond the Basics   In this section, you will begin to perform tasks and use features such as layers, channels, paths, and text. You will also learn some efficient work methods that save time.

The Fun Stuff   In this section, you get to do the cool stuff and use selection, filters, and layer styles to produce eye candy and special effects.

The Real World   In this section, you'll use Photoshop for real-world applications, such as working with photographs, building web pages, and printing your work.

Behind the Scenes: A Gallery with Techniques from the Pros   This inspirational gallery features work by some of the biggest names in the graphic design industry. Not only will you see their art, you will learn how to accomplish some of the effects that they use.

I have interacted with over one and a half million visitors passing through our virtual doors of PhotoshopCAFE.com, the online Photoshop community I run. One thing I have learned is that not all Photoshop users are the same. In fact, there are few things that draw so many different types of people from different cultures, ethnic backgrounds, ages, and philosophies and unites them into one common purpose. There are so many types of people who use Photoshop, from hobbyists to professionals in the fields of graphic design, web design, photography, architecture, fine art, forensics, medicine, law, and other fields. I am not aware of any other graphics software that has such a diverse user base.

Whether you are brand new to Photoshop, or are already comfortable with the program and have picked up this book to brush up your skills and become familiar with the new features of Photoshop CS, this is the book for you.

Part I

Get to Know Photoshop CS

Chapter 1

Photoshop CS Primer

How to...

- Use palettes
- Use the toolbar
- Use the options bar
- Set rulers grids and guides
- Work with windows
- Navigate images
- Choose preset workspaces
- Create custom shortcuts
- Use the Preset Manager
- Set the preferences
- Understand common color modes
- Understand common file types
- Use the status bar
- Change views

At first glance, the interface in Photoshop CS can seem a bit intimidating, but all those complex-looking windows and palettes are soon going to become your friends. In this chapter, we will tame the interface tiger and quickly have you on your merry way. You see, there is method to the madness in all these palettes. Once you get the hang of one palette, you'll find it easy to conquer all the palettes, because Adobe has created an intuitive user interface that repeats functionality throughout the program. In other words, once you learn the basics, the rest will start to come naturally to you. The best way to approach learning a program with as many features as Photoshop is as the old saying goes: "How do you eat an elephant?" "One bite at a time." Don't look at everything you need to learn as one huge task; just take one task at a time, and before you know it, you will be soaring with the pros.

The Photoshop Workspace

When you launch Photoshop, you will see the Welcome Screen shown in Figure 1-1.

This screen will direct you to some valuable resources that will help you learn the program. You will find tutorials and techniques that will help you master Photoshop. If you don't want to see this screen every time you open the program, uncheck

Show This Dialog At Startup. You can access this screen from the Help menu at any time. When you are ready to proceed to the program, click the Close button.

When you are working in Photoshop, you will see a interface similar to Figure 1-2, depending on your platform.

Other than some differences in the onscreen user interface, and some keyboard shortcuts, the Windows and Mac versions of Photoshop features work in exactly the same way. This book will cover both versions and the keyboard commands will be provided for both. The

FIGURE 1-1 The Welcome Screen

FIGURE 1-2 The Photoshop Interface

A. In Windows

B. On the Mac

basic differences in shortcuts between the two platforms are
listed here.

PC Shortcut	Mac Shortcut
CTRL	CMD
ALT	OPTION
Right-click	CONTROL-click (If you don't have a two-button mouse)
BACKSPACE	DELETE

Palettes

A palette is a movable box that contains a variety of options
for a particular tool or for accomplishing a task. Photoshop is a
palette-driven program—almost everything you do will involve
palettes in one way or another. You can organize palettes in a
few different ways. If you need to be able to access more screen
space, you can, of course, close all the palettes and use the
menus to access and choose information as needed, but there
are better ways to get back some of your screen real estate.

A great way to maximize space is to use a two-monitor setup. This setup allows you to extend your workspace to a second monitor. You can drag all your palettes onto the second monitor, freeing up space on the main monitor for your image.

FIGURE 1-3 A group of palettes

When you first open Photoshop, you will find that related tools are grouped together in Palette groups similar to the one shown in Figure 1-3. To activate a palette, click its title tab.

Organizing Palettes

You can easily isolate a palette from the group by clicking and dragging its tab. You can then drop it onto the workspace by releasing the mouse button. The palette will appear exactly where you drop it.

Docking Palettes

You can *dock* columns of palettes together and build a "super palette." When you dock multiple palettes and move the top palette, all the palettes will move with it. Here's how it works:

A.

B.

1. Click and drag the palette's title tab.

2. Drag it over the bottom of another palette group.

3. You will see a double line appear in the bottom of the palette, as shown at the left in Figure 1-4A.

4. Release the mouse button and the palette will be docked, as shown at the right in Figure 1-4B.

Adding a Palette to a Group

You can also add a palette to a group by clicking and dragging its title bar into a current group, as shown in Figure 1-5.

FIGURE 1-4 Docking the palettes: (A) Drag the palette to the bottom of another palette (B) The new palette becomes docked to the group

A.

B.

Expanding and Contracting Palettes

You can also change the size of your palettes. Figure 1-6A-D shows four ways that you can expand and contract palettes. From left to right:

- Expand a palette by dragging the bottom corner.
- Click the minimize button to shrink the palette the minimum size that is needed to show all of its content.
- Click the minimize button again; only the options will be visible.
- Click the button once again and the palette will be reduced to just the title bar. This is as small as it gets.

FIGURE 1-5 Adding a palette to the group. (A) Drag the palette (B) It is added to the group

FIGURE 1-6 Minimizing the palette (A) Expands a palette (B) Shrinks to content (C) Shrink to options (D) Shrinks to title bar

A.

B.

C.

D.

The palette will keep cycling through these views as you click the minimize button.

The Palette Well

You can use the palette well to organize your palettes and free up screen space. You can drop palettes into the palette well, which is located in the top right of the options bar, as shown in Figure 1-7.

 The palette well is available only if you are using a screen resolution larger than 800×600.

Here's how you add a palette to the well:

1. Drag any palette tab to the well, as shown in Figure 1-7A.

2. Release the mouse and it will be added to the well, freeing up precious screen space, as shown in Figure 1-7B.

3. Click the tab in the well, and all the palette will open in the well, as shown in Figure 1-7C.

4. You can also add any palette to the well by clicking the little arrow at the upper-right corner of any palette and choosing Dock To Palette Well, as shown in Figure 1-7D.

FIGURE 1-7 The palette well
(A) Drag a palette to the well
(B) The palette in the well
(C) Use a palette in the well
(D) Choose the Dock To Palette Well option

Flyout Menu

The little arrow at the upper-right corner of all palettes is the Options flyout menu, which provides a quick way to access the most common tasks you will perform with the palette. Figure 1-8 shows the Options menu for the Layers palette. Particular options available for each palette are discussed throughout this book when each palette is discussed.

FIGURE 1-8 Options menu for the Layers palette

Resetting Palettes

You can reset the palettes to their default positions by choosing Window | Workspace | Reset Palette Locations, as shown in Figure 1-9.

The Toolbar

The toolbar, or tool palette, is the vertical bar from which you select all the tools you need to work with in Photoshop. To choose a tool, just click its icon on the toolbar. As shown in Figure 1-10, tools are grouped into four categories:

FIGURE 1-9 Resetting the palette locations

- **Selection** Use these tools to select objects.
- **Creative** Use these tools to draw objects and retouch photos.
- **Vector** Use these tools to work with vectors.
- **Navigation and Information** Use these tools to view the page and gather information.

Some of the icons in the toolbar show tiny triangles at their lower-right corners. If you click and hold your mouse on an icon with a triangle, a flyout

Visit Adobe.com

Marquee — Move tool

Lasso — Magic wand

Crop — Slice tool

Color replacement — Brush

Clone stamp — History brush

Eraser — Gradient

Blur — Sponge

Path tool — Type

Pen tool — Shape

Notes — Eyedropper

Hand tool — Zoom tool

Color swatches

Quick mask

Status bar toggle

Jump to ImageReady

FIGURE 1-10 The toolbar

menu will appear with additional tools. These tools are usually variations of the selected tool. Figure 1-11 shows you a complete list of all the tools in the toolbar. The single letter to the right of each tool in the group is the keyboard shortcut. Just press the corresponding key on your keyboard to access the tool.

Tools and Information

This section gives you a brief rundown of each tool and tells you where to look for more information regarding use of these tools. Most of the tools are covered in depth throughout the book.

Selection Tools

■ **Marquee tools**   Used to make selections. See Chapter 10 for information.

■ **Move**   The default tool used to drag objects on the page. See Chapter 10.

■ **Lasso**   Used to make irregular shaped selections. See Chapter 10.

■ **Magic Wand**   Used to create a selection based on color. See Chapter 10.

Creative Use Tools

■ **Crop**   Crop an image to a chosen size. See Chapter 12.

■ **Slice**   Cut an image into smaller pieces for use on the World Wide Web. See Chapter 13.

■ **Repair tools**   Make repairs and enhance photographs. See Chapter 12.

■ **Brushes**   Paint with color and to perform special effects in conjunction with other tools. See Chapter 3.

FIGURE 1-11 All the available tools in the toolbar

■ **Rubber Stamp** Sample a portion of the image and then "paint" with the sampled portion of the image. See Chapter 12.

■ **History and Art Brush** Paint and make enhancements with a previous version of the working image. See Chapter 3.

■ **Eraser** Delete portions of the image in the same way a traditional eraser works. See Chapter 3.

■ **Fill tools** Fill image areas with color and gradients. See Chapter 3.

■ **Blur and Sharpen** Blur and sharpen precise portions of an image. Good for fixing photos and also for special effects. See Chapter 12.

■ **Dodge and Burn** Lighten and darken select portions of an image. See Chapter 12.

Vector Tools

- **Path Selection**   Manipulate and adjust paths. See Chapter 7.

- **Type**   Used to create text. See Chapter 8.

- **Pen**   Create paths. See Chapter 7.

- **Shape**   Create paths or predetermined shapes. See Chapters 3 and 7.

Navigation and Information Tools

- **Notes**   Attach notes or audio messages to an image in the same way you would use "sticky notes." Useful for adding instructions for another designer, or to remind yourself of some settings or techniques used. Notes will not print, but they will travel with the document. See Chapter 1.

- **Eyedropper**   Sample colors and other information from images. See Chapter 12.

- **Hand**   Drag the canvas around in a window. You will use this tool when you have zoomed in on an image and need to navigate. See Chapter 1.

- **Zoom**   Change the magnification of the working document. You can zoom in or out with this tool. See Chapter 1.

Other Tools

- **Color Swatches**   Choose your foreground and background colors from here. See Chapter 3.

- **Quick Mask**   Make a selection with a brush and apply filters to the selection. See Chapter 10.

- **View**   Toggle the status bars on and off. See Chapter 1.

- **Jump to ImageReady**   Launch ImageReady, a web design program that ships free with Photoshop. See Chapter 13.

Options Bar

The options bar is a *context-sensitive* menu—whenever you select a tool, the options in the bar will change to the particular options available for that selected tool. Choose another tool and the options will change. This saves a lot of clutter and allows you to see only the options that you need. Whenever you select a tool, take a glance at the options bar and see what options are available. Figure 1-12 shows the options bar at the top of the screen with the Move tool selected. Notice that more options are available on the options bar, including alignment options, which are covered in Chapter 4.

FIGURE 1-12 The options bar

You can move the options bar to another location on the screen; if you click and drag on the dotted line on the far left of the bar, you can choose to have it floating like the other palettes, or drag it near the bottom and it will snap to the bottom of the screen. The default location at the top should work best for most users, however.

Rulers, Guides, and Grids

When it comes to laying out objects on a page, "eye-balling it" can sometimes be your best bet; however, to be really accurate, you need to use guides. Photoshop comes with rulers, guides, and grids to help make your layouts nice and even. A basic design principle, *alignment* means everything on the page relates to other objects in some way—this gives a sense of balance and order to a page.

Rulers

To help you take measure of a layout, you can choose to show the rulers. The rulers will be visible along the left and top edges of the image. The zero point for both rulers is at the top left corner of the image.

To show the rulers, press CTRL-R (CMD-R on the Mac) or choose View | Rulers. Figure 1-13 shows an image with the rulers.

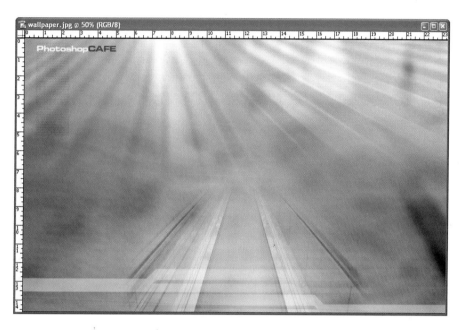

FIGURE 1-13 Showing the rulers

You can easily switch among units of measures in your rulers: pixels, inches, centimeters, millimeters, points, picas, and even percentage. To change the unit of measure, do one of the following:

■ Position your mouse over the units on one of the rulers. Right-click (CONTROL-click on the Mac) and choose a new unit of measure from the drop-down list.

■ Double-click the ruler and change the unit in the Preferences window that opens.

Guides

You can also use guides to measure and layout pages. A guide is a nonprinting line that can be positioned on the page to assist you in aligning objects. To add a guide:

1. Show the rulers.

2. Position your mouse over one of the rulers.

3. Click and drag. You will notice that you are dragging a dotted line.

4. Release the mouse to drop the guide on the page. Figure 1-14 shows three guides in place and one guide's placement in process.

FIGURE 1-14 Adding guides

 Guide Guidelines

Here are a few tips to keep in mind when using guides:

- To add a horizontal guide, drag down from the top ruler.
- To add a vertical guide, drag right from the left ruler.
- To reposition a guide, click it with the Move tool and drag it to another position.
- To remove a guide, drag it off the workspace.
- To hide and show a guide, choose View | Show Guides.
- To lock the guides so that they cannot be moved, choose View | Lock Guides.
- To delete all guides in a document, choose View | Clear Guides.

Snap-To Guides
A useful feature to help you lay things out with guides is the Snap To option. To turn it on, choose View | Snap To | Guides.

When the Snap To option is turned on, the guide will act like a magnet that attract objects as you move them to within a few pixels of the guide. This option is handy if perfect alignment is important to your layout.

Grids

When grids are turned on, they provide a visual system that helps you measure, align, and generally keep things in proportion. To turn on grids, as shown in Figure 1-15, choose View | Show | Grids. The grid size can be changed from the Preferences menu—choose Preferences | Guides, Grids And Slices, and enter new settings in the Grids section.

FIGURE 1-15 Grids visible

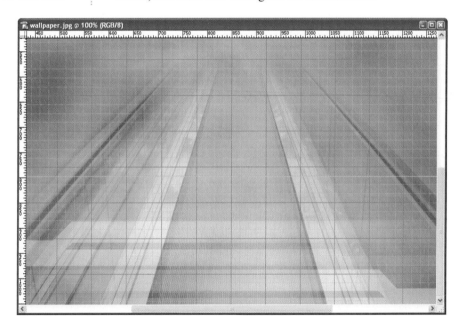

Working with Windows

Whenever you open a new image in Photoshop, it will appear in a window. While working, you can zoom in or out, navigate around the window, and arrange your windows on your screen to make it easier to work.

In Windows, you can maximize your workspace window so that it fills up the entire screen. To do this, click the maximize button. This button is similar to the maximize button that appears in most Windows applications. When you maximize the window, some gray area might appear around the image in your Photoshop workspace window, as shown in Figure 1-16. This gray area is part of your workspace, but it does not contain any images. You can, however, see bounding boxes in this area when you are scaling and transforming images.

FIGURE 1-16 Maximized window

Zooming

To zoom in and out of windows, you use the Zoom tool, which looks like a magnifying glass. After you choose the Zoom tool, you can do the following:

- To zoom in, click anywhere within an image window.
- To zoom out, hold down the ALT key (OPTION on the Mac) and click.
- To show 100 percent size, double-click the Zoom tool.

You can also select a portion of the image to zoom into by clicking and dragging the Zoom tool in a rectangle. The image will zoom into the selected area, as shown in Figure 1-17.

 To change the Zoom tool to zoom out, hold down the OPTION *key as you click.*

A.

B.

FIGURE 1-17 Zooming in to a selected area
(A) The selection is made
(B) The image is zoomed

When you choose the Zoom tool, you will notice that the following options appear in the options bar:

- **Actual Pixels**   Display images at 100 percent.
- **Fit On Screen**   Make the image as large as possible to fit on the screen.
- **Print Size**   Show an approximate size of the image if it were to be printed at the current resolution.

 To display an image at full-screen size, press CTRL-0 *(CMD-0 on the Mac).*

Navigating

Once you have zoomed in on an image, you will notice that scrollbars appear in the window. This means that all the image information cannot be displayed inside the current window size. You can move around the window in a few ways:

- Choose the Hand tool from the tool palette. Click and drag the image around the window.

- Click and drag the scroll bars to reveal other parts of the image.

- Hold down the SPACEBAR. The current tool will temporarily turn into the Hand tool. Use the Hand tool to move the image around onscreen.

Navigator Palette

The Navigator palette allows you to zoom in and out and move your zoomed selections in an image. When you zoom in to an image at a very high magnification, it can be easy to get a bit lost at times and not know where you are in the image as a whole—it's like being lost in a giant maze. The solution would be to have a bird's eye view. That's exactly what the Navigator palette, shown in Figure 1-18, does.

The little red box in the palette shows where the current window area is located on the image. To move to another part of the image, click and drag the red box and the window will follow.

You can also zoom in and out using the Navigator palette. You will see the slider that shows a small mountain on the left and a large one on the right. Drag this slider to change the magnification. The amount of magnification will appear in the Percent field.

FIGURE 1-18 The Navigator palette

The Current Magnification

Zoom In/Out

Location on the image

Arranging Windows

You are not limited to opening just a single image in Photoshop. Sometimes you'll want to have multiple image windows open at the same time—for example, you could be combining images by dragging and dropping, or comparing images to each other side by side. Or perhaps you are working on multiple projects at the same time. Whatever the reason, a few tools can help keep you from being overwhelmed by all these windows.

Cascade

Most of the commands to help you organize windows will be found by choosing Window | Arrange. If you choose Window | Arrange | Cascade, all the open windows will be stacked on top of each other at the current magnification, as shown in Figure 1-19.

FIGURE 1-19 Cascaded windows

FIGURE 1-20 Tiled windows

FIGURE 1-21 Match zoom

Tile

If you choose Window | Arrange | Tile, all the open windows will be tiled on the workspace, as shown in Figure 1-20. This is a good option if you want to see all the open images at once.

Match Zoom

If you choose Window | Arrange | Match Zoom, the magnification of all the open windows will be changed to match the currently selected window. This is a quick way to view all the images at any chosen size. Figure 1-21 shows all the images at 100 percent size.

Different Zooms

When you are retouching images, it's a good practice to zoom in to the image so that you can work with precision. The only drawback with this is that you can spend a lot of time zooming out again to see how your retouching is affecting the rest of the image. There is a solution to this dilemma. Photoshop will allow you to open multiple windows of the same image and set these for different magnification. Because the windows all show the same image, you will see a real-time preview as you work. It's common, for example, to open a copy at 100 percent and use it as a reference, while working on an image zoomed up to a maximum of 1600 percent. Figure 1-22 shows working on a zoomed copy of a window.

To open a new working window, choose Window | Arrange | New Window For (the name of your document will appear here).

To snap the new windows to the current working area, as shown in Figure 1-23, choose Window | Arrange | Match Location.

FIGURE 1-22 Working with multiple windows

Preset Workspaces

Now that you have gone to all this trouble to customize your palette locations and set up your workspace exactly how you like it, wouldn't it be great to be able to save your workspace and recall it at any time? You can, with the Workspace commands.

To save your settings:

1. Choose Window | Workspace | Save Workspace.

2. A pop-up naming field will open. Type in a name for your workspace.

3. Click OK.

FIGURE 1-23 Match Location

Whenever you want to recall the settings, choose Window | Workspace and choose from a list of named workspaces. This is really helpful if you are using Photoshop for various tasks; you can set up a custom workspace for each task with only the necessary palettes open for each one. Switching between setups is fast.

To remove any of the saved workspaces for the list, choose Window | Workspace | Delete Workspace.

To go back to the original factory settings, choose Window | Workspace | Reset Palette Locations.

Custom Shortcuts

Keyboard shortcuts are handy when you're working in Photoshop. You can save time by pressing a keyboard combination instead of working from menus and palettes. Another great thing about shortcuts is that don't have to wait for the screen to redraw before pressing the next shortcut key. You can press a combination of shortcuts and Photoshop will zip through the tasks.

Photoshop CS is the first version of Photoshop that allows you to choose your own keyboard shortcuts for just about any task you can imagine.

Creating a New Shortcut

You can assign custom shortcuts using the Keyboard Shortcuts dialog box shown in Figure 1-24. To open the Keyboard Shortcuts dialog box, choose Edit | Keyboard Shortcuts.

 Even this dialog box has a keyboard shortcut! Press CTRL-ALT-SHIFT-K (CMD-OPTION-SHIFT-K *on the Mac).*

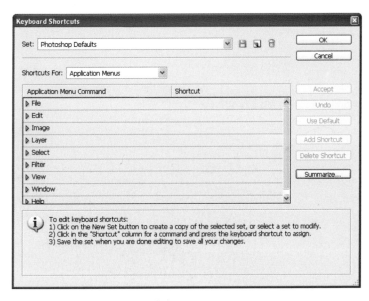

FIGURE 1-24 Keyboard Shortcuts dialog box

If you find yourself performing a particular task a lot in Photoshop, first check the list of shortcuts to see whether a current shortcut is already assigned to the task. If not, you can create your own shortcut using this method:

1. Open the Keyboard Shortcuts dialog box.

2. Choose the category of shortcut from the Shortcuts For drop-down list.

3. Drill down the list of commands until you find the one you want.

4. Open the chosen group, as shown in Figure 1-25.

FIGURE 1-25 Finding the command

5. Choose the command you are looking for by clicking it.

6. Click the Shortcut field, as shown in Figure 1-26.

FIGURE 1-26 New Shortcut field

7. Type in the shortcut on your keyboard. You must include the CTRL key (CMD on the Mac) in the combination.

◼ If the shortcut is already in use, a warning will appear, as shown in Figure 1-27A. You can try using different keys (recommended) or overwrite the existing shortcut.

■ If the shortcut is not yet in use, it will display
without a warning, as shown in Figure 1-27B.

FIGURE 1-27 Choosing shortcuts
(A) An error reports a conflict
(B) The shortcut is assigned

A.

B.

8. Click Accept.

9. Use the shortcut whenever you like.

Three categories of shortcuts can be assigned, as shown in
Figure 1-28:

■ **Application Menus**   The menus at the top of the
workspace window

■ **Palette Menus**   The menus in the palettes

■ **Tools**   Shortcuts for the tools

FIGURE 1-28 Categories to which you can assign shortcuts (A) Application Menus (B) Palette Menus

A.

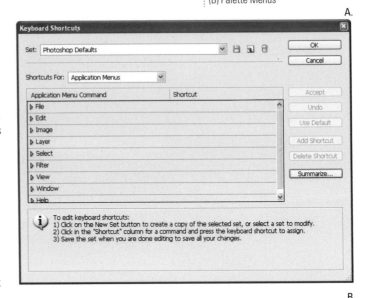

Printing Out Shortcuts

In the Keyboard Shortcuts dialog box, you will see a button called Summarize. Click this button to produce a current list of all the shortcuts assigned in Photoshop.

1. Click the Summarize button.

2. Choose a location to which you want to save the list of shortcuts.

3. An HTML document will be generated.

If you want to print the list, choose Print from your browser commands.

Preset Manager

As you read this book, you will learn that many of the Photoshop tools have *libraries* attached to them. When Photoshop is loading, a line of text tells you what is loading up. The libraries will need to load before Photoshop is ready for use.

To minimize load time, it's a good idea to keep all the loaded libraries to a minimum. As you progress through the chapters, you'll find tips for loading and saving items from the libraries. All the libraries can be managed from one place called

B.

the Preset Manager, which is accessed from the Edit menu. The Preset Manager is shown in Figure 1-29.

Here is where you'll find more information about each library:

FIGURE 1-29 Preset Manager

- **Brushes**   Chapter 3
- **Swatches**   Chapter 3
- **Gradients**   Chapter 3
- **Styles**   Chapter 11
- **Patterns**   Chapter 3
- **Contours**   Chapter 11
- **Custom Shapes**   Chapter 7
- **Tools**   Chapter 9

Preferences

In the Preferences dialog box, you can choose how Photoshop will operate; the default settings are for the average computer, but you'll find it helpful to be able to customize Photoshop for your needs. You may want to make some tweaks if you have a slower or more powerful than average machine.

Rather than discuss each preference, I will focus on those that you should be aware of. I'll make suggestions for changing certain settings.

If you want a complete rundown of each and every setting, refer to the online help that comes with Photoshop.

To launch the Preferences dialog box, choose Edit | Preferences. You'll see a list of nine categories, beginning with General. Choose any of the categories and then cycle through them all by choosing the Prev and Next buttons.

General

- **History States**   This is your "undo memory." If you have a lot of RAM and a fast processor, consider increasing the History States. If you use a slower machine or never use the history options, reduce the History States to 10 or 15. This will free up some resources. You can always use the Edit | Purge command to get back some resources, too.

- **Interpolation**   Bicubic is a good multipurpose setting. This setting will be used whenever you are scaling images. If you are reducing images in size, choose Bicubic Sharper; if you are increasing the size of images, choose Bicubic Softer.

- **Export Clipboard**   Consider turning off this option unless you are going to paste your images into another program once you close Photoshop.

- **History Log**   Turn on this option only if you want to log all your Photoshop use. Otherwise, it will just slow things down for nothing.

File Handling

- **Image Previews**   If you are working on the Web only, turn off this option; it will reduce the file size of your images ever so slightly.

- **Enable Large Document Format**   Turn on this option if you are working with images larger than 4 GB.

- **Name of the Option**   It's a good idea to increase the Recent File List Contains: (x) files list to 25.

- **Maximize PSD File Compatibility**   This saves a composite image (flattened copy) with the layers. This option will increase the file size but allows you to open the images in Photoshop 2.5 and also some other graphics editing programs. Ask is a good option because you will want to allow compatibility only with images that need extra flexibility.

Display and Cursors

The default setting will work well for most cases. You don't need to turn on Precise Cursors because if you press the CAPS LOCK key, the Precise Cursors will be toggled on and off. The Precise Cursors work with the drawing tools and allow for pinpoint accuracy, but they are not always the best option because you cannot see the brush sizes with this option turned on.

Transparency and Gamut

No changes are needed for transparency unless you prefer to change the indicator for transparency.

The gamut warning tells you an image cannot be printed with the chosen color. Gray is a good color because the "out of gamut" warning will usually appear in bright portions of the image. These can be seen in dialog boxes such as the Variations dialog box.

Units and Rulers

This was covered earlier in the "Rulers, Guides, and Grids" section of this chapter.

Guides, Grids, and Slices

You can change the appearance of your grids and guides. You can also change the appearance of slices. Slices are covered in Chapter 13. No changes are recommended to these options.

Plug-Ins and Scratch Disk

- **Plug-ins**   Specify a location for additional plug-in filters. Choose this option if you are using filters from a previous version of Photoshop. You can enter the serial number in the Legacy field to help you get around serial number verification problems.

- **Scratch Disk**   A scratch disk is your hard drive. When Photoshop runs out of physical RAM, it copies information to the hard drive and processes the images on the drive. You can use up to four drives. If you can afford a separate hard drive or partition a large portion of your main drive to be used as a scratch disk, this will help speed up Photoshop. Generally, Photoshop will need ten times the image size to process a number of tasks.

Memory and Image Cache

- **Cache For Histogram Levels**   If you turn on this option, the histograms will not be accurate in the Levels dialog box. The "Cache" is on by default in the Histogram palette.

- **Memory Usage**   This assigns how much memory is available for Photoshop. If you have a decent amount of RAM (more than 256 Mb) or you don't use other programs much while Photoshop is running, turn it up to around 75 percent or more.

File Browser

- **Do not process**   100 MB is the default, but you can make it smaller if you want to speed things up and increase the stability of the file browser.

- **Custom Thumbnail size**   Set the size here for the custom display. You can also set this for the preferences in the file browser. (Which just happens to be the same Preferences dialog box we are looking at in this section.)

- **Turn off High Quality Preview**   Select this to speed things up if you are on a slow machine.

Common Color Modes

A color mode determines the way that Photoshop will process an image. Each color mode has a different color channel configuration. (Channels are covered in Chapter 6.) You can choose different color modes for different tasks. The official name is a *color space*. You can change the color mode by choosing Image | Mode.

- **Grayscale**   This has only one channel and has a maximum of 256 shades of gray (65,536 in 16-bit mode). No color information appears while in Grayscale. Use this mode for printing black-and-white and duotone images.

- **RGB (Red, Green, and Blue)**   These are the primary colors used on a monitor, and this is the color space to be used for online and multimedia work. Also the best working mode for most color images.

- **CMYK (Cyan, Magenta, Yellow, and Black)**   This is the best color mode for offset printing (commercial printing press). If you are not printing on a commercial press, don't use this mode.

- **LAB (Luminosity A and B channels)**   This mode puts all the grayscale information on the L channel and splits the colors onto the A and B channels. This is an excellent mode for performing image correction.

Common File Types

Whenever you open or save a file, you are dealing with some kind of file format. When you are saving a file, you will have to choose the best file format for your image. This list will help you decide what to choose.

- **TIFF (Tagged Image Format)**   This is the most common file format for printing and saving a flattened image without any loss of quality. Photoshop TIFFs can now contain layers and channels.

- **EPS (Encapsulated Postscript)**   This is the language designed by Adobe for print. Use this file format if you want to include a clipping path on your image or you are printing to a PostScript printer.

- **PSD (Photoshop Document)**   This is the native working format for Photoshop. Use this for all your working files; it will save all the layers, channels, notes and color profiles. You can also use this format for printing through Adobe InDesign. (Be sure to convert to CMYK mode for commercial printing.)

- **PSB (Photoshop Large Format)**   Use this format to save an image up to 300,000 pixels. Use this option for images larger than 2 GB.

- **GIF (Graphical Interchange Format)**   This was invented by CompuServe for saving images for the Web; it's limited to 256 colors. This is the best format for images that have repeating patterns or are cartoon-like. It also supports transparency and animation. GIFs compress images by throwing away colors and repeating simple patterns—this is known as a *lossy* format. (See Chapter 13 for more on the lossy format.)

- **JPG (Joint Photographic Experts Group)**   This is the most popular format for images on the Web. This format reduces the quality of the image (often undetectable to the human eye). This lossy compression can greatly reduce the file size of an image.

- **PNG (Portable Network Graphics)**   Lossless format for the Web that support up to 16 million colors and 256 levels of transparency. This was supposed to be the "miracle" file format, but it hasn't taken off yet because the file sizes are larger than JPG or GIF and older browsers do not support it. (See Chapter 13 for more on the lossless format.)

Status Bar

Along the bottom of the main Photoshop window, you will see a bar with information on it. This is called the status bar, and it offers interesting information. For example, whenever you choose a tool, its description is displayed in the center of the status bar.

The bulk of the information appears on the left side of the bar. At the bottomleft is the image magnification. If you type figures here, Photoshop will change the magnification of the image to match. Figure 1-30 shows the status bar at the default settings.

If you click over the document information on the status bar, as shown in Figure 1-31, you will see a print preview that shows how large your image is compared to the default page size of your printer—usually 8.5×11 inches in the United States and A4 in other countries.

FIGURE 1-30 Status bar

FIGURE 1-31 Print preview

FIGURE 1-32 Image information

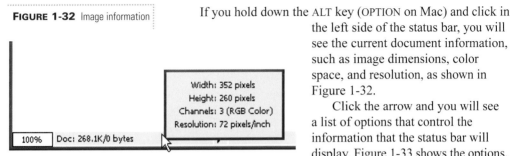

If you hold down the ALT key (OPTION on Mac) and click in the left side of the status bar, you will see the current document information, such as image dimensions, color space, and resolution, as shown in Figure 1-32.

Click the arrow and you will see a list of options that control the information that the status bar will display. Figure 1-33 shows the options.

FIGURE 1-33 Status bar options

Changing Views

Photoshop has three modes for viewing and working on images:

- **Standard View**   This is the default view, as shown in Figure 1-34A.

- **Full Screen With Menu Bar**   Hides all the window "chrome." All the borders and title bars will be hidden, as shown in Figure 1-34B.

- **Full Screen**   Hides the menu and turns the workspace black, as shown in Figure 1-34C. This is the Presentation mode. Notice that the menu is now available from the top of the toolbar.

To change the modes, click the View buttons on the bottom of the toolbar, or just press the F key. Each time you press the F key, the view will cycle through the modes. For the ultimate in viewing pleasure, press the TAB key while in Full Screen mode. The TAB key toggles the palette on and off. You can have a full screen with nothing but your image showing, as shown in Figure 1-34.

A.

B.

C.

D.

FIGURE 1-34 Toggling through the view modes (A) Standard view (B) Full screen with menu bar (C) Full screen (D) Full screen with palettes toggled off

Chapter 2

Get Documents into Photoshop

How to...

- Create a new document
- Use preset document sizes
- Open images
- Import PDF images
- Place images
- Scan images
- Use the file browser

- Rotate and organize images
- Change thumbnail sizes
- Open multiple files at once
- Understand image resolution
- Calculate the output resolution
- Choose different interpolation methods
- Change the size of a picture

We are used to the word *document* when it is used in a text or office setting. A document is also the name given to an image in Photoshop. There are many ways to bring documents into Photoshop. Documents can be created in Photoshop or in other programs, or images can be brought into Photoshop from a scanner or by opening existing image documents.

In this chapter, we look at the basic Photoshop document.

Creating a New Document

Whenever you open a new document in Photoshop, all the grayed-out options come to life, and you have the opportunity to play around a bit and find your bearings. The best place to start this chapter, then, is to create a new document.

1. Choose File | New, and you will see the New dialog box shown in Figure 2-1. Here, you can set up several options for the new document, as shown in the list that follows. When you're satisfied with your settings, click OK.

   - **Name** Type in a name for your document.
   - **Preset** Choose an option from the drop-down list of preset document sizes for different types of uses (more on presets in the next section).

Document name
Choose a preset size
Document width
Document height
Resolution
Color mode
Background color

FIGURE 2-1 The new document
dialog box

■ **Width and Height**   You can choose from various
measurement units—points, centimeters, and inches.

■ **Resolution**   Choose the desired resolution.
Typically, 72 pixels/inch (ppi) is fine for online
presentation and 300ppi is used for print. (See the
section "Understanding Image Resolution" later in
this chapter for more information on resolution.)

■ **Color Mode**   Typically, RGB will be the best
choice for color images, and Grayscale is fine
for noncolor images.

■ **Background Contents**   Choose a background
color or a transparent background.

*If you are designing for video, click the Advanced button in the New dialog box. In the
dialog box that opens, choose a new pixel aspect ratio, because video uses rectangular
pixels as opposed to the square pixels used for most graphic uses.*

Creating Custom Preset Document Sizes

You may find that you use the same document specifications on
a repeated basis. To save time, you can save the settings as a
document preset. Here's how it's done:

1. Choose File | New.

2. In the New dialog box, choose Custom from the Preset
drop-down list and enter your custom settings.

3. Click Save Preset.

4. In the New Document Preset dialog box, shown in Figure 2-2, type in a name for your document preset.

5. In the Include In Saved Settings area, click to select all the boxes to keep all the settings you set earlier. (These boxes relate to the features explained in Figure 2-1.)

6. Click OK.

FIGURE 2-2 Saving as a preset

Your settings are now saved. You may want to create a custom preset if you often need to create documents using a particular size and resolution, such as documents used for a PowerPoint presentation or a web page.

Using Presets

In the future, if you want to use the preset, click the Preset field from the new document palette. The list of available presets will display, as shown in Figure 2-3. You can see our preset is now in the list. Select the desired preset and the new document will be created to meet the preset specifications. A number of presets ship with Photoshop, and these can be used to create all kinds of things, from web banners, to 4×6 photos, to letter-sized pages.

Opening Documents

You can also open an existing document in Photoshop.

1. Choose File | Open. You will see the Open dialog box, shown in Figure 2-4.

2. By default, all file types appear, but if you want to limit the display to one type, choose it from the Files Of Type drop-down list.

3. Locate your document and select it. You will see a small preview of the image.

4. Click Open.

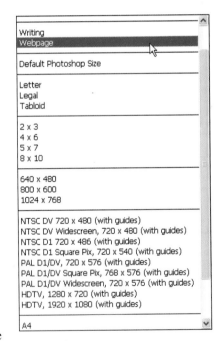

FIGURE 2-3 Choosing the custom preset

A.

B.

Working with Images

You can import images into Photoshop—even those created from other applications. Photoshop has a robust set of import filters and can open images created from a variety of sources.

Import PDF Images

1. PDF (Portable Document Format) is a growing technology that is fast becoming the standard for e-paper. You can open images from within a PDF document in Photoshop, even if it is a multiple-page document. Choose File | Import | PDF Image.

2. Navigate to the PDF image and click OK.

3. You will see a PDF Image Import dialog box like that shown in Figure 2-5. Choose the image(s) you want to import.

4. Click OK, and the image will open in Photoshop.

FIGURE 2-4 The Open dialog box in Windows (A) and on the Mac (B)

You can use this import process to import either a single or a group of images from a PDF document. You can get some pretty good-quality images by importing them from PDF, as shown in Figure 2-6.

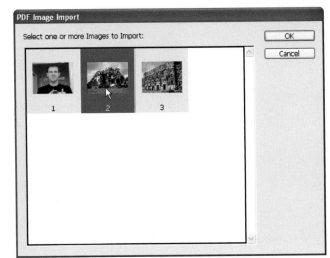

Place an Image

When images are created in programs such as Adobe Illustrator, Macromedia Freehand, or CorelDRAW, they can be placed into a Photoshop document and still retain their sharpness. That is because these types of images are made of *vectors*. (Chapter 7 explains vectors in depth.) These types of images typically use the filename extension .ai (this is native to Illustrator) or .eps (Encapsulated PostScript). We use a process called *placing* to transfer images to Photoshop from another program.

FIGURE 2-5 PDF Image Import dialog box

 For more information on PDF and Photoshop, see Chapter 15.

When we place an image, it will be shown as a *proxy image* (a low-resolution representation of the final image). You will see a box around the image with eight little squares on the corners and edges; these squares are called *handles*. You can drag these handles to enlarge or reduce the image. Once you press the ENTER key, the image will be *rendered*— a full-resolution image will be drawn in place of the proxy image.

Here is how you place an image in Photoshop:

1. Create a blank document at the size you want the final image to be.

2. Choose File | Place.

FIGURE 2-6 Image imported from a PDF document

FIGURE 2-7 Placing an image into a Photoshop document

FIGURE 2-8 Final rendered image

3. Choose the image you want to place.

4. You will see the image and a bounding box, as shown in Figure 2-7. Make size and position adjustments by dragging the handles.

5. Click OK to render the final placement, as shown in Figure 2-8.

Scan Images

Because each scanner has its own particular settings and user interface, the explanation in this section will be a bit general and will mainly deal with the Photoshop end of scanning. Before you scan, read the documentation that came with your scanner. You will also have to install the software that comes with the scanner before you use it. If you have installed Photoshop after installing the scanner, you may need to reinstall your scanner software before it will work with Photoshop.

After installation, your scanner software may have installed a little plug-in called Twain. This Twain driver is what allows Photoshop to communicate with many scanners.

To scan an image into Photoshop:

1. Choose File | Import | Twain (or your scanner software name).

2. The scanners software will open. Make the adjustments according to your scanner's documentation.

3. Click Scan. Your scanner will now scan the image and transfer it to Photoshop.

Scanning Tips

Here are a few tips that should help you achieve better scans.

- Keep the scanner's glass plate clean at all times.

- Scan the images larger than you think you may need. (Enlarging images later will cause loss of quality.)

- Make as many tonal adjustments on the scanner's software as you can before scanning.

- If you are scanning from a magazine or printed page, choose the scanner descreen options or you will see moiré patterns in the scanned image.

 Moiré patterns are patterns of dots that will be created if you scan an image from a magazine or printed page without using the descreen option on your scanner. If your scanner doesn't support descreen, try scanning the image on an angle to reduce the effects.

Use the File Browser

Photoshop comes with its own File Browser that's jammed with so many features, it's almost a program in itself. It's so useful that I open almost all my files in the File Browser. The File Browser is even useful for organizing and renaming images.

You can launch the File Browser in several ways:

- Choose File | Browse.

- Press CTRL-SHIFT-O (CMD-SHIFT-O on the Mac).

- Click this icon, located to the right of the options bar.

The File Browser has four main windows, as shown in Figure 2-9.

- **Navigation Window**   Navigate all your disk drives.

- **Preview**   Adjustable window that shows the currently selected file. The right screens in Figure 2-9 show a different view of the File Browser. To adjust the view, simply click and drag the windows to the sizes and locations that you want.

- **Image Information**   Shows all the information about the selected image. You can also assign search keywords in this window.

- **Image Thumbnails**   View the images and their filenames in the current directory.

A.

Flag (mark image) ————— Search   Delete image

Rotate image

Navigation window

Image thumbnails

Preview selected images

Image information

Expand/Collapse information panels ———   ——— Folder information

B.

FIGURE 2-9 The File Browser in two views

On the bottom status bar, you will see a double-sided arrow. Click the arrow to collapse all the windows except the thumbnails window, which will take up the full screen.

Here's how to open a file in the File Browser:

1. Launch the File Browser.

2. Navigate to your image directory.

3. Double-click the thumbnail of the image you want to open.

Rotating and Organizing Images

The File Browser is more than just a means of opening images. You can organize and rotate your thumbnails, too. When you take a picture with the camera turned sideways, you will need to rotate the image in Photoshop for it to display in the correct orientation.

To organize the thumbnails, simply click and drag the thumbnails to new locations.

To rotate a thumbnail:

1. Click the thumbnail you want to rotate. To select more than one image, CTRL-click (CMD-click on the Mac) each image.

2. Click either the rotate clockwise or counter-clockwise icon, as shown in Figure 2-10. The thumbnail will rotate.

FIGURE 2-10 Rotating an image counterclockwise

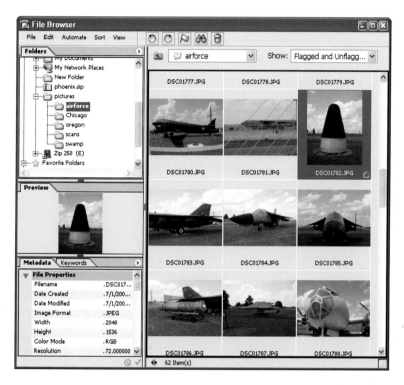

The source image will not be altered, but every time you view the image in the File Browser, it will appear rotated, as shown in Figure 2-11. A little icon appears in the bottom-right corner of the rotated image. When you open the image in Photoshop, it will open in the orientation in which it appears in the File Browser.

FIGURE 2-11 Thumbnail showing the image has been rotated.

Changing the Thumbnail Sizes

You can change the size of the thumbnails in the File Browser . Five options can be selected from the View menu.

- Small
- Medium
- Large
- Custom
- Details

With the Details view selected in Figure 2-12, you can see a lot of extra image information displayed, including the size, type, filename, and date.

When we choose Small thumbnail view, as shown in Figure 2-13, all the images are displayed in a column with a tiny thumbnail and the file name next to it. This is a good option to use when you are organizing and renaming groups of pictures.

FIGURE 2-12 Thumbnail details displayed

FIGURE 2-13 Small thumbnail view

To change the name of an image, click its name to highlight it. Then type in a new name.

Setting a Custom Thumbnail Size

You can also choose your own custom thumbnail size:

1. In the File Browser, choose Edit | Preferences.

2. In the Preferences dialog box, under Custom Thumbnail sizes, enter a size.

3. Click OK.

4. Choose View | Custom. Your thumbnails will now be displayed in your chosen size.

Automating Options

Figure 2-14 shows the Automate menu options. You can use these options to apply automatic image processing to folders of images from within the File Browser. For a complete rundown of features and instructions, see Chapter 9.

FIGURE 2-14 The automation options

Opening Multiple Files at Once

You can open multiple images at once from the File Browser.

1. Launch the File Browser.

2. Select the first thumbnail by clicking it.

3. To select a group of contiguous thumbnails, hold down the SHIFT key and click the last thumbnail in the group. For nonadjacent thumbnails, CTRL-click each thumbnail (CMD-click on the Mac). The selected thumbnails are highlighted in color.

4. Double-click any selected thumbnail to open all the selected images. The images will open in Photoshop, as shown in Figure 2-15.

FIGURE 2-15 The open images in Photoshop

Understanding Image Resolution

Resolution is one of those words that you hear a lot in the computer world. That is because every digital image displayed has a resolution, whether it be on screen or in print. Understanding and using the correct resolution for your images will ensure the sharpest output for every occasion.

Images created in Photoshop are made up of tiny squares called *pixels*, each a single color. With enough of the tiny colored pixels clustered together, the image appears very smooth. If you view your image on a computer screen, it's using pixels to display the image.

Figure 2-16 shows an image zoomed to 1600 percent, to show the actual pixels that make up the image. Notice that each pixel is uniform in size and shape and that each pixel contains a single color.

Resolution refers to how many pixels are present in an image. A typical 17-inch monitor displays pixels at a resolution of 1024×768. To figure out how many pixels are present on the monitor at 1024×768 resolution, you would multiply 1024 × 768, which comes to 786,432 pixels on your screen. We measure resolution by how many pixels fit into each inch. This is know as ppi (pixels per inch) A typical computer monitor displays pixels at 72ppi.

FIGURE 2-16 Image zoomed in to see pixels (image courtesy of Ablestock.com)

Calculating the Output Resolution

To determine the size of an image in inches, we divide the pixels by the ppi. Here are the sizes of an image 1024 pixels wide at different resolutions:

- **72ppi**   1024 / 72 = 14.2 inches
- **150ppi**   1024 / 150 = 6.9 inches
- **300ppi**   1024 / 300 = 3.4 inches

Figure 2-17 illustrates the same image displayed at three different resolutions. Notice that the images appear smaller at higher resolutions. This is because the pixels are packed in much tighter (that is, a higher count of pixels are needed to fill the same space).

Another way to look at it would be to take three images and make them a set size at 3 inches wide. To figure out the pixels present in the image, we would multiply the size by the ppi and this would give us the numbers of pixels in an image.

- **72ppi**   3 inches × 72ppi = 216 pixels wide
- **150ppi**   3 × 150 = 450
- **300ppi**   3 × 300 = 900

As the image resolution drops, so does the output quality of the image. If the resolution is insufficient for the purpose, then a problem called *pixelization* occurs. Pixelization occurs when the resolution is so low that the edges of the pixels begin to appear. Figure 2-18 shows an image printed at various resolutions. You can see that the image with the lowest resolution (72ppi) is less sharp than the image at the highest resolution (300ppi).

The more pixels present, the sharper the image will appear. More pixels mean smoother color transitions, more detail, and a sharper output.

FIGURE 2-17 Images Displayed at different resolutions; from top, 72ppi, 150ppi, and 300ppi

2

FIGURE 2-18 Images at 100 percent size; from top, 300ppi, 150ppi, and 72ppi

The higher the resolution, the larger the file size. At times, you will want to minimize the file size; for instance, an image to be posted on a web page would require as small a file size as possible so that the image takes less time to load. Similarly, when you output an image to a printer, a larger file will take a longer time to output and print.

The obvious solution is to use the correct resolution for each task. Here are the most common uses for images and the recommended resolutions:

- **Multimedia**   72ppi
- **Web pages**   72ppi
- **CD-ROM**   72ppi
- **Inkjet printer**   150ppi
- **Photo printer**   200ppi/360ppi on an Epson
- **Commercial printing press**   300ppi

Resizing

When preparing images, it's a good idea to create them at a size larger than you think you will need; when you enlarge an image in Photoshop, you will lose quality, because the number of pixels does not increase as the image is enlarged—and large pixels mean rougher images. You can get away with a little bit of enlargement, but it will begin to show pretty quickly. You can, however, safely reduce the size of images without losing much, if any, quality.

Interpolation Methods

When you enlarge or reduce an image's size, it's called *resampling*. When the image's dimensions are changed, pixels have to be added or subtracted from the image. When these pixels are altered, Photoshop calculates what the new pixels should look like based on the existing pixels. This process is called *image interpolation.* Five interpolation methods are available in Photoshop. When you check the resample option, as we did in Figure 2-19 in the Image Size dialog box, you will see the following options:

- **Nearest Neighbor**   The quickest method, with the lowest quality
- **Bilinear**   Best for line art
- **Bicubic**   Default mode, high quality and best for most purposes
- **Bicubic Smoother**   Best when you are increasing the size of an image
- **Bicubic Sharper**   Best when you are reducing the size of an image

FIGURE 2-19 Interpolation options in Photoshop

Changing the Size of a Picture

Here is how you change the size of your pictures:

1. Open an image.
2. Choose Image | Image Size. You will now see the Image Size dialog box.
3. Click the Resample Image button.
4. Choose Constrain Proportions to maintain the image's proportions. Or, enter the desired sizes into the image fields. (The other fields will adjust automatically if you choose Constrain Proportions, as shown in Figure 2-20.)
5. Click OK. The image will be changed to the desired size.

Changing Image Resolution

Sometimes you may want to change the resolution only, and not change the image's pixel size:

1. Open the image.
2. Choose Image | Image Size. You'll see the Image Size dialog box.

FIGURE 2-20 Changing the image's size

FIGURE 2-21 Changing the resolution of the image

3. Uncheck the Resample Image box and enter the desired resolution, as shown in Figure 2-21. The Height and Width fields will be automatically adjusted to compensate for the new resolution setting.

4. Click OK.

Using the Resize Image Wizard

FIGURE 2-22 Choose Print or Online in the Resize Image Wizard.

Another way to resize your images is to use the Resize Image Wizard. This takes care of all the technical resizing issues for you. You just complete a short interview, and based on the answers, Photoshop will make all the decisions for you. Here's how to use the Resize Image Wizard:

1. Open an image.

2. Choose Help | Resize Image. You will see the dialog box shown in Figure 2-22.

3. Choose Print or Online, and then click Next.

4. If you chose Online, enter your pixel dimensions. Then click OK twice. Photoshop makes a copy of the image for you and leaves the original intact.

5. If you choose Print in step 3, choose the desired size of the image, and then choose a halftone screen. Hints are displayed in the Description box, as shown in Figure 2-23.

5. Choose the image quality, as shown in Figure 2-24. Choose the lowest quality for a draft quality or the highest quality for final print.

6. Click OK and you're done.

FIGURE 2-23 Choose the halftone screen.

FIGURE 2-24 Choose the quality

Chapter 3

Draw and Paint

How to...

- Choose colors and color swatches
- Use the Color Picker
- Use the drawing tools and brushes
- Use the Eraser tool
- Create and modify brushes
- Use the Smudge, Sharpen, and Blur tools
- Use the Dodge, Burn, and Sponge tools

- Apply and create a gradient
- Use the Shape tools
- Transform, rotate, and flip
- Use Free Transform
- Use and create patterns
- Use the History palette and History brush
- Create art with the Art History brush

Photoshop includes some powerful drawing tools. Its brushes are packed with features that allow you to touch up photos or even create your own works of art. You can simulate the real world or create fantasy with a host of drawing and painting tools in Photoshop.

Choosing Colors

We can choose color in Photoshop by clicking on a Color Picker, a visual way for you to choose colors; you simply locate the color you want and click it, and it will become your new foreground color. Color Pickers are located in several places in Photoshop, and you'll find yourself using these again and again.

One of the keys to the success of Adobe products is the common user interface. Once you have learned to use one Adobe product, you have a head start on using all the other products. Because of this commonality, if you learn how to use the Color Picker here, you are ready to use every Color Picker in Photoshop—more than that, you are pretty much ready to use the Color Picker in every Adobe product.

Color Swatches

The illustration shows the tool palette with the color swatches highlighted. All color swatches in Photoshop look this way.

Here is how the color swatches work:

- The top swatch is the foreground color (black by default).
- The bottom swatch is the background color (white by default).
- To switch the foreground and background colors, press the X key.
- To reset the colors to default, press the D key.

Whenever you use the Eyedropper tool, it will replace the currently selected color. Click with the eyedropper anywhere inside an image to sample (or pick up) the color.

Color Picker

To choose a new color, double-click any of the color swatches and the Color Picker will open, as shown in Figure 3-1.

FIGURE 3-1 The Color Picker

You should be aware of the following features in the Color Picker:

- **Hue Selector**   Slide this up and down to choose a color (hue).

- **Currently Selected Tint** Click and drag to choose a tint of the selected color (hue). This shows the actual color that you are choosing.

- **New Pick** Shows the color you are choosing from the selected new color.

- **Current Color** Shows the current color you are replacing.

- **Gamut Warning** Tells you that the color cannot be reproduced; click the warning icon to choose the closest reproducible color.

- **Snap to Web** Changes the color to the closest color in the web-safe palette (see Chapter 13).

- **Color Values** These are the numerical values of the chosen colors. These values help you to identify and reproduce colors. They break down the mix of individual colors to make the final color.

- **Hexadecimal Number** A six-digit number commonly used for web colors.

- **HSB Values** Hue, saturation, and brightness values.

- **LAB Values** Separate grayscale and color values that are commonly used for color correction.

- **RGB Values** Red, green, and blue values that are commonly used for screen and multimedia color.

- **CMYK Values** Cyan, magenta, yellow, and black values, commonly used for print.

To choose a color:

1. Double-click a color swatch.

2. The Color Picker will open. Click and drag the hue selector to the desired hue.

3. Click and drag inside the Color Picker window to choose the exact tint of the color you want to choose.

4. Click OK. The color swatch displays your new color.

Filling with a Color

You can fill either the entire page or just a portion of an image with color. To fill a portion, you must first make a selection. See Chapter 10 for more information on selections.

To apply the color to the image, do one of the following:

- Choose the Paint Bucket tool and click anywhere in the image to apply the current foreground color.

- Choose Edit | Fill and choose either Foreground or Background Color to fill with the currently chosen colors.

 To open the Fill dialog box, press SHIFT-F5 *or* SHIFT-BACKSPACE (SHIFT-DELETE *on the Mac). To fill with the current foreground color, press* ALT-BACKSPACE (OPTION-DELETE *on the Mac). To use the background color, press* CTRL-BACKSPACE (CMD-DELETE *on the Mac).*

 About Graphics Tablets

Drawing with a mouse has been likened to drawing with "soap on a rope." It can be quite clumsy and requires lots of practice to master. Some people have become extremely efficient at this skill, but if you plan to use Photoshop for a lot of brushwork and freehand drawing, you might consider investing in a graphics tablet. These tablets are plastic slates that you draw on with specially designed pens. They can help you achieve your artistic vision more easily than using a mouse. The tablets also open up some extra features in Photoshop—the *pressure-sensitive tools*. These tools detect how hard you are pressing with the pen and respond to the pressure by varying the opacity, line thickness, and color of the brush stroke.

Some of the newer tablets even have a feature that allows Photoshop to detect the angle of the pen's tilt and react accordingly. The most popular of these tablets are manufactured by a company called Wacom. They range from the $99 Graphire through to the Intuious range that cost a few hundred dollars more. Other companies, such as Calcomp, also manufacture graphics tablets.

Drawing Tools

Photoshop comes with various drawing tools. With a little patience and practice, you can master these tools and use them to transform your work from the ordinary to the extraordinary.

Pencil Tool

When it comes to drawing tools, the Pencil tool is about as straightforward as it gets. Choose the Pencil tool, and then click

and drag your mouse to draw. As long as you hold your finger
on the mouse button, you will continue to draw a trail of pixels.
The Pencil tool draws with the current foreground color.

To draw with the Pencil tool:

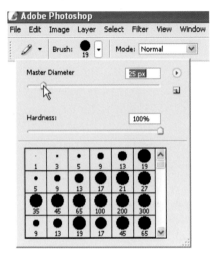

FIGURE 3-2 Choosing the size of
the pencil tip

1. Choose the Pencil tool from the tool palette.

2. Choose the foreground color.

3. Choose the pencil tip thickness from the
   options bar, as shown in Figure 3-2.

4. Click and hold the left mouse button.

5. Drag the mouse with the button still depressed.

You are now drawing freehand with the foreground
color. To draw a straight line:

1. Click the mouse.

2. Hold down the SHIFT key.

3. Click the mouse again in a different location. A
   straight line will be drawn between the two points.

Auto Erase

When you select the Pencil tool, you will see a box in the options
bar that says Auto Erase.

The secret to using this option lies in the location of the
mouse pointer when you first click. When you are drawing
and click in the background area, the pencil will draw with
the foreground color as normal.

If you first click over the foreground color, the Pencil
tool will erase to transparent, unless you are working on a
background layer. In this case, the tool will draw with the
currently selected background color instead.

Brush Tools

Brushes are the main drawing tools that you will use in
Photoshop. Because the brushes are versatile and extremely
customizable, you will use them for everything—from touching
up photos to creating your own works of art from scratch. You
can also use brushes in conjunction with other tools, such as the
Dodging and Burning tools, Eraser tool, and the Sharpening and
Blurring tools for special effects. You can choose from preset
brushes or create your own.

Using and Modifying the Brush Tool

When you choose the Brush tool, you will be offered a plethora of options. Figure 3-3 shows the options bar when the Brush tool is selected.

FIGURE 3-3 Brushes options bar

Selected brush   Blending mode   Transparency   Flow   Airbrush

These are the top level options:

- **Brush**   The currently active brush.

- **Mode**   Choose between blending modes to achieve different effects—see Chapter 5 for more details on these modes. The default is normal.

- **Opacity**   Adjusts the transparency of the brush.

- **Flow**   Controls how fast the paint flows from the brush.

- **Airbrush**   In Airbrush mode, paint will continue to flow as you hold down the mouse button, causing the paint to build up in a layered, airbrushed fashion.

FIGURE 3-4 Brush modifier drop-down menu

To change the style or type of brush you want to use, click the little arrow to the right of the Brush modifier on the options bar. You will see a drop-down menu, as shown in Figure 3-4, that presents the essential brush options.

The main options are as follows:

Brush size

Hardness

Brush type

- **Brush Size (Master Diameter)**   Adjust this slider to increase/decrease the diameter of the brush.

- **Hardness**   This adjusts the Hardness of the brush, as shown in Figure 3-5A.

- **Brush Type**   Scroll through the list to choose

the brush you want to use. To make it easier, you can switch to thumbnail view by clicking the arrow at the top right corner and choosing Thumbnail from the drop-down menu. Figure 3-5 shows the thumbnail view.

To draw with a brush:

1. Choose the Brush tool from the tool palette.

2. Choose the brush type, size, and hardness.

3. Select the foreground color.

4. Choose the opacity and blending mode.

5. Choose the airbrush option if desired.

6. Draw with your mouse in the same way you did with the Pencil tool.

 To adjust the size of a brush while painting, press the [and] keys.

Modifying and Creating Brushes

Photoshop lets you extensively modify your brushes. This is great news for artists and others who want to have precise control over the tools they are using and will allow them to mimic natural media and thus produce less "digital" looking art.

You will see a couple of terms used often in discussions of the Brushes palette, and we will talk about them briefly before we open the palette.

- **Jitter** Sets the randomness of an attribute. 0 percent has a value of no randomness; as you increase the jitter amount, you will increase the randomness of the chosen attribute of the brush stroke.

- **Control** The control sets how Photoshop will interact with your drawing device. If you are using a drawing tablet, you'll want to turn these options to the pen options to make the most of the pressure-sensitive tools in Photoshop.

- **Off** Turns off the selected control feature and defaults to the selected setting of the feature.

- **Fade** The tip will fade to transparent at the size you specify.

FIGURE 3-5 Brush options: (A) 0 percent (top) and 100 percent (bottom; (B) Hardness settings, thumbnail view

A.

B.

FIGURE 3-6 The Brushes palette
(A) Tip shape
(B) Texture
(C) Dual brush
(D) Color dynamics
(E) Other dynamics

A.

B.

Pen Tilt   When you tilt your pen, attributes will change. (This works only with graphics tablets equipped with tilt ability, such as the Wacom Intuios 2 tablets.)

Pen Pressure   How hard you press with your pen will affect the attributes, just like drawing in the real world. (Only graphics tablets offer this option, such as the Wacom Graphire or Intious series.)

Stylus Wheel   Controls the flow of "paint," similar to a traditional airbrush. (Available only for graphics tablets equipped with an airbrush.)

Modifying Brushes

To make modifications to the brush attributes, you will first need to open the Brushes palette. This palette is not the same palette available from the options bar; it's the larger Brushes palette you open by choosing Window | Brushes or by pressing F5. The Brushes palette is shown in Figure 3-6.

You will notice quite a few brush options. To choose a different brush, choose the Brush Presets option. You can scroll through all the available brushes. To make modifications to an attribute, click its name in the Brushes palette and make adjustments. To turn on an attribute, check the box next to the attribute name. If the box is unchecked, that particular attribute will not be applied to the working brush tip.

Brush Tip Shape   Controls style, size, angle, and spacing of brushes.

Shape Dynamics   Controls the shape of the brush.

Scattering   Sprays multiple instances of the brush tip at different sizes.

Texture   Allows you to add texture to your brush tips, as if drawing on a textured surface (see Figure 3-7).

Dual Brush   Allows you to mix two brush tips together.

C.

D.
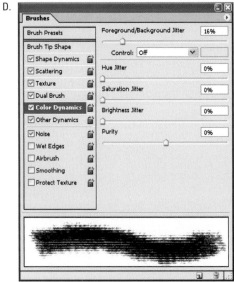

- **Color Dynamics**   Allows you to mix the foreground and background together to achieve a two-colored stroke.
- **Other Dynamics**   Allows you to adjust the random flow and opacity of the brush tips.

You will also notice five options with checkboxes at the bottom of the palette. These options have no adjustments—they are either on or off:

- **Noise**   Speckles the semi-transparent edges of a brush.
- **Wet Edges**   Simulates the effect of a wet brush drawing onto a damp surface.
- **Airbrush**   Turns on the airbrush option. Paint will continue to flow as you hold down the mouse button or the pen on a graphics tablet. This causes the paint to build up in an airbrush fashion.
- **Smoothing**   Smooths the curves when you are drawing with the brush.

E.

FIGURE 3-7   Painting with a brush with the Texture option turned on

3

FIGURE 3-8 Preparing to draw a dotted line

FIGURE 3-9 Maple leaves preset

- **Protect Texture**   If you are using more than one brush with the Texture option turned on, this option keeps consistency across brushes.

Creating a Dotted Line   Adjusting the spacing of the brush tips will allow you to create dotted lines. When you change the spacing, you are telling the brush how often to repeat the brush stroke when you are painting.

1. Choose a brush.

2. Select a brush tip.

3. In the Brushes palette, change the spacing to any number greater than 100%, as shown in Figure 3-8.

4. Draw with the brush and you'll see the dotted line.

Creating Brushes

Brush tips don't have to be restricted to random shapes and textures; you can use an image or a portion of an image and create a brush shape based on the grayscale information. Brushes cannot be created in color, however. An example of a useful brush shape is the maple leaves preset tip that ships with Photoshop and appears on the Brushes palette, as shown in Figure 3-9.

These types of brushes are excellent brushes to use with scattering and color jitter options. Figure 3-10 shows this brush tip painted as a scatter brush.

Creating Your Own Brush Tip   Brushes are not limited to basic shapes. You can select portions of images and turn them into custom brushes, too. This can open up a whole new world of creative options.

1. Open an image.

2. Using a marquee tool, select a portion of an image that you want to use as a brush tip, as shown in Figure 3-11.

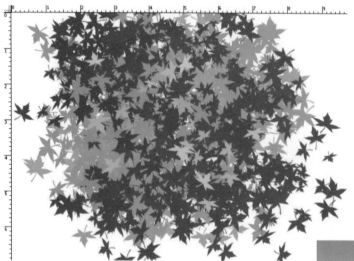

FIGURE 3-10 Maple leaves with the Scatter Brush option

FIGURE 3-11 Selecting a portion of an image

3. Choose Edit | Define Brush Preset. The Brush Name dialog box will open.

4. Type in a name for your brush. The brush is now ready for use.

5. Open the image you want to work on, or create a new image file.

6. Choose the Brush tool.

7. Scroll through the brushes in the Options palette until you find the new brush you just created.

8. Choose a size, as shown in Figure 3-12.

9. Choose the foreground color.

10. Begin to draw, as shown in Figure 3-13, by either

   ■ Clicking once in the image to make a single reproduction of the shape

   ■ Dragging the mouse to make a trail

FIGURE 3-12 Choosing the custom brush size

Master Diameter				353 px	

Use Sample Size

Hardness:

13	14	16	17	18	21
21	24	27	28	35	36
45	48	60	65	100	200
300	100	145	836		

FIGURE 3-13 Drawing with the new brush

FIGURE 3-14 The Eraser tool: (A) Brush mode, (B) Pencil mode, (C) Block mode

Eraser Tool

The Eraser tool functions exactly like the Brush tool, except instead of drawing, you use the Eraser tool for...*erasing*. If you are working on a flattened image, the Eraser tool will erase to the current background color. If you are working on a layer, the tool will erase to transparent.

The Eraser tool works in three different modes, as illustrated by Figure 3-14:

- **Brush mode**   Use the currently selected brush as an eraser that takes on the brush's attributes.

- **Pencil mode**   Use the currently selected brush with 100% hardness.

- **Block mode**   The eraser is a 15×15 pixel square with hard edges.

A.   B.   C.

Smudge, Sharpen, and Blur Tools

These three painting tools don't create any paint (with the exception of the Smudge tool with Finger Painting turned on). Instead, these tools simply modify existing pixels in various ways. They are useful drawing tools that, when used in conjunction with the paint brushes, let you create some interesting effects.

The Smudge Tool

The Smudge tool achieves the effect of dragging an object or your finger through wet paint. You can use it in standard mode, in which it will smudge the existing pixels, or you can choose the Finger Painting mode.

 When using the Finger Painting mode, some of the foreground color will initially be added to the stroke. The amount will depend on the Strength setting.

Figure 3-15 shows the result of using the Smudge tool used to create the illusion of fire. To create this effect, simply make a ring of color and then drag with the Smudge tool, wiggling the mouse on the way out to create the wavy flames.

FIGURE 3-15 Fire created with the Smudge tool

The Sharpen Tool

The Sharpen tool will sharpen any areas that you brush over. It is best to start with a softer setting and build up the sharpness. Adjust the Strength to change the intensity of the effect.

The Blur Tool

The Blur tool is the exact opposite of the Sharpen tool; you use it to soften pixels you paint over. You can work either on the selected layer or check Use All Layers to work on the entire image. This is a good tool to use for touching up wrinkles or other blemishes on faces. In Figure 3-16, the Blur tool was used to soften lines around the subject's eyes. In a real-word situation, you probably wouldn't want to blur quite as much as I did here, but I wanted to emphasize the effect.

Dodge, Burn, and Sponge Tools

These three tools alter the tonality and color saturation of the pixels to which they are applied. They are favorites for touching up photographs.

The Dodge and Burn tools derive their names from the photographic darkroom. These tools both share the same options and allow you to affect either the highlights, midtones,

A.

B.

FIGURE 3-16 The lines around the eyes, before and after blurring
(A) Before
(B) After

or the shadows in an image. Use these tools to brush over portions of the image to increase shadow or highlight detail.

■ **Burn tool**   In the darkroom, photographers will cup their fingers over the light to concentrate it on certain areas to "darken up" parts of the image. You use the Burn tool to darken up areas of images.

■ **Dodge tool**   In a darkroom, objects are placed in front of the developing light to lighten the images in certain places. When you use the Dodge tool on an image, it will lighten the tonality of the areas to which it is applied.

FIGURE 3-17 Dodging and burning an image: (A) the original image; (B) result of the Burn tool; (C) result of the Dodge tool

A.

Sponge tool The Sponge tool allows you to change the saturation (the amount of color used) of the brushed area of an image. The middle image in Figure 3-18A shows an image with the tool set to Saturate—notice how the brushed portion of the image has denser color than the rest of the image. In the opposite manner, the rightmost image in Figure 3-18B shows the same image with the option set to Desaturate; notice that virtually no color appears in the brushed areas.

B.

C.

A.

B.

C.

FIGURE 3-18 The Sponge tool, (A) original image; (B) Saturate; and (C) Desaturate

Gradient Tools

Gradients are the gradations between colors or blends that you see. Gradients add a lot of visual interest to images and break up flat color. They can also give the illusion of light falling on a surface.

To use the gradients, click the Gradient tool in the tool palette. The options bar will show all the Gradient options, as shown in Figure 3-19.

FIGURE 3-19 Gradient options bar

- **Current Gradient**   Shows a preview of the currently selected gradient.

- **Linear, Radial, Angle, Reflected, Diamond**   Types of gradients. We will look at these in a moment.

- **Blending Modes**

- **Opacity**   Indicates how solid or transparent you want to make the gradient.

- **Reverse**   Flips the gradient.

- **Dither**   Adds some "noise" to the gradient to reduce banding. *Banding* occurs when the color changes are abrupt and you can see the bands of separate colors.

- **Transparency**   Makes a part of the gradient transparent.

Applying a Gradient

Let's apply a gradient to an image.

1. Choose the Gradient tool from the tool palette.

2. Select the options.

3. Choose a gradient from the options. If you click the gradient preview, you will see the available gradients, as shown in Figure 3-20.

▦ Note that two standard options work off the current foreground and background colors. These are "foreground to background" and "background to transparent."

▦ The rest of the presets are custom presets based on actual colors.

4. Choose a gradient type. The types are shown in Figures 3-21A-E.

FIGURE 3-20 Gradient chooser

A.   B.   C.   D.   E.

5. Click and drag the mouse in the direction you want the gradient to flow.

6. Release the mouse and the gradient will be drawn.

FIGURE 3-21 Gradients: (A) Linear; (B) Radial; (C) Angle; (D) Reflected; (E) Diamond

Creating a Gradient

You can create your own custom gradients. It's useful to be able to modify gradients and create custom gradients that will work perfectly for your needs.

FIGURE 3-22 Gradient Editor

1. Open the Gradient Editor shown in Figure 3-22 by double-clicking the gradient preview in the options bar.

2. Choose a Gradient Type from the drop-down list.

3. The gradients are controlled by *color stops*. Each stop has a color assigned to it. The gradient will produce a smooth blend between the color stops. Now create a color stop by clicking anywhere beneath the gradient bar in the middle

FIGURE 3-23 Adding a color stop

FIGURE 3-24 Changing the color of a stop

FIGURE 3-25 Creating more color stops

of the Gradient Editor. In Figure 3-23, a new color stop is being added.

4. Click the color stop to select it.

5. Click the color swatch next to the word Color and choose a color; or choose Other to open the Color Picker.

6. Choose a color from the Color Picker. The color is now applied to the color stop and affects the gradient, as shown in Figure 3-24.

7. Add more color stops and colorize each one, as shown in Figure 3-25. You can also add a transparent stop by reducing the opacity to 0.

8. You can slide the color stops along the gradient by clicking and dragging them.

9. Move the Color midpoints to adjust the fall-off on the gradients, as shown in Figure 3-26.

10. The midpoints will appear as small diamonds on each side of the selected color stop. These midpoints control the middle point of the blend.

11. Name your gradient in the Name field.

12. Click New to save your new gradient. You will see your gradient in the thumbnail library.

Using Blending Modes

By using the blending modes, you can create some interesting effects with gradients. See Chapter 5 for more complete information on all the blending modes. Figure 3-27 used the new gradient created in the previous section. The blending mode was set to Multiply and the same gradient was applied multiple times in different directions.

FIGURE 3-26 Adjusting the Color midpoints

Shape Tools

Photoshop lets you draw basic shapes quickly by using the shape tools, which are accessed from the tool palette. After you have selected one of these tools, you can easily switch among different shapes from the options bar, as shown in Figure 3-28. To draw with these tools, click and drag in your document and the shapes will be created using the current foreground color.

FIGURE 3-27 The gradient applied multiple times in Multiply mode

FIGURE 3-28 Shape tool options

There are five basic Shape tools:

- **Rectangle** Produces rectangles and squares.

- **Rounded Rectangle** Creates a rectangle with rounded corners. You can set the radius of the corners in the options bar. This tool is excellent for creating buttons for web pages.

- **Oval** Creates ovals and circles.

- **Polygon** Draws different polygon shapes; you can draw polygon with three (triangle) to 100 (circle) sides.

- **Line** Draws straight lines; choose the thickness from the options bar. You can also add arrowheads to one of both ends.

Using the Shape Tools

Using the shape tools is a simple process:

1. Choose the foreground color.

3

2. Choose one of the shape tools.

3. Choose the Pixels option from the options bar.

4. Click and drag inside your image.

5. Release the mouse, and the shape will be drawn in the foreground color.

Hold down the SHIFT *key to constrain the proportions of the shape tools to draw precise squares and circles.*

Creating Custom Shapes

FIGURE 3-29 Select a shape

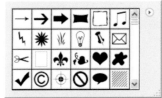

If you want to create something a bit more complex than the simple shape tools allow, use the custom shape tools. Photoshop ships with a few shapes ready for your use, but you can load more and even create your own. See Chapter 7 for more details and options on shape tools.

1. Choose the Custom Shape tool.

2. Click the arrow to the right of the Shape box to select a shape, as shown in Figure 3-29.

3. Choose a foreground color.

4. Click and drag the mouse in the document, and you will see an outline of a shape. Release the mouse and the shape is drawn, as shown in Figure 3-30.

FIGURE 3-30 Drag the mouse to create the shape (A), and the finished custom shape (B)

A.

B.

For more on using shapes, see Chapter 7.

Transform Tool

When you create any object or open an image in Photoshop, you can transform them later using two levels of transformations: basic and advanced.

Basic transformations include scaling, rotating, and flipping. Advanced transformations include skewing, perspective, and distortion. We will look at each of these techniques and how to create them in this section.

Basic: Rotating and Flipping

The controls for rotating and flipping images can be found by choosing Image | Rotate Canvas.

We will walk through each of these options, using Figure 3-31 as a visual guide.

Four rotate options are available: three set rotations and one customizable rotation. The main three rotations are used mainly for images that have been scanned upside down or at the wrong orientation.

- **180** Rotates image 180 degrees, as shown in Figure 3-32

- **90 CW** Rotates image 90 degrees clockwise

- **90 CCW** Rotates image 90 degrees counter-clockwise

Arbitrary lets you enter the angle of the rotation. When you choose this option, you will see the Rotate Canvas dialog box like the one shown in Figure 3-33A.

Choose the angle and the direction you want to rotate the image. Click OK and your image will be rotated, as shown in Figure 3-33B.

FIGURE 3-31 The image before any transformations are applied

FIGURE 3-32 Rotated 180 degrees

B.

A.

The final settings are Flip Canvas Horizontal and Flip Canvas Vertical. Choose these options to flip the image. Figure 3-34 shows the image flipped on the horizontal axis.

Free Transform Tool

A more advanced tool for transforming your objects in Photoshop is the Free Transform tool. This tool works only on layered objects. You can do a variety of transformations using the Free Transform tool.

FIGURE 3-33 An image rotated 25 degrees clockwise
(A) Enter your settings
(B) The result of rotation

 Refer to Chapter 4 for more information on basic layers.

FIGURE 3-34 Flipping the canvas horizontally

Press CTRL-T (CMD-T on the Mac) to enter Free Transform mode. When Free Transform is activated, a *bounding box* appears around your object. You will also see eight little squares on the corners and sides of the bounding box; these are the *adjustment handles*. Figure 3-35A shows the bounding box and adjustment handles. By clicking and dragging these handles, you can perform the following transformations:

- **Rotate**   When you hover your mouse outside the bounding box on one of the corners, you will see a double-sided, curved arrow that indicates that you are ready to rotate. Click and drag your mouse in either a clockwise or counter-clockwise direction to rotate the layer, as shown in Figure 3-35B.

- **Scale sides**   Click and drag on any of the side handles to adjust the width or height of the object, as shown in Figure 3-35C.

■ **Scale a corner** If you adjust one of the corner handles, both the height and width will be adjusted at the same time, as shown in Figure 3-35D. This is a good way to resize an image. If you hold down the SHIFT key while dragging, the proportions will remain even.

More advanced transform options are also available:

1. Press CTRL-T (CMD-T on the Mac), or choose Edit | Free Transform to enter Free Transform mode.

2. Right-click (CONTROL-click on the Mac) anywhere inside the free transform bounding box.

3. You will see the drop-down menu as shown in Figure 3-36.

4. Choose any option from the menu to control how the adjustment handles will work.

A.

B.

C.

D.

A.

Free Transform

Scale
Rotate
Skew
Distort
Perspective

Rotate 180°
Rotate 90° CW
Rotate 90° CCW

Flip Horizontal
Flip Vertical

FIGURE 3-35 Free transform options
(A) Free Transform mode
(B) Rotate
(C) Scale Side
(D) Scale Corner

FIGURE 3-36 Advanced Free Transform options
(A) Menu
(B) Skew
(C) Distort
(D) Perspective

B.

C.

D.

- **Skew**   Drag any of the side handles, and the shape will be distorted into a parallelogram.

- **Distort**   Choose Distort, and each adjustment handle will operate independently, which allows for a free range of distortion.

- **Perspective**   Drag one corner, and the opposite corner will also move to mirror your transformation; this creates the perspective effect that is useful to achieve the illusion of size in an object.

 Transformations can also be performed by changing the settings in the options bar; this provides a way for you to achieve precision results.

Patterns

Repeating patterns make a good alternative to color and gradients for filling objects. Any image can be turned into a pattern, and Photoshop ships with a number of patterns. Patterns are fairly simple to use and easy to create.

Using Patterns

The most common place to use patterns is from the Fill dialog box (choose Edit | Fill), shown in Figure 3-37. The available patterns can be seen in the pattern library, which is accessed via the Custom Pattern drop-down list. Here's how you use a pattern.

FIGURE 3-37 The Fill dialog box's pattern library

1. If you don't want to apply the pattern to the entire page, make a selection.

2. Choose Edit | Fill.

3. From the Use drop-down box, choose Pattern.

4. Open the Custom Pattern drop-down list by clicking the arrow. You will see the library.

5. To apply a pattern, click any of the thumbnails.

6. Click OK to apply the pattern as shown in Figure 3-37.

 Notice that the pattern repeats and fills the page or the selection in a seamless way. All the patterns that ship with Photoshop will repeat seamlessly.

Creating Patterns

You can also create your own patterns. This is a useful way to customize the appearance of objects and backgrounds. By using patterns, you can save a lot of time, because you don't need to re-create the same object or shape over and over again. Here's how to create your own pattern:

FIGURE 3-38 Creating a new Document

1. Create a new document; for this example, make it 2×2 pixels. This will make a pattern with very fine detail.

2. Zoom into 1600%, as shown in Figure 3-38.

3. Create your pattern. For this exercise, the Pencil tool was set to 1 single pixel width, and used to create a black-and-white stripe, as shown in Figure 3-39.

FIGURE 3-39 Creating a pattern

4. Press CTRL-A (CMD-A on the Mac) to select the entire document.

5. Choose Edit | Define Pattern.

6. In the Pattern Name dialog box shown in Figure 3-40, enter a name for your pattern.

FIGURE 3-40 Defining a pattern

7. Click OK; your pattern will be saved to the pattern library. Close the pattern document.

Figure 3-41 shows the pattern we created in the Fill dialog box and displayed on a page.

FIGURE 3-41 (A) The pattern in the Fill dialog box and (B) on its own page

A.

B.

Figure 3-42 shows an example of what you can do with patterns. This grid pattern was created and used for the background.

FIGURE 3-42 Example of a pattern in use

FIGURE 3-43 The Preset Manager

Loading and Saving Patterns

You can save your pattern sets or load new ones. Extra patterns come with Photoshop, and you can also find them from third-party products, such as on the CD PhotoshopCAFE Live, available from http://www.photoshopcd.com.

To manage your patterns (and a lot more), open the Preset Manager by choosing Edit | Preset Manager. You will see the dialog box shown in Figure 3-43.

Loading Patterns

Let's load some patterns in the Preset Manager.

1. Open the Preset Manager.

2. Choose the Patterns Preset Type.

3. To load the sets that come with Photoshop, click the arrow at the top right to open the drop-down menu. Choose any of the pattern sets from the list to load them.

4. To load the sets from an external source, click Load. Navigate to the location of the pattern sets. Then click Load again.

5. Choose Append or Replace: Append will add the pattern to your existing library, and Replace will reset your library with only the new patterns.

You can also perform the same tasks from the Fill dialog box, as shown in Figure 3-44.

FIGURE 3-44 Managing patterns from the Fill dialog box

Saving Patterns

To save your patterns in the Preset Manager:

1. Open the Preset Manager.

2. Choose the Patterns Preset Type.

3. Select the patterns you want to save. You can CTRL-click (CMD-click on the Mac) to select multiple patterns.

4. Choose Save Set from the menu.

5. Save the pattern set to your hard drive.

You can also save the patterns from the Fill dialog box; however, you can save only the entire library, you cannot save individual patterns from this dialog box.

History

Who said that time travel isn't possible? It is possible in Photoshop, via the History palette, which saves the most recent versions of the image. Each version is called a *history state*. You can choose the number of history states to save in the Preferences dialog box. Whenever you make any changes to the image, a new state is created with the name of the edit next to it.

FIGURE 3-45 History Palette

FIGURE 3-46 A new snapshot

FIGURE 3-47 Hue/Saturation history state (A) and original history state (B)

History Palette

Figure 3-45 shows the History palette with an image that was opened and then had a Hue/Saturation adjustment applied to it.

The only drawback with the History palette occurs when you have reached the set number of history states: each new edit will replace the oldest state in the palette—in essence, your history states are cycled. Fortunately, a solution to that problem is available. It's called *taking a snapshot*. A snapshot is a state that is saved independently from the revolving history states. In the History palette, click the camera icon and a new "snapshot" of the image will be taken. In the top frame of the History palette in Figure 3-46, you can see the original image and a new snapshot.

To view the history states, click the names of the states, as shown in Figures 3-47A and B. Notice that the current state will be displayed in the main window and the selected state is highlighted in blue in the History palette.

When you have chosen a history state, you can either

- Continue working on the image from the selected history state—in essence, performing a multiple undo.
- Take a snapshot of the history state.
- Click the button on the upper-left corner of the History palette to create a new document from the history state. This new document will be totally independent from the working image. All layers will be preserved in this new document.

History Brush

To paint with the History brush, you will need to choose a history state to work from. To choose a state, click in the well to the left of the history state in the History palette. You will see an icon of a brush with a circular arrow around it, as shown in Figure 3-48. This indicates that you are painting from this state. You can now paint just as you would with any other brush. Unlike other brushes, though, instead of painting with color, you will be painting with a previous version of the image. This is like the selective undo tool in Photoshop.

Let's do some work with the History brush:

1. Open an image.

2. Choose Image | Adjust | Hue/Saturation.

3. Click Colorize and slide the Hue slider to the color red.

4. Open the History palette.

5. Choose Create Snapshot of the Hue/Saturation state.

6. Select the original image state with the painting indicator.

7. Choose the History brush.

8. Select the appropriate size.

9. Begin painting on the image. You should see the full-color image come back to the areas you are painting, as shown in Figure 3-49.

FIGURE 3-48 Choosing a state for the History brush

FIGURE 3-49 Painting with the History brush

Roayfty Free Images from Hemera™

You can use the History brush for all kinds of things. Experiment with running filters over the image and painting back in portions of the image. Also, try painting from several history states into one image.

Art History Brush

This brush works the same as the History brush except it lets you specify different types of brush strokes that mimic Impressionist art brushes.

FIGURE 3-50 A new snapshot in the History palette

1. Open an image you want to turn into a painting.

2. If you have resized the image, such as the image shown in the History palette in Figure 3-50, you will have to create a new snapshot. (The History brush will not work from a resized or rotated image without a new snapshot.)

3. Choose the snapshot as your source image (history state).

4. From the tool palette, choose the Art History brush.

5. Choose one of the brush strokes from the options bar. You can experiment with the strokes to find the best one to use for your image.

6. Choose a fairly large brush and paint over the entire image.

7. You should see the image start to form as a painting, similar to the image shown in Figure 3-51.

FIGURE 3-51 Using a large brush size

8. Choose a smaller brush and paint over the detailed areas. The smaller the brush, the more detail will show in the image.

Figure 3-52 shows the completed image.

FIGURE 3-52 Painting with the Art History brush

Part II

Beyond the Basics

Chapter 4

Use Layers
in Photoshop

How To…

- Understand layers
- Change the thumbnail sizes
- Rename layers
- Create and delete layers
- Duplicate layers
- Show and hide layers
- Work with multiple layers
- Link layers
- Align and evenly distribute objects
- Center objects on a page
- Manage your layers
- Use layer sets
- Merge layers

In the pre-Photoshop 3 days, artists and designers with change-happy clients had to produce everything without the luxury of layers. I was one of those lucky designers who would complete a job, only to have a client then ask something like, "Could you increase the size of the font on the heading?" With layers, it takes just a couple of clicks to make such as change. Before layers, making this kind of change was a major undertaking. Before layers, everything was one, flat image—like a photograph. If you tried to cut and move an object, it would leave a ghastly hole, much as if you were to take a pair of scissors to a photograph.

Layers Explained

Imagine a pile of photographs lying on top of each other—layers of photographs. As you move a photo to the top of the pile, it hides the other photos underneath it. Now imagine each

FIGURE 4-1 Three images showing three layers in a Photoshop document Layers window

photo in the stack mounted on a sheet of glass a bit larger than the photo. As you move the glass-mounted photos around, you'll notice that even a photo that's not on top may become visible through or around other photos above it, while other photos are still obscured. Think of each photo as being part of a separate layer, and each layer can be moved to hide or show other layers below and around it.

Now imagine that rather than photos mounted on sheets of glass, you are using images in a Photoshop document, as shown in Figure 4-1. In Photoshop, a layer is always transparent until you put something on it. In this case, we have imported three photos and placed them on three separate layers—that is, "image data" now appears on each layer. Each layer remains transparent where no image data appears, and other layers will show through.

Using Layers in the Layers Palette

You deal with layers via the Layers palette, which is shown in Figure 4-2. In a nutshell, the order of the thumbnails on the Layers palette represents the order that the layers appear in the layer "stack" in the Workspace. Later in this chapter, you'll learn to change the order of the layers by moving a thumbnail image on the palette; as you do this, the image itself will change position on the stack in the Workspace.

In the Layers palette, each layer's name appears next to a thumbnail, as shown in Figure 4-2. (Don't worry too much about all the other options, as we will get to most of them in this and future chapters.)

Blending mode
Locking options
Thumbnail
Show/hide layer
Layer indicator

Palette options menu
Opacity slider
Fill transparency slider
Active layer
Locked layer

New layer set
Create mask
Layer effects

Adjustment layer
New layer
Delete layer (the trash can)

FIGURE 4-2 The Layers palette

Changing the Thumbnail Sizes

You can adjust the size of the thumbnails in the Layers palette, making them larger so their contents are easier to see and making them smaller (if you are working with a lot of layers) so that they take up less space. Here's how:

1. Click the arrow at the top right of the Layers palette. This is the palette options button.

2. From the drop-down menu that opens, choose Palette Options.

3. In the Layers Palette Options dialog shown at the top of the following page, choose the radio button of the new size for the thumbnails. For this example, choose the largest thumbnail size option, and then click OK.

4. The Layers palette appears with large thumbnail previews, as shown in the second illustration.

Note that in the Options dialog in step 3, you can choose None to save screen real estate if you are working on a small screen or using a lot of layers. This will default to a name only, and no thumbnail image will appear on the Layers palette.

Creating and Deleting Layers

You can create new layers in Photoshop in several ways:

- Click the new layer button in the Layers palette (see Figure 4-2).
- From the main menu, choose Layer | New | Layer.
- From the Layers palette's palette options menu, choose New Layer.
- Press SHIFT-CTRL-N (SHIFT-CMD-N on the Mac).
- Drag a layer from another document.

To delete a layer, drag it to the Delete layer (the trash can) at the bottom of the Layers palette.

Renaming Layers

When you create a new layer, it will have the default name "Layer *x*" (*x* being the next incremental number). After you have created ten or more layers in an image, it can be tricky trying to remember what "Layer 6" means, even with the thumbnail preview. To help you keep track of your layers, you

can give them meaningful names. The kind folks at Adobe listened to users, and in version 7 they brought back the simple renaming technique that was removed from version 6. To change the name of a layer, simply double-click the layer's name in the Layers palette and type in the new name. Figure 4-3 shows the palette with a rename in process.

FIGURE 4-3 Naming your layers will help you keep track of them.

Changing a Layer Color

You can also choose colors for the layers. This color coding is useful, for example, if several people are working on the same image—each worker could use a particular color. Or you could use the colors to identify revision versions or portions of an image, for example. You can also color code the layers to help keep track of them.

To choose a color for a layer:

1. Right click (Control-Click on the Mac) on the layer in the layer palette.

2. Choose "layer properties" from the pop-up menu.

3. Click the colors option and choose a color.

4. Click OK.

Duplicating Layers

You can duplicate layers in several ways:

- To make and exact copy of a layer, drag the layer to the new layer icon at the bottom of the Layers palette. The duplicate layer will have the same name as the original with the word *copy* appended to the end of its name, as shown in the first illustration:

- Use the keyboard shortcut: Highlight the layer on the Layers palette, and then press CTRL-J (CMD-J on the Mac).

- Copy all or part of a layer's contents onto a new layer (discussed in the next section).

- Cut and paste a layer (discussed on the following page).

Copying a Selection of a Layer

You can copy the entire layer or a portion of a layer onto a new layer without changing the contents of the existing layer. (For more information about selections, see the section "Selecting Layers" later in this chapter.)

1. Choose the target layer (the layer you want to copy) by clicking the layer's thumbnail to highlight it, as shown in the second illustration. (You can edit only the selected layer.)

2. From the document window, make a selection on the layer, using any of the selection tools, as shown in the illustration at left.

3. From the Main menu, choose Layer | New | Layer Via Copy, or press CTRL-J (CMD-J on the Mac).

Only the selected portion of the layer will be *copied* to a new layer, as you can see in the illustration on the right. (Note that I moved the new layer contents so you could see the result; the copied layer appears in the same position as the original— so you can't really see it until you move it.)

Cutting and Pasting a Duplicate Layer

To cut a selection from a layer, you mark the selection with any marquee tool. Then choose Layer | New | Layer Via Cut shown in the illustration, left.

When you *cut* a selection from a layer, instead of making a *copy* of the selection, it will actually *move* the selected area to a new layer. This means that the pixels are removed from your existing layer and pasted onto a new layer, as shown here.

Changing the Layer Stacking Order

To change the order of layers, just click and drag a layer in the Layers palette.

1. Click and hold down the left mouse button over the name of the layer you want to move.

2. Without releasing the mouse button, drag the layer to the desired location in the palette. Choose the space at the top or bottom of an existing layer to target the new location.

3. Let go of the mouse button and the layer will move to the desired order in the thumbnail layers and in the stack.

To move a layer up or down the stack in the Layers palette, you can press and hold CTRL (CMD on a Mac) over the layer, and then press the left and right bracket keys on the keyboard.

Working with the Background Layer

In the Layers palette, the background layer is identified by the word *Background* in italics and displays a small padlock icon. The background layer is flattened by default. Its position is fixed and it does not support any transparency.

The background functions much like other layers, in that you can fill it with color and place images on it. However, the background layer has a few limitations:

FIGURE 4-4 The background layer cannot be moved to another level.

- The background layer is always at the bottom of the stack, and you cannot move it. If you try to move it, you will see the "no" icon, as shown in Figure 4-4.

- Transparency is not available for the background layer, and you cannot adjust the opacity (transparency).

- The background is always locked; you cannot change the position of objects on the background.

- Blending modes may not be applied to the background.

Changing the Background to a Normal Layer

You can change a background layer into a normal layer.

1. Double-click the Background layer in the Layers palette.

2. In the "New Layer" dialog box that opens, click OK or press ENTER.

3. The background will be converted to a regular layer, and you can then manipulate it as a regular layer.

Showing and Hiding Layers

A great feature in Photoshop is the ability to hide layers temporarily without deleting them. This allows for great artistic experimentation, because you can include as many layers as you want in your project and display only the ones you choose. In this illustration, all three layers are displayed.

The key to hiding or displaying is the little eye icon, called the layer visibility icon, that appears to the left of each thumbnail in the Layers palette. To hide or show a layer, you simply click the icon to toggle the layer visibility off and on. In the illustration at left, the city layer is being hidden in the Layers palette.

The result of hiding this layer is shown in the second illustration. As you can see, one of the images is now hidden.

Partially Hiding Layers with the Opacity Slider

You can also hide layers by using the opacity slider in the Layers palette.

By using the opacity slider, shown in Figure 4-5, you can reduce the opacity of a layer to hide it.

Reducing the opacity of layers can have both creative and practical uses. You can use the opacity slider to blend images together in interesting ways. You can also reduce the opacity of an image to "ghost" it for practical purposes. For example, suppose you are working on a layer and need to show a hint of the underlying layers to help you position the layer. Figure 4-6 shows the Document window, with the top layer set at 50 percent opacity. You can see the layer below it.

FIGURE 4-6 By dragging the slider, you control the opacity of a layer's contents.

FIGURE 4-5 A layer at 50 percent opacity allows the layers beneath to show through.

Note *Because opacity is the opposite of transparency, the terms are interchangeable as far as the results of the slider go. (So, 100 percent opaque is the same as 0 percent transparent, 0 percent opacity equals 100 percent transparency, and 50 percent opaque is identical to 50 percent transparent.)*

To hide all the layers except for the layer you are currently working on, right-click the working layer's visibility icon and choose Show/Hide All Other Layers.

Working with Multiple Layers

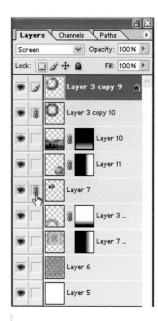

We have looked at the basics of working with individual layers, but you can also perform tasks on multiple layers at once. Many tools in Photoshop can help you save time by allowing you to work with multiple layers at once.

Linking Layers

Once you delve into Photoshop and create more complex images, you may need to reposition, align, and transform more than one layer at a time. The ability to link layers lets you do this with ease.

To link layers, you simply click one of the layers to start the link. This is called the *active* layer. To link any other layer to the active layer, you simply click the little box directly to the left of the thumbnail and a chain icon will appear there, indicating that the layers are linked. Figure 4-7 shows some linked layers in the Layers palette. Figure 4-8 shows the document window with a working background image; the layer showing a ring with the "Photoshop Café" label is linked to the camera layer. Although you can't necessarily see the links in the images shown in Figure 4-8, you can use Figure 4-8 for context as we move the images around in a bit.

FIGURE 4-7 Layers linked in the Layers palette

 You can link as many layers as you wish. To unlink a layer, just click its chain icon.

The two linked layers will now be treated as one single layer when you want to work on positioning and transforming. To move the layers at once, you simply click one of the linked images in the document window and drag it to a new location. Notice in Figure 4-9 that the two linked layers have moved as a single layer.

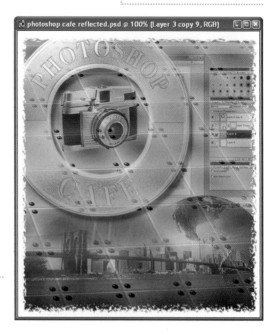

FIGURE 4-8 The working image with linked layers (although you can't really see this here)

FIGURE 4-9 The linked layers have been moved as a single unit.

FIGURE 4-10 Linked layers can be transformed together.

Similarly, as shown in Figure 4-10, the linked layers can be scaled, rotated, or distorted and they will all be transformed together. Here the linked images are reduced in size.

If your file size is getting too big and things start to grind to a slow crawl, you can merge some layers to lighten the computer's load a little. Be sure that you have saved a copy of the image first.

Aligning and Evenly Distributing Objects

When you're working with multiple layers, you may find that you need to line up several objects or space several objects evenly in the document. You could draw grids and guides and do the math to figure out exactly where to line up everything, but a better way is to take advantage of the align and distribute tools provided in Photoshop. These options appear in the options bar when the move tool is active. The tools will be dimmed unless two layers have been linked; at that point, the align tools are available. At least three layers must be linked to make the distribute tools available (see Figure 4-11).

Let's walk through these options.

1. We begin by opening a document with several objects that we can arrange. In this case, we'll use the document shown in the following illustration. We'll align all the colored buttons horizontally and space them evenly.

FIGURE 4-11 The align and distribute tools

2. We link only the layers that we want to be affected (see illustration at right).

3. Now we click the align top tool.

All the linked objects are now aligned horizontally.

4. Now we want to space the buttons evenly. We click the distribute horizontal center tool to do this.

The buttons in our document are now aligned horizontally and spaced evenly.

When linking several sequential layers, you can click and drag down the layer column to link the layers instead of clicking each one separately.

Centering Objects on a Page

Here is a little trick you can use to place objects exactly in the center of the page.

1. Click the background and link it with the objects you want to move.

 2. Choose the Align Vertical center button and click it.

Now all the objects are aligned to the center of the page.

 Being a successful designer requires more than just being good at design. You also have to be fast, and learning to use tools like distribute and align tools will save you lots of time.

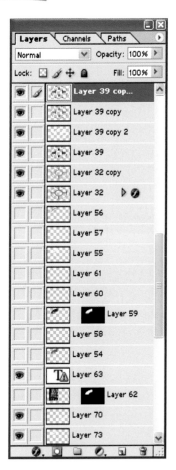

How does this work? Remember that the background cannot be moved. Because of this, when you choose the align vertical center tool, all the other layers are forced to move instead. All this aligning took only a few mouse clicks and produced a precise result.

Managing Layers

If you're like me, by the end of a working day your desk is covered in clutter—junk mail, notes, and unread mail are strewn all over the place. You start to feel choked by the mess until you clean it up. Some more organized people deal with paperwork by using the two-step rule: either file it or throw it in the trash. To be most effective in managing your projects, you can apply the same rule with your Photoshop documents. You can accumulate many layers in a document: some are failed experiments and others are changes. Fortunately, Photoshop has the tools to help you organize your layers.

In this section, we will learn to "file or trash it" with our Photoshop layers. At left is a typical Layers palette during a reasonably sized job. You can see how large it can grow.

Deleting Unused Layers

You can easily delete all unused layers in one click in the Layers palette by opening the Palette options menu and choosing Delete Hidden Layers, as shown next.

This will trim down the file size and free up your computer's resources.

Before you delete, make sure that you really won't need to use these layers, because once you delete them and turn off your computer, they're gone forever.

Empty layers do not take up any space; it is only the content in the layers that adds to the file size.

You can also use a couple of other methods to delete layers:

- Drag individual layers to the trash can at the bottom of the Layers palette.

- Link the unwanted layers and choose Delete Linked Layers from the Palette options menu.

Creating Layer Sets

The Layers palette can be treated much like a file cabinet for your layers. You can create folders called *layer sets* that hold your layers, much like a manila folder holds documents in your file cabinet. Let's create a layer set.

1. On the Layers palette, click the new layer set button.

2. On the palette, you will see a folder with a downward facing arrow, named Set 1, shown in the bottom illustration. This is our layer set. It is currently empty.

3. To move layers from other parts of the Layers palette into the layer set, simply drag and drop them into the Set 1 folder. Each of the layers in the set will be displayed below the folder.

4. To change the stacking order in the set, drag the layers into new positions. Remember that if you change stacking order, the order of image layers will change in the document (see first illustration).

5. To save space in the Layers palette, you can collapse the expanded layer set. Click the downward-facing arrow, and it will become a right-facing arrow (see second illustration). All the layer thumbnails in the set are hidden away. To expand, just click the arrow again.

Nested Layer Sets

A welcome new feature added to Photoshop CS is the ability to nest layer sets. By using nested layers, you can drag sets inside other sets to organize your work better. You can also nest folders inside nested folders. You can nest folders up to five levels deep. This will help you keep your files organized in a logical way.

Here's how to nest layer sets:

1. Create several layers.

2. Link the layers you want to include in the set.

3. From the Palette options menu, choose New Set From Linked.

4. A new folder will appear in the Layers palette with the linked layers inside. The folder will be named Set 1.

5. Add more layers to the set by dragging and dropping their folders into the new folder.

6. Remove layers from the set by dragging them out of the new folder to different locations in the Layers palette.

 You can reposition layer sets in the Layers palette by dragging the entire set, just as you would with a single layer. You can even drag a set into another Photoshop document and the entire set and its contents will be copied there.

Merging Layers

You might want to combine several layers into a single layer. This is called *merging* layers. When you merge layers, the contents of the merged layers become a single image on the *target* layer.

For example, you might find it handy to merge layers as you're linking together the parts of a logo. At right is an ad and logo for a fictitious guitar string company.

The logo is made up of three separate layers called Rectangle, DOGPAW, and Layer 2. Let's merge them into one single logo layer.

1. In the Layers palette, we first click the DOGPAW layer to indicate that it's the target link.

2. Then we link the layers that we want to merge with it: in this case, we link DOGPAW and Layer 3 shown in the lefthand illustration.

3. From the Palette options menu, choose Merge Linked shown in the center illustration.

4. The layers are now combined into one, and they take on the name of the target layer, DOGPAW, shown in the righthand illustration.

Merge Down

You can also merge layers by using the merge down option, which combines a layer with the target layer directly beneath it in the stack. To merge two layers, first select a layer in the Layers palette and then, from the Palette options menu, choose Merge Down, shown at left.

Notice that the layer took on the name and attributes of the target layer—the layer directly beneath it (see illustration directly below).

You can also press CTRL-E (CMD-E *on the Mac) after selecting a target layer to merge down.*

Selecting Layers

You can also create selections from layers. You can use selections to define parts of an image. All the image data inside the selection can be manipulated, while the area outside the selection is protected. Selections operate independently of the layers; after a selection is active, you can switch between layers and the selection will stay active until you turn it off. (Selections are so important that Chapter 10 is dedicated to the subject.)

I created the image shown at left in Photoshop. Notice the *51* on the door; it is on its own separate layer, and in this example, we'll make a selection around it.

The easiest way to load the selection is to CTRL-click (CMD-click on the Mac) the layer thumbnail in the Layers palette. Photoshop will automatically create a selection around the opaque areas of the layer in the document window.

When you hover your mouse over the thumbnail with CTRL (CMD on the Mac) key pressed, you will notice that a dashed square appears around the thumbnail (see top illustration). This indicates that you are about to create a selection.

You will now see what Photoshop users affectionately call "marching ants." These "ants" are not the kind that typically spoil a picnic; they are moving dotted lines that indicate that a selection has been applied to the document (see center illustration).

 To load a selection, you can also right-click the layer thumbnail and choose Select Layer Transparency.

Now that we've made a selection, let's explore what we can do with it.

1. Create a new layer.

2. Drag the layer to the top of the stack.

3. Fill the layer with gray. To do that, choose Edit | Fill and choose 50 percent gray from the "Contents" menu.

4. Drag the new layer onto the document.

The bottom illustration is another variation using selections.

We will get more into special effects in Part III of the book, "The Fun Stuff."

 For information about making a copy of a selection of a layer, see "Copying a Selection of a Layer" earlier in this chapter.

Chapter 5

Work with Advanced Layer Techniques

How to...

- Use special types of layers
- Create text layers
- Use shape layers
- Add adjustment layers
- Use layer masks
- Create clipping groups
- Use layer comps
- Understand layer blending modes
- Use blending modes for creative results

So far in this book, we have dealt with standard layers. These are all called *raster* layers because they are made out of *pixels*—the tiny squares that fill your screen and make up the images you see.

Photoshop images can be two types: *raster* (or *bitmapped*) and *vector* images. Raster images are made up of patterns of light and dark or various colored pixels arranged in a rectangular array. Vector images contain no pixels. Vectors are made of mathematical instructions that determine the position, length, and direction in which lines are drawn. Images are created with lines rather than with individual pixels. For example, to draw a line, you tell the program, "Place a point here, and now place one there." You then specify how thick you want the line and what color to use, and the line is drawn.

We will be getting deeper into the difference between the two types of images in Chapter 7. For now, you should know the following four points:

- A vector can be scaled without any loss of quality.
- A vector has a very sharp edge.
- The file size of vectors is very small.
- Most of the filters and transformations in Photoshop will not work with vector images.

These points are important to know because layers behave differently, depending on whether they're raster-based layers or vector-based layers. The manipulations you can make to objects on layers depend on their type. Let's look at some special layer types to see how this works.

Special Layer Types

Some Photoshop layers have special features that make them easier to work with. Some of these special features also help produce higher quality images than can be produced using standard layers alone.

Text Layers

A text layer is simply a layer that contains text. These are marvelous little inventions because they keep the text in an editable vector format. Text layers have three main advantages:

- Vectors are sharp, so the text is clear.
- You can scale text vectors up and down, with no loss of quality.
- If you make a typo, you can go back and change it later.

To create a text layer:

1. Click the Text tool from the tool palette.

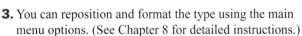

2. Click anywhere in the document window and begin typing.

3. You can reposition and format the type using the main menu options. (See Chapter 8 for detailed instructions.)

4. When you are done typing the text, you can apply it either by choosing any other tool from the tool palette or by clicking the checkmark from the right of the top toolbar.

FIGURE 5-1 A text layer is indicated by the letter *T*

When you add text to a document, Photoshop automatically creates a new layer. The layer is called a text layer and is indicated in the Layers palette by a large *T* next to the layer thumbnail, as shown in Figure 5-1. Whatever you type, up to 256 characters, becomes the layer name. A text layer can be linked, moved, and grouped exactly like a regular layer in Photoshop. It cannot have certain transformations and filters applied to it because it is in vector format, but you can apply the text warp and type on a path.

 If you merge a text layer with other layers, it will cease to be a text layer and the contents will be merged just like any other layer. This means you won't be able to edit misspellings or change any particular characters in the text.

Converting a Text Layer to a Regular Layer

As we already discussed, type in Photoshop is a vector object and is *resolution independent*. That means you can change the type size at any time without getting *jaggies* (pixelization or jagged edges). The type also remains editable as long as it's in a text layer. If you want to change the font, color, or your text characters, you can do that even after the document has been saved and re-opened.

When you rasterize type, it changes it from the mathematical vectors into pixels. The text layer changes to a *regular* layer. Once you have made that change, the text is no longer editable and behaves like a regular object layer. When you convert text to a rasterized type, you get a chance to rethink your options before you convert (shown right) once text is rasterized, it can no longer be edited.

To rasterize the text, right-click the layer name in the Layers palette and choose Rasterize Layer from the pop-up menu, as shown in Figure 5-2.

Once rasterized, the text layer will perform exactly like a regular layer, and the *T* indicator will be replaced by a regular thumbnail image, as shown in Figure 5-3.

For the most part, you could get away with keeping text layers. But sometimes you will need to rasterize the text to apply certain transformations. Some effects can be applied only to rasterized layers. These kinds of effects change the pixels, and they include the majority of plug-ins, filters, and shape transformations available in Photoshop.

FIGURE 5-2 Layers pop-up menu

If you always rasterize a duplicate of your text layer and keep the original text layer intact as a vector, you can hide the original and work with the copy. You could make a layer set and store all the original text in the folder. Then if you need to change the text in any way later, you will always have the original to go back to (more on text in Chapter 8).

FIGURE 5-3 After rasterizing

Shape Layers

Shape layers are similar to text layers in that they use vectors, and the same rules of vectors apply. A variety of tools can be used to draw vector shapes—from primitive shapes to custom shapes. Figure 5-4 shows the tools on the tool palette that can be used to create shape layers. To access the options, click and hold your mouse on the shape icon on the tool palette and the flyout menu will open.

Note *We look into all the features of shapes in Chapter 7.*

When one of the shape tools is selected, the options bar at the top of the Photoshop window will display all the options for the particular shape. The following illustration shows the available options.

FIGURE 5-4 The vector shape drawing tools

You will notice that you can change shape types from the options bar. Also take note of these three options:

- **Shape Layer**   Creates a new shape layer
- **Path**   Creates a path that follows the shape (see Chapter 7)
- **Fill Pixels**   Creates pixels like a brush would

To create a shape layer, first select the Shape Layer icon in the options bar. Then simply draw in the image area as you would using the regular tools. A new layer will automatically be created. Figure 5-5 shows a shape created with the Polygon tool. The shape will be filled with the foreground color and the edges will appear as a thin stroke. The stroke will not print and disappears when you select another layer. It appears only when the shape layer is active.

  You can also create rectangles, rounded rectangles, lines, circles, and custom shapes with the shape tools. These are covered in detail in Chapter 7.

When you create a shape with the shape tools, the Layers palette will display a special type of layer called a *shape* layer. Figure 5-6 shows a shape layer in the Layers palette.

A shape layer has two main parts:

- **Background** This contains the color of the object. This is an adjustment layer, and you can use a gradient, pattern, or any adjustment for this layer.

- **Vector shape** This can be easily modified. The vector can be distorted, rotated, scaled, and adjusted with no loss of quality. This shape clips out the background.

Shape layers can be organized much like other layers. Shape layers add practically nothing to the file size.

You can easily convert a shape layer to a regular layer, the same way you convert a text layer, by rasterizing it:

1. In the Layers palette, right-click (CONTROL-click on the Mac) on the layer name.

2. Choose Rasterize Layer from the drop-down menu. The shape layer is now a regular layer.

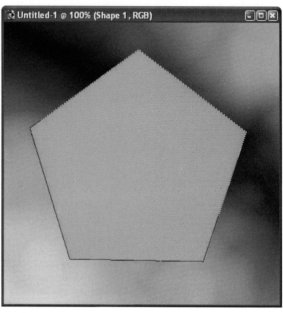

FIGURE 5-5 A vector polygon shape in a document

FIGURE 5-6 A shape layer in the Layers palette

Adjustment Layers

You use adjustment layers to make alterations to the tone and color of layers beneath the adjustment layer. An adjustment layer is *nondestructive*. This means that although the adjustment visually affects a layer, it will not alter the pixels in the actual image. This is good news, because every time you alter the pixels in an image you lose some quality.

If you make a change and then change your mind, you can make further adjustments or simply delete the adjustment layer and the original image will be preserved.

The primary uses for adjustment layers are enhancing and correcting photography, but they also have many creative uses. When you apply an adjustment layer, *it will affect all the layers*

FIGURE 5-7 The adjustment layers

Solid Color...
Gradient...
Pattern...

Levels...
Curves...
Color Balance...
Brightness/Contrast...

Hue/Saturation...
Selective Color...
Channel Mixer...
Gradient Map...

Invert
Threshold...
Posterize...

underneath it. The layer will also affect the entire image unless you make a selection before adding the adjustment layer. If you make a selection, only the selected portion will be affected.

To create an adjustment layer:

1. Click the Create Adjustment Layer button in the Layers palette (shown in Figure 5-7), or choose Layer | New Adjustment Layer.

2. You will see 14 possible options.

3. When you choose an option, its dialog box will open.

4. Make the adjustments and click OK.

The adjustment layer dialog boxes are the same dialog boxes you would find when you choose commands on the Image menu. Space limits us from looking at them all here, so you can experiment and look at them yourself. The main ones you will be using will be covered in depth in Chapter 12.

When an adjustment layer is applied to the document, it appears in the Layers palette with an icon showing what kind of adjustment was made.

- **Color**   Fills the layer with a solid color
- **Gradient**   Fills the layer with a color gradient
- **Pattern**   Fills the layer with a repeating pattern
- **Levels**   Adjusts the tones in an image
- **Curves**   Similar to levels, adjusts the tones, but with more precise control
- **Color Balance**   Handles basic color correction and shifting
- **Brightness/Contrast**   Brightens an image and adds contrast across the board
- **Hue/Saturation**   Controls color shifting and effects
- **Selective Color Options**   Adjusts process colors for printing
- **Channel Mixer**   Exercises precise control over the color channels
- **Gradient Map**   Replaces the color table in an image with a gradient

- **Photo Filter**   Creates photographic colorizing effects that resemble lens filters
- **Invert**   Inverts the colors and produces a negative effect
- **Threshold**   Converts to solid black and white and sets the shift point
- **Posterize**   Reduces the number of colors in each channel

Advanced Layer Features

By now, you should be getting the hang of layers and you should be ready to start with experimenting with them. This section introduces some of the more creative features of layers. A lot of the cool collages and images that have caught your attention were created using these tools. (Perhaps these are even the reason you have chosen to learn Photoshop.)

Layer Masks

Layer masks are among the most useful and misunderstood features of the Layers palette. These masks give you amazing control over the way layers interact with each other. Layer masks allow you to blend all or part of an effect or image to underlying layers. You can even adjust the opacity to just a section of a layer.

A layer mask can be filled with solid black or white and can contain up to 254 levels of gray. By default, a layer mask is filled with white, as shown in Figure 5-8, which has no effect on the parent layer.

If you were to fill the layer mask with solid black, as shown in Figure 5-9, its parent layer would be completely transparent. The layer mask will alter the transparency of the layer to which it is attached.

FIGURE 5-8 A layer mask filled with white has no effect.

The transparency is directly related to the amount of gray in the layer mask. For example, if the mask were filled with 50 percent gray, the layer would be 50 percent transparent, as shown in Figure 5-10. When you fill the mask with a solid shade of

FIGURE 5-9 A layer mask filled with black makes the parent layer transparent.

FIGURE 5-10 A layer mask with 50 percent gray is 50 percent transparent.

gray, you are performing the same task performed when you use the Opacity slider.

So why use a layer mask? Because it lets you control where and how much of the transparency is applied. For example, you could fill the mask with a black-to-white gradient, and this would produce a smooth "fading away" of the image. This is a popular use for layer masks.

Another example of using a mask would be to use a black or gray brush to paint away sections of the masked layer, allowing portions of the layer underneath to show through, as shown in Figure 5-11.

The flipside in Figure 5-12 fills the mask with black and uses a white brush to paint in only the areas you want to keep.

Notice that the brush icon changes to a square with a circle in it when you are editing a layer mask. This indicates that you are working on a layer mask. To work on the layer itself, click

FIGURE 5-11 Painting on a mask with black produces transparency.

FIGURE 5-12 Painting on the mask with white paints the layer back in.

the layer thumbnail in the Layers palette. You will see the brush icon that indicates that you are editing a layer, as shown in Figure 5-13. To go back to the layer mask, click the mask thumbnail.

FIGURE 5-13 This icon indicates you are editing a layer mask.

Let's walk through some layer masking to give you an opportunity to grasp some of the layer skills.

Using layer masks, we will combine the satellite dish and the woman (see Figure 5-14). We are going to create an advertising poster for a communications company.

1. Begin with two pictures of roughly the same size. In this case, we're combining the two images shown in Figure 5-15.

2. Click and drag one image into the other image window. You will see an arrow with a plus sign, indicating that you are adding a new layer to the image.

Hold down the SHIFT key while dragging to center the new image in the window.

Royalty Free Images from Hemera™

FIGURE 5-14 Using layer masks

FIGURE 5-15 Attaching a layer mask to the selected layer

3. You now have two images in one document. Each picture is on its own layer.

4. In the Layers palette, click the Create New Layer Mask button.

5. A layer mask will now be attached to the selected layer. You can see the mask is filled with white and currently has no effect on the image.

6. Now we'll apply a black-to-white gradient to the layer mask. This will create a smooth blend between the layers. Press the D key to reset the foreground and background colors to black and white.

7. Choose the Gradient tool from the tool palette, and set the options to Foreground To Background and Linear.

8. Starting at the top-left corner of the image, click and hold down the left mouse button and drag diagonally to the bottom right corner of the image.

9. Release the mouse button and a gradient will be created in the mask, resulting in a smooth blend of images, as shown in Figure 5-16.

Notice that the layer mask is highlighted (the mask icon is showing) and you can see the gradient in the mask thumbnail on the Layers palette, as in Figure 5-17.

Now we'll paint directly onto a mask with a brush to demonstrate the versatility of masks. We will paint the woman's chin back into the picture. Remember that the darker the gray, the more opaque the image will be. If you notice on the layer mask shown in Figure 5-18, the gray is around 50 percent in the area of the chin. Because we want to bring back the top layer, we will use lighter than 50 percent to paint.

FIGURE 5-16 Smooth blend of images

FIGURE 5-17 The gradient depictd in the mask thumbnail

1. Choose a large soft brush—a 100 pixel brush will work. Make the foreground layer white.

2. Make sure the layer mask is selected, and begin to paint around the woman's chin. Notice the pixels are returning, as in Figure 5-19.

3. Continue until you have painted all the pixels back in the chin area, as in Figure 5-20.

Let's practice masking out details. We will paint back some of the satellite dish on the right of the chin. This time, we want to make the image semi-transparent. Remember that setting the mask layer to black will hide the top layer. We don't want to paint the background in solid, we just want a hint, so we could choose a gray shade—30 percent gray would work. Another option is to choose black and reduce the opacity of the brush from the top tool palette.

1. Choose 30% and begin to paint out part of the top layer. Notice that the layers are blending smoothly (see Figure 5-21).

FIGURE 5-18 The gray is around 50 percent gray on the mask at this point, amounting to 50 percent opacity on the layer.

5

FIGURE 5-19 Pixels returning

FIGURE 5-20 All pixels are back in the chin area

FIGURE 5-21 Painting out the top part of the layer

2. Now let's finish our artwork and add some type with the Text tool. You can add a drop shadow if you choose by clicking on the little *f* symbol at the bottom of the Layers palette and choosing Drop Shadow, as shown in Figure 5-22. Accept the default settings.

Now let's blend the bottom part of the top text to transparent. Normally, you would have to rasterize the text layer to apply a gradient to it. But this isn't true when you're using masks (see Figure 5-23).

1. Create a layer mask on the text layer.

2. Using the same gradient technique we just used, create a gradient that goes from the top of the text characters to the bottom, as shown in Figure 5-24.

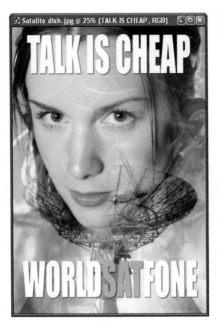

We have finished our poster. We have a professional-looking design that really wasn't more complicated than a few layer masks. Figure 5-25 shows the layers of the completed image. Notice that everything happened on only four layers.

FIGURE 5-22 Adding a drop shadow

FIGURE 5-23 Layer mask on the text layer

FIGURE 5-24 Creating a gradient

Clipping Groups

Clipping groups are an underused and interesting effect. You can them to looking through binoculars. When you look through binoculars, you see only what's available in the confines of the lenses' view area. There is much more than what you can see through the lenses, but everything else is "clipped" away. Imagine that the binocular lenses are the base layer and the view is the clipped layer.

FIGURE 5-25 A layer mask applied to an adjustment layer

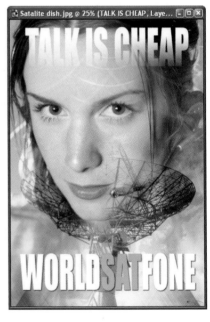

To create a clipping group, you must start with a layer other than a background. This layer must contain a combination of solid and transparent areas. Shape layers and text layers are ideal. This will become our base layer. Anything we apply to this layer as a clipping group will fit into the shape of the base layer.

Note *You can combine layer masks with clipping groups for interesting results.*

Let's demonstrate this effect.

1. Begin with some text, a background, and a layer that you want to clip to the text, as shown in Figure 5-26.

FIGURE 5-26 Choose a layer (A) to clip to the the text (B)

A.

B.

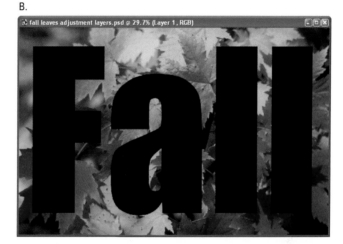

FIGURE 5-27 Arranging layers in the Layers plaette

2. In the Layers palette, move the image layer above the text layer. Remember that the base clipping layer must be underneath the layers you want to clip, as shown in Figure 5-27.

3. Here is where it all happens (see Figure 5-28). Place your mouse between the two layers you want to clip and hold down the ALT key (OPTION on the Mac). Your cursor will turn into a little figure eight. This means that the two layers will be converted into a clipping group.

4. Click, and the clipping group will be created. Notice that the clipped layer is indented, as shown in Figure 5-29.

Figure 5-30 shows what happened to our image after we finished this procedure. Notice that the leaves now appear inside the text. Because nothing is finalized yet, you can still ungroup the layers; repeat step 3, or drag the clipped layer to another location on the Layers palette.

FIGURE 5-28 A clipping group

FIGURE 5-29 Clipped layers are indented

FIGURE 5-30 Image after clipping

Figure 5-31 shows an example of a clipping group dressed up a little. We used a duplicate of the leaves layer for the background and faded it out using a levels adjustment layer. We then clipped an unmodified copy to the text. Finally, we added a drop shadow effect.

FIGURE 5-31 Dressing up the clipping group

Layer Comps

Photoshop CS has a wonderful new feature called Layer Comps, which is designed to free the graphic designer from the shackles of creating and saving multiple versions of a file. Graphic designers using Photoshop can work in various ways: perhaps you love the way a layer style works with a font, or the arrangement looks good more than one way and you might like to show someone else the different versions of the image. You may want to show two or three different layouts to a client and let him decide which he likes best. Experimenting with different layout options is called *comping* (a *comp* is short for *composition*).

Before now, to create comps, you would have to save the file, make the changes, and save it again under a different name. By the time you have finished a few comps, many versions could be stored on your computer. It might get difficult to determine which one is which.

Layer comps remembers the position, visibility, blending modes, styles, and transparency of every layer in your image. It allows you to save multiple layouts of your image all in the same file. You can save layouts and preview them all with the click of a button. What's more, when you save the file, the layer comps are saved, too.

Let's look at the way this little toy works. Figure 5-32 shows the Layer Comps palette.

When you are designing and like what you have created, but you want to explore a bit further, press the New Comp button in the Layer Comps palette and your layout will be saved. Experiment a little and then save another comp. Experiment still more—perhaps hide a layer and create a new one with a new element—and save that, too. If you want to make some changes to a particular comp, first select it and then click the Update Comp button.

When you want to view the saved layouts, just click the area to the left of the comp's name and the associated layout will be displayed.

The Layer Comps palette also comes with a slide show feature. Clicking the two arrow buttons at the bottom of the Layer Comps palette lets you cycle through your saved comps.

FIGURE 5-32 The Layer Comps palette

Layer Blending Modes

If you want real interactivity and powerful creative effects, layer blending modes are the way to go. At the top of the Layers palette (also available in the Layers Styles palette) is a drop-down menu where you can select various blending modes, as shown in Figure 5-33. These incredibly useful modes affect the way layers interact with each other. The blending modes are also available from the options bar when the Painting and Gradient tools are selected.

Two layers are mainly affected by the blending modes: the *base color* layer, which is the existing image, and the *blend color* layer, which is the layer to which you are applying the blending mode, usually on top of the base color layer. (You can also blend multiple layers together; in this case, they would all become blend layers.) In this section, we'll discuss all the blending modes; because there are so many, we can't show them all, but you can experiment to see how they look when applied to your images.

FIGURE 5-33 The blending modes

Normal Modes

In Normal modes, color and opacity are unaffected.

■ **Normal** The standard mode in which images are blended without any special effects.

■ **Dissolve**   When you lower the opacity, the blend layer dissolves rather than turns transparent.

■ **Behind**   Available only with the painting tools. Paints only on the transparent pixels and ignores opaque pixels.

■ **Clear**   Available only with the painting tools. Erases opaque pixels and performs just like the Eraser tool.

Darkening Modes

Darkening modes will cause white to disappear on the blend layer.

■ **Darken**   Where the blend layer is darker, it becomes dominant. Where it is lighter, the base image becomes dominant.

■ **Multiply**   The white areas on the blend layer appear transparent. Only the darker areas affect the base color. This is commonly used for drop shadows, allowing the underlying color to bleed through.

■ **Color Burn**   Use to paint deeper shadows onto images by increasing the contrast on the base layer.

■ **Linear Burn**   Darkens the base color by decreasing the brightness.

Lightening Modes

The opposite of darkening modes, lightening modes will cause black to disappear on the blend layer.

■ **Lighten**   Where the blend layer is lighter, it becomes dominant. Where it is darker, the base image becomes dominant.

■ **Screen**   The dark areas on the blend layer appear transparent. Only the lighter areas affect the base color.

■ **Color Dodge**   Decreases contrast on the base layer.

■ **Linear Dodge**   Lightens the base color by increasing the brightness.

Light Modes

Light modes will cause 50 percent gray to disappear. They have no effect on black or white.

- **Overlay**   The shadows and highlights of the base layer are not affected; the colors are blended together.

- **Soft Light**   If the blend color is lighter than 50 percent gray, the colors are dodged; if the blend color is darker than 50 percent gray, the colors are burned.

- **Hard Light**   50 percent gray disappears and white and black are unaffected. Lighter than 50 percent gray screens and darker than 50 percent multiplies.

- **Vivid Light**   Same as Hard Light but the result is burned or dodged colors, depending on the percentage of gray.

- **Linear Light**   50 percent gray disappears and white and black are unaffected. Lighter than 50 percent gray increase brightness and darker than 50 percent reduces the brightness.

- **Pin Light**   If the blend color is darker than 50 percent gray, pixels are lighter.

- **Hard Mix**   Reduces everything to eight colors: cyan, magenta, yellow, red, blue, green, black, and white. If the blend layer is lighter than 50 percent gray, the color shifts the base hue to one of the eight colors; if it's less than 50 percent, the blend hue shifts to the closest of the eight colors.

Inverting Modes

Inverting modes are good to get radical and psychedelic effects.

- **Difference**   Inverts the color where the layers overlap. Black is ignored.

- **Exclusion**   Inverts the color where the layers overlap, but with less intensity than Difference.

Color-Based Modes

These are more practical modes. They affect only certain aspects of the image at a time and affect the underlying image.

- **Hue**   Change the color of an image. When you apply the Hue mode, only the color is affected in the underlying image; all the other properties are unaffected.

- **Saturation**   Affects only the amount of color in the underlying image. When you overlay with a strong color, the color itself is ignored and only the strength of the color is applied. If the top color is black, white, or gray, the image underneath will appear without color as a grayscale image.
- **Color**   This is like hue and saturation mixed together. This is the best mode for colorizing grayscale pictures.
- **Luminosity**   This is the opposite of the Color mode. The color will be preserved, but the grayscale values can be changed.

Using Blending Modes for Creative Results

The best way to get familiar with blending modes is to experiment and try different modes on different layers and see how they look. Some images will look better with certain blending than others. Let's look at a few common uses for blending modes.

Making White Disappear

You'll recall that the darkening modes cause white to disappear altogether and leave black intact. This is an excellent mode to use when a layer has unwanted white areas around the image. For example, suppose you have a page of black text on a white background, and you want to overlay a colored image with it. You would like the white to be invisible so that it looks like the black text is on top of the image. You could select all the white and remove it using several tools, but why bother when you can accomplish exactly the same result using the Multiply blending mode?

To change the blending mode, select a layer and choose a mode from the top-left, drop-down menu in the Layers palette. Figure 5-34 shows the layer converted to Multiply mode; the text looks as if it were typed directly onto the background.

To experiment with different blending modes, choose a layer, select the Move tool, and then press SHIFT-+ *(plus sign) to cycle through the modes. To cycle backward, press* SHIFT- – *(minus).*

A.

FIGURE 5-34 Using blending modes to make white invisible: (A) the base layer; (B) the text layer; (C) the text layer changed to Multiply mode.

B.

bg2.psd @ 100% (Layer 22, RGB/8#)

(3)The Light Modes - Will cause 50% gray to disappear. No effect on black or white.

- Overlay: The shadows and highlights of the base layer are not effected, the colors are blended together.

- Soft Light: If the blend color is lighter than 50% gray then the colors are dodged, if the blend color is darker than 50% gray then the colors are burned.

- Hard light: 50% gray disappears and white and black are unaffected. Lighter than 50% gray screens and darker than 50% Multiplies.

- Vivid Light: Same as Hard Light but the result is burned or dodged colors depending on the percentage of gray

- Linear Light: 50% gray disappears and white and black are unaffected. Lighter than 50% gray increase brightness and darker than 50% reduces the brightness

- Pin Light: If the blend color is darker than 50% gray, pixels lighter

C.

bg2.psd @ 100% (Layer 22, RGB/8#)

(3)The Light Modes - Will cause 50% gray to disappear. No effect on black or white.

- Overlay: The shadows and highlights of the base layer are not effected, the colors are blended together.

- Soft Light: If the blend color is lighter than 50% gray then the colors are dodged, if the blend color is darker than 50% gray then the colors are burned.

- Hard light: 50% gray disappears and white and black are unaffected. Lighter than 50% gray screens and darker than 50% Multiplies.

- Vivid Light: Same as Hard Light but the result is burned or dodged colors depending on the percentage of gray

- Linear Light: 50% gray disappears and white and black are unaffected. Lighter than 50% gray increase brightness and darker than 50% reduces the brightness

- Pin Light: If the blend color is darker than 50% gray, pixels lighter

Making Black Invisible

Instead of making white disappear, let's make black disappear. We'll work with a darker background and reversed text—that is, white text on a dark background. (This works for any pixel content—not just text.) In Figure 5-35, we have converted the top layer to Screen mode and all the black has disappeared, leaving us with nice clean white type on the background.

FIGURE 5-35 Making black disappear: (A) the background image and (B) the text layer in Screen mode

A.

B.

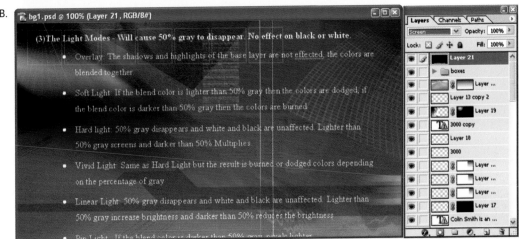

Changing Image Color Without Losing Detail

When we change a layer to color mode, all the image detail is retained from the base layers and the image takes on the color of the blending layer. This is a great trick for a fast change to a collage, and it's a popular and useful layering trick that produces stunning results with very little effort.

Notice how we create three totally different options with two mouse clicks. Figure 5-36 shows the following three steps:

1. Start with a blue collage.

2. Reveal a colored layer that is more of a salmon color; this overrides a lot of the detail in the collage.

3. Switch the layer to Color mode; changing to Color mode allows all the detail to show through while retaining the colors of the blend layer.

FIGURE 5-36 Using color blend mode: (A) the original collage; (B) a colored layer is revealed; and (C) changing to Color mode

A.

B.

C.

Making Objects Overlay in a Natural Way

When we apply text objects on top of other objects, they tend to look a little unnatural. This is because the base image has highlights and shadows that are not apparent in the text. By changing to overlay mode, you will allow the shadows and highlights to show through to the blend layer, as shown in Figure 5-37. This makes the text look like it is a part of the object and blends in nicely with its surroundings.

FIGURE 5-37 Blending text into textures: (A) the text before blending; (B) the text with Overlay mode applied

A.

B.

Removing the Layer Color

The Luminosity mode will cause a layer to shed its color and allow the base colors and textures to come through. In Luminosity mode, the image will retain its highlight and shadow information.

FIGURE 5-38 Luminosity mode

In Figure 5-38, we added a face on top of an image and changed it to Luminosity mode. To enhance the organic effect further, we lowered the opacity to 50 percent. You will find that changing the opacity will make a big difference when you are blending images. Use the opacity with different blending modes to achieve surrealistic results.

Chapter 6

Demystify Channels

How to...

- Understand channels
- Use RGB channels
- Use CMYK channels
- Convert color to grayscale
- Use the Channels palette
- Use alpha channels
- Create spot colors

Channels sound really complicated, and to be honest they can be. Before you say "forget this" and skip to the next chapter, though, let me tell you a couple of things about these little beasts.

You don't have to understand everything about channels to use them. For example, most of us have no idea how they put a movie onto a little plastic disc called a DVD. But that doesn't stop us from slipping *The Matrix* into our DVD players and watching Neo do his thing.

By leveraging the power of channels, you will find that they make everyday tasks easier and more accurate. For example, by using channels, you can make better selections, your line art will look better than ever, and all kinds of cool special effects will be at your fingertips. So have I sold you yet? How about I break channels down into plain English and leave out all the techno mumbo jumbo? Deal? Good; then read on.

Channels Explained

Channels are the raw information that Photoshop uses to produce color. As you know from messing around with a paint box as a child, the paint box doesn't come with all the colors you need, but you can mix colors to create new ones. For example, mixing red and yellow will create orange. You may also remember hearing about *primary colors*, which are yellow, red, and blue. By mixing combinations of these primary colors, you can create a range of new colors. The range that you can create is called the *color gamut*.

In Photoshop, you work with channels using a handy user interface call the Channels palette, which is similar to the Layers palette you used in Chapter 4 and is described in its own section a little later in this chapter. Before we get into technicalities of use, though, you need to understand a little bit about the two kinds of channels that you use in Photoshop: CMYK channels and RGB channels.

CMYK Channels

In Photoshop, you can think of the channels as the primary colors, and by mixing them together you can create a new gamut of colors. In *CMYK mode*, the colors are similar to their paint-box cousins. CMYK stands for *c*yan (blue), *m*agenta (red), *y*ellow, and blac*k*. Black is added because mixing the other three colors produces a muddy brown rather than a pure black, and there's no way to render a full-color image correctly without using black. In the painting world, artists also use pure black and pure white pigments. In Photoshop, we don't need white because the paper is usually white.

FIGURE 6-1 A CMYK image showing the Channels palette and a strip in CMYK colors

Figure 6-1 shows a color image with the Channels palette open. (For more on the palette, see "The Channels Palette," later in this chapter.) The figure includes a test strip in cyan, magenta, yellow, and black so that you can see the effect that the channels have on the image.

Because each color has its own channel, you'll see four channels in the Channels palette for a CMYK image. You can see how each channel is separated and how the ink will disperse in Figure 6-2, screens A through D. To look at just one channel, click its name in the Channels palette. If, for example, you click the Cyan channel, the preview displays only the parts of the image that use cyan ink (as shown in the leftmost image in Figure 6-2).

 By default, the previews appear in black and white because it's easier for you to see the channel contents in black and white. You can change the channel previews to appear in color by checking the box Edit | Preferences | Display & Cursors | Check Color Channels In Color.

Previewing your color channels in the default black and white is a good idea, because when you are preparing the color plates for printing, the plates are in black and white. The appropriate colored ink will be printed in the black areas of each plate (see Figure 6-2D). Notice how the test strip on each channel in the figure is solid black for its respective color.

When printing in CMYK, colors are printed as tiny dots at different angles and shapes, which are arranged together in such a way that it fool the eyes into seeing colors that really are not present at all. If you take a loupe (a magnifying device, not unlike a mounted magnifying glass) and look at a *process printed* piece (another name for a four-color print), you will be able to see these tiny dots. Even without using a loupe, you can sometimes see the dots on a low-line screen image, such as a newspaper photo. (A *line screen* tells how many lines of dots per inch are present.)

When these colors are arranged and printed in the printing process, the new colors are created. When the piece is printed on a printing press, only four ink colors are used, and they combine to make all the colors you see on a finished printed piece. Because of this, *CMYK mode* should be used *only* if you are preparing files to be printed on a *commercial printing press.*

Tip *When creating CMYK documents, it's best to work in RGB first and convert to CMYK at the end for the following reasons: CMYK doesn't support all the Photoshop filters; RGB has more colors available; and because CMYK has an extra channel, the file size will also be almost a third larger, which can slow down system performance. You'll learn about RBG colors shortly in the section "RGB Channels."*

A. Cyan channel

B. Magenta channel

C. Yellow channel

D. Black channel

FIGURE 6-2 An image's color dispersal as represented by each channel

Note *The reason we began with CMYK channels and not RGB channels is simple. CMYK channels are the easiest to understand when relating to the "real world." CMYK colors are subtractive colors, which means that if you take all the colors away, only white will remain. The more color you add, the darker the image will be. That's easy to understand!*

The Prepress Process

When a document is printed on a commercial printing press, the file must pass through a few phases. The first stage is called "ripping," where film or negatives are made from your file. These negatives are not that different from what you get from a normal camera, except the printing negatives are much larger, and each negative caters only to one color. Four individual "film plates" are made, one for each color of cyan, magenta, yellow, and black. The film is then "burned to plates"—chemicals are applied to an aluminum, rubber, or paper sheet, called a plate. The chemicals react to the film and cause indentations on the plate. The plates are then loaded onto the printing press, where the indentations pick up inks and apply them to the pages that are being printed.

Current printing trends are moving to DTP, direct-to-plate, printing. In DTP, the film process is eliminated and the electronic files are sent directly to the plates.

RGB Channels

RGB stands for *r*ed, *g*reen, and *b*lue. This is the main color space you will use most of the time in Photoshop. Remember what you just learned about mixing color for CMYK? In RGB, everything is the opposite! RGB mode is called *additive color* because the three colors *combined* make white. "How can this be?" you may ask. Think of CMYK as inks and RGB as light. With RGB, we are painting with light. RGB is the standard color space used for monitors, where the three primary colors are used; they are called *monitor primaries*.

 Green is used instead of yellow because cleaner colors can be produced on monitors using green.

You may remember a high school science experiment for which you used different colored markers to mark up a round piece of cardstock. You then spun the card really fast until all the colors blended into pure white. How did this happen? Because the human eye also sees in additive color. White light is a combination of all the colors of the spectrum—just look at a rainbow as it splits the light into individual colors, which were really there all the time, even though we couldn't see them. (For more on color theory, see Chapter 1.)

Figure 6-3A shows several preview images: Starting at left, you see an RGB image with a test strip. The *test strip* contains pure colors for each of the channels, which allows you to see how each color interacts with each different channel. Figure 6-3B through D show each individual color channel. In RGB channel previews, whenever a solid color is used, the test strip and channel shows as white. For example, look at the red channel image (second from left) in Figure 6-3B. Imagine that instead of white, we are showing red light; so where there is no red light, it is shown as black, and where there is intense red light, it is shown as white. It makes sense, then, that *no* light would mean *no* color and *a lot* of light would mean *a lot* of color. Study the test strip for each of the channels shown in the figure.

FIGURE 6-3 RGB channels— notice that each color channel shows as white.

A. The composite of all channels

B. Red channel

C. Green channel

D. Blue channel

Each channel is also capable of displaying 256 levels of gray (8-bit color).

FIGURE 6-4 Mixing the blue and red channels produces a purple image

We can mix channel views by first choosing a color channel by clicking its name in the palette and then showing a second channel by clicking the visibility icon—the little eye to the left of the channel thumbnail, as shown in Figure 6-4, just like the icon on the Layers palette. In Figure 6-4, the red and blue channels both show the visibility icon. Notice how the combined channels display as a purple color? Guess what? If you mix blue and red together, you get purple.

Changing Grayscale Mode to RGB Mode

Figure 6-5 shows an image in grayscale. Grayscale is the term for an image that has no color present. You may have called it "black and white." Notice that only one channel appears in the Channels palette. That is because no extra color information is needed for a grayscale image. If you wanted to add color to this image, you would first have to convert to RGB mode so that channels would be available in which to store the color. To convert from grayscale to RGB mode, choose Image | Mode | RGB from the main menu.

After you change to RGB mode, the actual image would still look exactly the same, and the information copied would be exactly the same for each channel. But we

FIGURE 6-5 A grayscale image contains only one channel on the palette would now be able to *add* some color so that Photoshop could display it.

Converting Color to Grayscale

You can also convert a color image to grayscale by using one of several methods:

- With the image open in Photoshop, press CTRL-SHIFT-U (CMD-SHIFT-U on the Mac).
- From the main menu, choose Image | Adjustments | Desaturate.
- Convert to grayscale mode.
- Create a new document with new channel information.

The first two methods will *equalize* the channels; in other words, the channels will all display the same image even though the palette now includes color channels, as shown in Figure 6-6.

FIGURE 6-6 Grayscale Channels palette settings in RGB mode

The third method, convert to grayscale mode, will just "throw away" all the color information and transfer all the grayscale information into the grayscale channel. If you want to print a single-color image, you will first need to convert your image to grayscale. Then you can apply whatever color you want to the image.

Finally, you can also use the channels to your advantage when converting to grayscale. Rather than just convert to grayscale and let Photoshop make all the decisions, you can choose which channel you want to use as your new grayscale image and convert the single channel into a new document.

This is a superior conversion method, because you get to make all the decisions. Here's how it's done:

FIGURE 6-7 The blue channel produces the cleanest preview with the most detail.

1. Open an image that's in a color mode, and click each of the channels until you see one that looks better than the rest. For our example, we'll use the blue channel, as shown in Figure 6-7, because it looks best on this image.

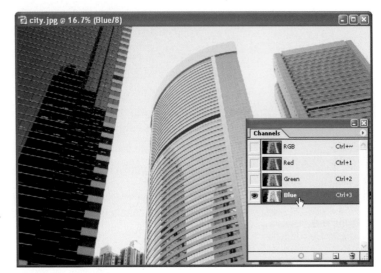

2. Click the arrow at the top right of the Channels palette to open the flyout menu, as shown in Figure 6-8A. Choose Duplicate Channel:

A. The flyout menu from the channels palette

B. Choose a new document

FIGURE 6-8 Creating a new document from a channel

3. The Duplicate Channel dialog box, shown in Figure 6-8B. In the Document field, choose New. This will create a new document from this channel. You can name it whatever you want.

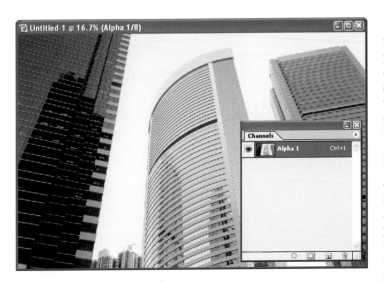

FIGURE 6-9 The new image and its Channel palette

Figure 6-9 shows a new document Channel palette showing only one channel, called Alpha 1. (More in the section "Alpha Channels.") The new channel looks exactly like the old one shown in Figure 6-7, except this image is now in *multi-channel* mode, which is a special mode that lets you add or delete channels as you wish. A multi-channel image with a single channel looks the same as an image in grayscale mode. You should convert the image from multi-channel to grayscale mode by changing to grayscale: choose Image | Mode | Grayscale from the main menu.

In Figure 6-10, you can see the difference using this method makes compared to just converting to grayscale mode. It's worth the little bit of extra effort. The image in Figure 6-10A is the image we converted from a channel. The image in Figure 6-10B is the result of converting to grayscale. Notice how much better Figure 6-10A looks.

FIGURE 6-10 The image converted from a channel (A) and the same image converted to grayscale (B).

A.

B.

 With the latest release of Photoshop, a document can contain up to 56 channels.

The Channels Palette

Now that you have some understanding about channels, let's take a closer look at the Channels palette—particularly its functionality.

The Channels palette behaves pretty much like the Layers palette (as discussed in Chapter 4). Choose Window | Channels for the main menu to open the Channels palette, if it isn't already visible on the workspace.

The icons on the Channels palette are similar to the Layers palette, and the two palettes' appearance is almost the same. If you want to display individual channels, you can click the channel name. To show all the channels, click the topmost channel, which is called a *composite* channel.

Figure 6-11 shows the Channels palette with several channels, including two alpha channels. An *alpha* channel is an extra channel used to aid us in special tasks. (Alpha channels are discussed in the next section.)

At the bottom of the Channels palette, you will notice four buttons. The function of these buttons are listed here:

FIGURE 6-11 The Channels palette

- **Load Channel as Selection**   Loads the contents of a channel into a selection. This button is used mostly in conjunction with an alpha channel (discussed next).

- **Save Selection as Channel**   Creates a channel out of a selection. This is a good way to save a selection for later use. This button is handy when you're masking objects.

- **New Channel**   Creates a new channel.

- **Delete**   Drag an unwanted channel to this trash can to delete it.

 You can also load a channel as a selection by pressing CTRL *(*CMD *on the Mac) and clicking the thumbnail.*

Alpha Channels

Alpha channels are storage channels. They are useful for saving specific, selection information and special effects information. As you will have discovered by now, once you turn off a

FIGURE 6-12 Create an alpha channel and the dialog box for a new channel opens.

selection (deselect) or close the document, the selection is gone. You can use alpha channels to save and reuse selections, even after you close a document. All the selection information is saved in this alpha channel for later use (see Figure 6-12).

Alpha channels are used mainly for image manipulation. They do not print with the file. They are saved with the file and can be turned into selections at any time. But more than that, an alpha channel can store a soft or feathered selection. A feathered selection will create a soft faded transition as opposed to a hard-edged transition. An alpha channel can contain up to 256 levels of grayscale, just like a regular channel.

 Because an alpha channel is used for the main purpose of image manipulation, alpha channels will not print or affect the appearance of your printed images.

When you create an alpha channel, it holds a *mask* of your selection. When you load a selection using a channel, black is loaded while white is ignored. Gray is treated as a *soft selection*, meaning that the selection contains some transparency. You can even save and load a selection that has areas using different transparencies on sections of the channel.

Creating Alpha Channels

To create an alpha channel, do one of the following:

- Click the New Channel button.
- Make a selection, and click the Save Selection as Channel button.
- With a selection active, choose Select | Save Selection. The Save Selection dialog box will open, asking for you to name the new channel, as shown here:

Figure 6-13A shows how a new alpha channel looks in the preview. Notice that the new channel contents in Figure 6-13B are solid black and white, creating a very sharp selection.

A.   B.

Royalty Free Images from Hemera™

FIGURE 6-13 Creating an alpha channel (A), and the alpha channel displayed (B)

Loading the Contents of an Alpha Channel

Once you have created an alpha channel or opened an image that contains an alpha channel, you can load the channel as a selection in several ways:

- CTRL-click (CMD-click on the Mac) on the channel thumbnail you want to load, as shown in Figure 6-14.

- While working in the Main image window, choose Select | LoadSelection, and then choose which channel you want to load from the drop-down menu in the Load Selection dialog box.

- Choose the target channel, and then click the Load Channel As Selection button in the Channels palette.

Note *For more information on selections and their uses, see Chapter 10.*

After you have loaded the alpha channel, you can use the selection for many purposes. For example, you could use a

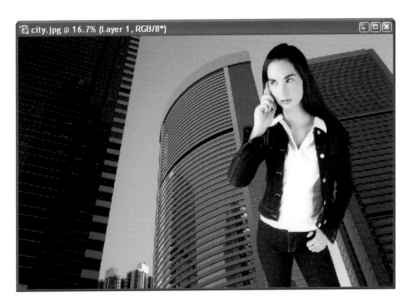

city.jpg @ 16.7% (Layer 1, RGB/8*)

FIGURE 6-14 The image on a new background after using an alpha channel to load a selection

selection as a mask to protect parts of an image while painting and applying regional effects. Another common use would be to lift the image off its background and drop in onto a new one, as shown in Figure 6-14.

Here's how you place an object into a new document using an alpha channel:

1. Open an image that contains an object saved in an alpha channel. This is your source document.

2. Open the document that will serve as the background into which you want to place the object. This is your destination document.

3. On the source document, load the selection from the channel.

4. Click on the layer thumbnail in the Layers palette. Making sure the correct layer is active (if a multi-layered image is used), drag the selected object to the destination document.

5. Release the mouse and position the object to suit your tastes.

Spot Colors

CMYK offers a relatively small palette of colors. Very bright colors, for example, cannot be reproduced in this format, and color accuracy is not guaranteed. When you need bright, accurate colors, you would use *spot color*, an extra color that is printed at the same time as the CMYK inks. Unlike CMYK color, spot ink is a solid color and is not printed as dots.

Generally, a special ink brand called Pantone color is used in the United States. These inks are part of a matching system that helps you choose accurate colors, similar to a paint chip you would pick up from a paint store. Each country has its preferred ink matching system. Check with your printer to determine which system is preferred.

The color will match exactly the colors you see in a special printed color chip called a Pantone color guide. Typically, you would need to use one or more spot colors in the following situations:

- You need an exact match of a color
- You want to use metallic inks
- You want to use florescent inks
- You want to use a spot varnish
- You want to print a two- or three-color project

No matter what your need for spot color, the creation process in Photoshop is the same. You will need to leverage the power of spot channels.

 Some printers have eight-color printing presses that are capable of printing CMYK plus four spot colors at the same time.

FIGURE 6-15 For this advertising piece, we want to make the logo a spot color.

Creating Spot Colors

You can create a spot color using the spot channels in Photoshop. Figure 6-15 shows a color postcard that requires a spot color for the logo. Assume that compuFIX is a large company, the color of the logo is very important, and budget is not an issue (since it's expensive to print a five-color job).

FIGURE 6-16 The logo selected

FIGURE 6-17 Creating a new spot channel

FIGURE 6-18 Choosing a custom color

6

1. Convert the RGB image to CMYK by choosing Image | Mode | CMYK. Choose No when a dialog box asks whether you want to flatten the image.

2. To select the object that we're turning into a spot color, CTRL-click (CMD-click on a Mac) the layer thumbnail that contains the logo. This will load the selection, as shown in Figure 6-16.

3. Open the Channels palette by clicking on its tab in the main window. If the palette is not displayed, choose Window | Channels for the main menu.

4. To turn the selection into a spot channel, click the flyout menu at the upper-right corner of the palette and choose New Spot Channel, as shown in Figure 6-17.

5. The New Spot Channel dialog box will open automatically. Click the color swatch in this dialog box to open the Custom Colors dialog.

6. Click the custom color button to launch the options and In the Book field, choose PANTONE Solid Coated. Two types of paper can be used: plain *uncoated* paper (such as newsprint) and *coated* paper (such as the finished paper used in art books and magazines). Coated paper is coated with chemicals that prevent the paper from absorbing too much ink (blotting). This results in crisper images and cleaner colors. Generally, with a high-quality color job, you will be using coated paper.

7. Choose a Pantone color, as shown in Figure 6-18. Then click OK.

8. Photoshop will return you to the New Spot Channel dialog box; you'll notice the information that appears in the Name field is the same as the color you chose in step 7 (see Figure 6-19).

Make a note of the color and give it to your printer. He will need to know the ink number so the color can be correctly matched.

9. Now let's set Solidity. Unless you want the color to be *screened* back (printed semitransparent) choose 100%.

FIGURE 6-19 Setting the solidity

10. Click OK to create your new spot channel (shown in the Channels palette in Figure 6-20). Notice that the name of the channel is the Pantone color name. The logo in the image has also been changed to this color.

FIGURE 6-20 The Channels palette and image showing a spot channel and color

Knocking Out Colors

When we create a spot color, we can either have the printer *overprint* the color, or we can create a *knockout.* In an overprint, the spot color ink is printed directly over the other inks. This works well for varnishes, metallic inks, and very dark spot colors.

Imagine, for example, that you

need to add a bright red spot color over the top of some very dark inks. The red ink would not show up too well—at best it would look dirty. If you are printing with a light color over dark colors, you can create a *knockout*, for which you remove any ink behind the spot color and print directly on the paper. A knockout "knocks out" all the color behind it. Figure 6-21 shows the difference between printing an overprint and a knockout.

FIGURE 6-21 Printing an overprint and a knockout

Overprint

Knockout

Creating a Knockout

Follow these steps to knock out color:

FIGURE 6-22 Selection loaded in the Layers palette

1. In this example, we're going to deal with the logo again, so we choose the logo channel. In the Channels palette, CTRL-click (CMD-click on a Mac) the spot channel thumbnail. This will load the selection and open the Layers palette, as shown in Figure 6-22.

2. Create a new layer, and move it to the top of the layer stack.

3. Choose the new top layer and fill the selection with white. The white will hide the color from the rest of the layers and leave a nice, clean base over which our spot color will print.

What Is Trapping?

When you create a knocked out image, you also need to consider *trapping*. During a printing operation on a printing press, the paper can sometimes slip a little bit. This causes a problem called *misregistration*, which occurs when the paper slips and the ink doesn't quite cover the exact area where it's supposed to cover. The result is that little white gaps can be seen on the edges of the spot color area.

This problem can be corrected by a process called *trapping*. To use trapping, you'll make the knocked out area slightly smaller than the actual ink area. This way, if the paper slips slightly, because you've left a little leeway to work with, the ink still covers the empty space.

To create trappings in Photoshop, you simply contract your selection a little bit so that a pixel or so of ink leeway is removed from the knocked out area.

To do this, choose Select | Modify | Contract and enter a setting of 1 pixel, as shown in the illustration. To accommodate multiple spot colors, just repeat the steps for each knocked out area.

Saving the File

To enable your printer to reproduce the spot color and other colors and images, you must save the file correctly. You can use the following file formats:

- **PSD (Photoshop Document)**   Photoshop native file. This will work if you are printing directly from Photoshop or assembling your files in Adobe InDesign.

- **TIFF (Tagged Image File Format)**   The new Photoshop TIFF supports, layers, channels, and spot channels. You can print these files directly from Photoshop or InDesign.

- **DCS 2.0 (Desktop Color Separation)**   An Encapsulated Postscript (EPS) file. Postscript is the language most printers use. This format is supported by QuarkXPress and Adobe InDesign. If you save as DCS 2.0, when the pop-up menu appears, choose the ASCII format. Choose a single file with color composite. (Also use an 8-bit preview.) This way, the image will look halfway decent in your page layout software. It will print much better, too.

Chapter 7

Create and Understand Paths

How to...

- Understand raster graphics
- Understand vector graphics
- Create paths
- Use the Pen tool
- Convert a curve to a straight line
- Convert a straight line to a curve
- Use the Freeform Pen tool
- Convert a selection to a path
- Use custom shapes
- Create a path from a shape
- Fill and stroke paths
- Edit paths
- Turn a path into a selection
- Manage and load shapes
- Create custom shapes

Apples and oranges are used as a cliché for trying to compare two totally different things. The truth is, they really are not so different—they are both fruit, they are both round, and you can mix them together into a fine salad. Like apples and oranges, graphics in Photoshop come in two flavors: raster graphics and vector graphics. Both are graphical formats that work together to produce what you see on screen, but they function in totally different ways.

In this chapter, we look at these two types of graphics. By the end of the chapter you will not only know the difference between the two, but you will also be able to create graphics using both technologies—a sort of graphics salad, if you will. You'll also jump into the world of paths, which are useful for all kinds of tasks, from drawing to cutting out objects cleanly.

Apples and Oranges: Raster vs. Vector Graphics

Because you probably use them all the time on your computer, you're likely already familiar with raster or bitmap graphics. Most of Photoshop is based on this format. Raster graphics are made up of pixels, tiny squares that each contain one color.

FIGURE 7-1 A close-up of the pixels that make up a raster graphic

When colors are applied to these pixels and they are mixed together on your viewing screen, you no longer see the individual pixels—instead, you see the entire image. Back in Chapter 6, you read about using a loupe to view the dots of color on a printed color image. Pixels work in a similar way to "blend" colors on your computer screen.

Figure 7-1 shows part of an image zoomed up to 1600 percent. You can see the individual pixels that form the image. To give you an example of how tiny these pixels are, the average 17-inch screen contains 800,000 of them!

Photoshop is essentially a raster-based program. Most of the graphics and just about all the images you output are based on pixels. Vector graphics, on the other hand, are based on math. To those of you who are mathematically challenged: don't worry, because all the math happens behind the scenes, and you don't have to be a scientist to use vectors.

Think of vectors as "joining the dots." A minimum of two dots (called *anchor points*) are necessary for any vector image to happen. When you create two points, Photoshop will draw a line between the points, as shown in Figure 7-2. You will then tell Photoshop whether you want a straight line or a curved line to be drawn. If you move one of the points, Photoshop will adjust the curve to fall between the lines so that they are still connected.

FIGURE 7-2 A vector showing two points joined

In an illustration program such as Adobe Illustrator, were we were to draw a circle, the first point would mark the center, and the second point would mark the radius. The program would then know to draw a circle based on this information. Such programs are based on vector graphics.

Vectors have several benefits:

- Easily edited at any time
- Small file size

■ Because they are based on math, you can scale them
up and down (resize) without any loss of quality

The features in Photoshop that use vectors are

■ Paths

■ Text

■ Shape layers

Paths Explained

Paths are made of curves, lines, and points. Think of them as the
lines you would draw with your ink pen to connect the dots. The
technical name for the curves created by lines are *Bézier curves*,
named after their inventor, Pierre Bézier.

A path in Photoshop has four basic components, as shown
in Figure 7-3.

FIGURE 7-3 Anatomy of a path

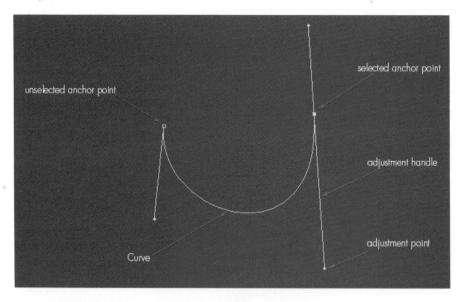

■ **Anchor points**   These points tell the curves where to
begin and end. When selected, the anchor point is solid,
or filled. The point will display as unfilled (or hollow)
when it's not selected. You can edit only selected points.

■ **Adjustment handles**   These join the anchor points
and adjustment points, as a visual reference.

■ **Adjustment points**   Click these to make changes to the shape of the curves.

■ **Curve**   The shape that is being drawn.

Paths do not print and they are not visible in the final image. They appear as reference points to help you draw complex shapes and perform other operations. You can, however, draw shapes with paths and then fill them with color or images, and these colors or images will print and are visible in the final image. You can create a precise outline around an image using paths, which could then be used to "cut out" the image. A path will create the cleanest edge possible in Photoshop, so it lends itself well for such purposes. You can also save the path with the final image, which makes it possible to reuse the path later. You can even use paths as guides to curve text (which is covered in Chapter 8).

Creating Paths

Now that you have a basic understanding of what paths are, we are going to examine some techniques for creating them.

The Pen Tool

The "mother" of the path is the Pen tool. Most paths begin their existence when the Pen tool renders them. The concepts of the Pen tool are not difficult to grasp, but the execution is another thing altogether. Because the Pen tool requires some practice to master, you should experiment with it before you tackle any important projects. Mastery of the Pen tool will help you work successfully in Photoshop for years to come.

Drawing a Straight Line

Drawing a straight line is fairly straightforward (excuse the pun):

1. Choose the Pen tool from the tool palette.

2. Click anywhere on your canvas.

3. Click at another spot, and a straight line appears between the two clicks.

4. Press CRTL (CMD on the Mac) and click as many times as you want to connect the line to the next point(s) and finish drawing the path.

You can hold down the SHIFT key as you click to draw vertical lines, horizontal lines, or perfect 45-degree angles.

Drawing an S Curve

Now let's create an S curve. This is a bit more difficult that a straight line. Figure 7-4 illustrates the process.

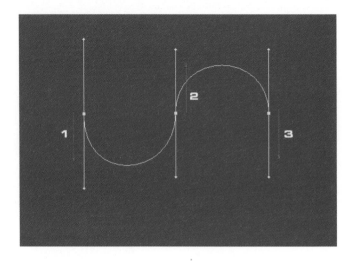

FIGURE 7-4 Drawing an S curve

1. Select the Pen tool. Click, and then drag down with the Pen tool. Dragging defines the direction of the curve.

2. Click and drag up for the second point. You will see your first curve begin to form into the shape of a *U*.

3. Click and drag down for the third point, and notice a nice *S* shape.

You will probably have to try this a few times to make your curve look even.

 Turn on Show Grid to assist in drawing paths. To turn on this option, choose View | Show | Grid from the main menu.

Drawing a W Curve

Sometimes you will need to draw a sharp curve, as in a *W* shape. You'll use a new tool for this, called the Convert Point tool.

Figure 7-5 shows several pen types, with the Convert Point tool at the bottom of the list in the tool palette.

You can also access this tool by pressing the ALT key (OPTION on the Mac). The Pen tool will switch to the Convert Point tool until you release the key; at this point, the tool will revert back to the active Pen tool.

Now let's draw the W curve, as illustrated in Figure 7-6.

1. Click and drag down with the Pen tool; this defines the direction of the curve.

FIGURE 7-5 Pen types

Pen Tool		P
Freeform Pen Tool		P
Add Anchor Point Tool		
Delete Anchor Point Tool		
Convert Point Tool		

CHAPTER 7: Create and Understand Paths   **161**

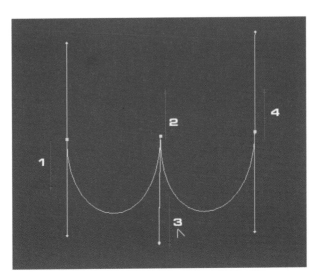

FIGURE 7-6 Creating a W curve

FIGURE 7-7 Converting a curve to a straight line

2. Click to set the second point and drag up. This makes an S curve. Hover the mouse over the second anchor point you just created. Press the ALT key (OPTION on the Mac) and you will see the cursor change to the *convert point logo* (a little V shape).

3. Drag in the direction you want the next curve to go—in this case, drag down. You will notice an adjustment handle is created, but no path. You are now "telling" the path to change direction.

4. Click and drag up, and you will see a W curve.

You have now created two types of curves; keep practicing drawing curves with the Pen tool until you become comfortable with its use.

Converting a Curve to a Straight Line

Once you have created a curve, you can change it to a straight line anytime. The technique is illustrated in Figure 7-7. Begin with either an S curve or a W curve that you've already created.

1. Choose the Convert Point tool (press the ALT key, or press OPTION on the Mac).

2. Click the first point. It will now become a straight point, and the end of the line will still be a bit curved because the second point is still a curve.

3. Click the second point and the curve will become a straight line.

Converting a Straight Line to a Curve

This is the opposite of the preceding instruction. To convert a
line to a curve, you will need a path with a straight line on it.

1. Choose the Convert Point tool.

2. Click the first point, and drag either up or down to
begin a curve.

3. Click the second point and drag again. You will now
have a curve.

4. Don't forget to CTRL-click (CMD-click on the Mac) to
finish drawing the curve.

Using the Freeform Pen Tool

This tool is simple to use. Just choose the tool and begin to draw
on the page, just as you would with an ink pen in the real world.
The Freeform Pen tool will add all the anchor points for you
and clean up the path a little bit to reduce the number of points.
The disadvantage of using this tool is that you have no control
over where the points are created. However, you can edit them
just like all the other path tools. (See the sidebar "Adding and
Deleting Anchor Points.") Figure 7-8 shows the result of using
the Freeform Pen tool.

FIGURE 7-8 Freeform Pen tool
drawing

Add and Delete Anchor Points

In Figure 7-5, two pens in the pen group show a plus sign and a minus sign. These are the pens you use to add and delete anchor points.

To delete an anchor point:

1. Choose the Delete Anchor Point tool, or just hover the Pen tool over an existing anchor point. You will see a minus sign.

2. Click to delete the anchor point.

To add an anchor point:

1. Choose the Add Anchor Point tool, or just hover the Pen tool anywhere over part of a curve that doesn't already have an anchor point. You will see a plus sign.

2. Click to add the new anchor point.

Creating a Closed Path

So far, all the paths we have discussed are called *open* paths—*open* meaning that a distinct start and end point appears. Think of these paths as being similar to pieces of string—you can curve them or pull them straight, but no matter what the shape, the string has a beginning and an end.

In Photoshop, you can use another type of path, called a *closed* path, an example of which is shown in Figure 7-9. In a closed path, the start and end points are the same, and the path forms a closed loop. Any path can be turned into a closed path.

When you are creating a path, hover the mouse over the start point and a little

FIGURE 7-9 Creating a closed path

circle will appear, like that shown in Figure 7-10. This circle lets you know that you are at the start point, and if you click, you will close the path.

Converting a Selection to a Path

You can now breathe a sigh of relief, because the hardest part is over. Not all path making is difficult. Following is an easy way to create a path. Photoshop has a great feature called *make a path from selection*. All you need is an active selection and you can turn it into a path in a jiffy.

In Figure 7-11, we have loaded one of the layers as a selection. Here's how you can turn it into a path:

1. Load the selection.

2. Choose Window | Paths from the Main menu to open the Paths palette, if it's not already visible.

3. Do one of the following:

   ■ Click the Make Work Path From Selection button, as shown in Figure 7-12.

   ■ Click the flyout menu at the upper-right corner of the Paths palette and choose Make Work Path. You will see an option asking for a tolerance setting. This determines how tightly you want the path to follow the selection. Choose a smaller number to make a more accurate path, but with more points. Choose a larger number to make a smoother path, but less accurate. The default setting of 2.0 works for most situations, so leave it at that for now.

4. You now have created what is called a *work* path. This is a temporary path used to create quick edits and effects. When you choose another path, the work path will be replaced. Save this path, click the flyout menu, and choose Save Path.

FIGURE 7-10 The start point of a path

FIGURE 7-11 An image showing an active selection

Illustration courtesy of www.photoshopcafe.com

FIGURE 7-12 The Paths palette

Path thumbnail

Fill path

Stroke path

Load path as selection

Make work path from selection

Delete path

New path

FIGURE 7-13 The path created from the selection

FIGURE 7-14 Various shape tools

The default name is path 1. After you have saved the path, it will stay with the document, even after you turn off your computer and then turn it back on; the path will still be available for the document as long as it's saved as a PSD, TIFF, or EPS format (which is covered in Chapter 1). You can even transfer the path to other documents just by clicking and dragging. Figure 7-13 shows the path created from the selection in Figure 7-12.

 You'll learn to convert a path to a selection a little later in this chapter.

Creating Paths Using Shape Tools

Another quick way to create a path is to use one of the shape tools, set to a path option. Several shape tools are available from the tool palette, as seen in Figure 7-14.

■ **Rectangle**   Makes rectangles and squares

■ **Round rectangle**   A rectangle with rounded corners; choose the corner radius (how round the corners are) from the tool options bar (see Figure 7-15)

■ **Ellipse**   Draws circles and ellipses

■ **Polygon**   Creates everything from triangles to icosahedrons (a shape with 20 faces) and beyond; choose the amount of sides from the tool options bar

■ **Line**   Draws straight lines; choose the line thickness from the options bar

■ **Custom Shapes**   Lets you create your own shapes; choose a shape from the drop-down list in the options bar

Note *We will create a custom shape at the end of this chapter.*

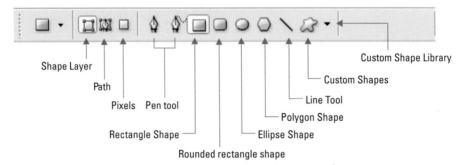

Shape Layer
Path
Pixels   Pen tool
Rectangle Shape
Rounded rectangle shape
Ellipse Shape
Polygon Shape
Line Tool
Custom Shapes
Custom Shape Library

FIGURE 7-15 Tool options bar

Creating a Path from a Shape

Here is how to create a path from a custom shape. Figure 7-16
illustrates all the steps required to perform this task.

1. Choose the Custom Shapes tool.

2. Choose the Path option from the left of the tool
   options bar.

3. Choose the shape you want to create from the Custom
   Shapes Library drop-down menu.

4. Click and drag to draw the shape's path.

5. The shape becomes the work path in the Paths palette.

 Hold down the SHIFT key as you draw to constrain the shape's proportions.

Filling and Stroking Paths

Now that you have created a path, you can use it for a number
of things, including adding type to the path (see Chapter 8). For
now, we are going to add a fill and stroke path using the two
options on the Paths palette, as shown in Figure 7-12.

FIGURE 7-16 Creating a path from a custom shape

Filling a Path with Color

This is a simple one-click, one-trick pony. You can fill a path with the current foreground color.

1. Choose the *foreground color* from the *color picker* in the *tool palette*; this is the color you will use to fill your path.

2. Click the Fill Path button from the Paths palette, as labeled in Figure 7-12. This button will always fill the path with the current foreground color.

Stroking a Path

Contrary to public understanding, *stroking* is not just something you do with a puppy or kitten. Inside the mind of the Adobe engineers, *stroking* means *adding an outline,* so for us Photoshop experts, outlines are called *strokes*. Stroking is similar to the fill task, except Photoshop uses the currently selected brush to draw the stroke. Of course, it goes without saying that you will need an active path, but I will say it anyway.

1. Choose the Brush tool from the tool palette.

2. Choose Window | Brushes to open the Brushes palette, and choose a brush.

3. Set your foreground color to your desired color.

4. Click the Stroke Path button on the Paths palette, as shown in Figure 7-12, and the path will now show an outline around it.

Figure 7-17 shows an example of an icon with both a color fill and a color stroke applied.

FIGURE 7-17 A path filled with foreground and stroke color

Editing Paths

Whatever method you used to create your path is up to you; how you create paths depends on your current needs. No matter what method you use, once paths appear in the Paths palette, they are all treated exactly the same. You can edit and manipulate all the paths in exactly the same way.

You can use two main tools for editing paths after they are created, as shown in Figure 7-18.

- **Path Selection tool**   Click anywhere on a path with this tool, and the entire path is selected. Use this tool when you want to move, copy, or delete paths.

- **Direct Selection tool**   Use this tool to select individual anchor points. With this tool, you can reshape your paths, move anchor points, reshape curves, and control adjustment handles.

Selecting and Moving the Entire Path

When an anchor point is selected, it appears as a solid point; when it is not selected, it appears as a hollow point. This is the same when you use a selection tool to choose a path or point.

FIGURE 7-18 The path selection tools

FIGURE 7-19 The path selection tool selects the entire path.

To select the path, choose the Path Selection tool and click anywhere on the path. Notice in Figure 7-19 that all the anchor points are selected (they're all solid). You can use this tool to copy, delete, or move a path to a new location. To move the entire path, just drag it with the mouse.

Editing Individual Anchor Points

Choose the Direct Selection tool to select either single points or groups of anchor points. When you click a path with this tool, the path is activated, but no anchor points are selected. Figure 7-20 shows an active path with no anchor points selected.

To select a group of anchor points, click and drag the Direct Selection tool around a group of anchor points; they will become active and ready for editing.

To select a single anchor point, click it with the Direct Selection tool; the point will become filled and the adjustment handles will become visible. You can now edit the path.

FIGURE 7-20 An active path with unselected anchor points

Editing a Path

To edit a path

1. Choose the Direct Selection tool from the tool palette.

2. Click the path to activate it.

3. Click an individual anchor point or a group of points.

4. Either drag the anchor point, as shown in Figure 7-21, or click and drag the adjustment handles to edit the path.

FIGURE 7-21 Modifying the path

 By default, both sides of the adjustment handles move together. To move just one side of a handle, hold down the ALT *key (*OPTION *key on the Mac) while you drag.*

Converting a Path to a Selection

Because a path can present the cleanest edge out of any tool in Photoshop, it would make sense to be able to turn a path into a selection and take advantage of that sharp edge to cut out images or mask them for editing.

Some stock photography, such as Photo Objects from Hemera as shown in Figure 7-22, come with paths included to make it easy to lift an image off its background. Of course, you can always make your own path, too.

Here's how to create your own path:

1. Open the Paths palette by choosing window | Paths, if it is not already visible

2. Click the path's thumbnail to make the path active.

3. You can now use one of three ways to make a selection from a path:

FIGURE 7-22
An image with a path

- Click the Path To Selection button from the Paths palette.

- Click the flyout menu and choose Make Selection.

- CTRL-click (CMD-click on the Mac) the path's thumbnail to load it as a selection.

Choose whatever method is the most comfortable for you. Figure 7-23 shows the image with the active selection.

Working with Paths and Shapes

When you are drawing with the Pen tool, or any of the other shape tools, three types of options are available. Figure 7-24 shows the options on the tool options bar. Select one of these options before you begin to draw:

- **Shape Layer**   Creates a shape layer, which is a vector mask. See Chapter 5 for more on shape layers.

- **Path**   Creates an editable path.

- **Fill Pixels**   Creates a solid area of color using the current foreground color. This is not editable, and it is not a vector;

FIGURE 7-23
The image with a selection from a path

rather, it is treated just like a paint brush in a raster format. (See the beginning of this chapter for vector and raster details.)

FIGURE 7-24 Custom shape styles

Fill Pixels

Paths

Shape Layer

Managing and Loading Shapes

In Chapter 5, we discussed shape layers, the newest vector addition to Photoshop. Shape layers are useful for creating shapes that can be applied and modified quickly. At the heart of shape layers are custom shapes, which are stored in a library.

When you open the custom shapes library for the first time, you will notice that only a handful of shapes are available for use. Figure 7-25 shows a preview of the default shapes. More shapes ship with Photoshop, and you can access them with just a few clicks. If you can't find what you are looking for in the library, it's also easy to create your own shapes and save them to the library. In this section, we will look at managing and creating shapes.

FIGURE 7-25 The default set of shapes

To access the custom shapes, first choose the Custom Shape tool from the tool palette. You will then see a Shape drop-down menu in the options bar. Click this to reveal the shape library shown in Figure 7-25.

FIGURE 7-26 Loading extra shapes into the library

FIGURE 7-27 The library with extra shapes loaded

Loading Shapes

Here's how to load the extra shapes that ship with Photoshop:

1. Choose the Custom Shape tool.

2. Open the library from the Shape menu on the tool options bar.

3. Click the little arrow at the upper-right to open the flyout menu, as shown in Figure 7-26.

4. In the bottommost list, choose one of the categories, or choose All to load all available shapes.

5. An option box appears, asking whether you want to replace the current shapes. Click OK to replace the shapes in the library, or click Append to add the shapes to the current library without removing the existing shapes.

Figure 7-27 shows the library with all the shapes loaded and all ready for use.

Loading Shapes from an External Source

You can also load shapes from another source (for example, perhaps you have downloaded some shapes from the Internet). Here's how:

1. Choose the Custom Shape tool.

2. Open the library from the tool options bar's Shape drop-down menu.

3. Click the arrow at the upper-right to open the flyout menu, as shown in Figure 7-26.

4. Choose Load Shapes.

5. Navigate to the location in which your shapes are saved. You shapes will have a .CSH file extension.

6. Click OK.

Creating Custom Shapes

In the final section of this chapter, we will create a custom shape.
Before you start, you'll need a path to work with.

1. Either open an image that has a path, or create one.
   (Perhaps create a path from a selection.)

2. Click the path thumbnail in the Paths palette. Refer to
   Figure 7-22 to see a path selection.

3. Choose Edit | Define Custom Shape.

FIGURE 7-28 Creating a custom
shape

4. You will see a dialog box
   like the one in Figure 7-28,
   showing a thumbnail preview
   of the shape and requiring
   that you type in a name.

5. Type a name into the box.

6. Click OK.

That's all there is to it. When you open the custom shapes
library, your new shape will appear (see Figure 7-29). You can
apply this shape to any image in any size as a path, shape layer,
or fill pixels.

FIGURE 7-29 Our new shape in
the library

Chapter 8

Create and Manipulate Text

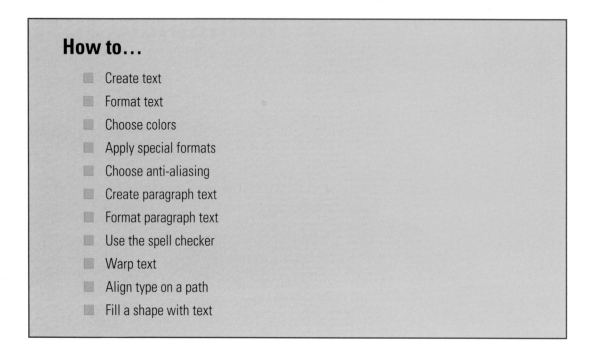

How to...

- Create text
- Format text
- Choose colors
- Apply special formats
- Choose anti-aliasing
- Create paragraph text
- Format paragraph text
- Use the spell checker
- Warp text
- Align type on a path
- Fill a shape with text

Although Photoshop is primarily an image editing program, the engineers at Adobe have realized that more and more people need to use text with the program. As a result, many text options are included in Photoshop, some simple and some complex. We can now create everything from fancy and wild type effects to readable paragraph text.

In this chapter, you will learn how to use all the text tools to make your p's and q's behave themselves, just like they should.

Creating Text

To create text in Photoshop, choose the Text tool from the tool palette, as shown in Figure 8-1. Then, when your mouse hovers over the document window, the mouse curser will show as an *I-beam* pointer, just as it does in a word processor program.

Click anywhere in the document window and type in some characters. The characters are displayed in the main document window.

FIGURE 8-1 The Text tool selected from the tool palette

You don't need to create a new layer to add text; when you begin to type, a new text layer will be created automatically.

Once you have finished typing the text, you will notice that the I-beam is still active. You need to tell Photoshop when you have finished typing in the text, which is called *applying the text*. If you press ENTER (RETURN on a Mac) as you type, the text will wrap to a new line. To *apply* the text to Photoshop, do one of the following:

- Click the checkmark at the far right of the toolbar.
- Click any tool other than the Text tool in the tool palette.

If you click and hold your mouse over the Text tool in the tool palette, you will notice that several Text tool options appear:

- **Horizontal Type Tool**   The standard type tool, which causes text to appear horizontally across the screen.
- **Vertical Type Tool**   The type runs vertically and text is stacked in a column; this is perfect for Asian type characters.
- **Horizontal Type Mask Tool**   This tool creates a mask selection in the shape of the type, aligned horizontally across the screen. It's useful for special effects and for filling the text selection with another image or other elements.
- **Vertical Type Mask Tool**   Creates the text as a selection mask rather than pixels, and displays the text vertically.

To use any of these tools, click in the document, choose your formatting from the tool palette, and begin typing.

 When using the type mask tools, you will type normally; the text will appear in a pinkish color.

Make your formatting changes and then apply the type by clicking the checkbox in the options bar or by clicking another tool in the tool palette. As soon as you apply the type, the pink will disappear and you will be left with just a selection. After the selection is active, you can no longer make any formatting changes, so it's important that you make these changes before applying the type.

 When creating text with either the Type or the Type Mask tools, you can switch from the type I-beam to a transform box by holding down the CTRL *key (*CMD *on the Mac). You can now use the transform box to reshape the text by dragging any transform handle, or you can reposition the text by clicking and dragging inside the transform box.*

Moving Text

After you have applied text to your document, it can be easily repositioned by choosing the Move tool and dragging it to a different position on the page.

At times, you may want to move the text while you're still in the process of typing it (for example, perhaps your text is running off the page). To reposition the text while you're typing, hold down CTRL (CMD on a Mac) and drag your text to a new location. As soon as you release the key command, the pointer will turn back into the I-beam and you can continue typing your text.

Formatting Text

What use is text if you can't format it? For instance, if you were creating an invitation, you would want to use a nice script font, or you'd want to use a solid headline style for a newsletter. Photoshop allows you to edit many attributes of your text. You can change the font size, style, color, alignment, and even the scaling.

Applying Fonts and Styles

Before you can format any text, you must first highlight it. To highlight text, choose the Text tool, click and hold down the mouse button at the beginning of the text, and then drag the curser through all the text that you want to format. Only highlighted text will be affected by the formatting. (You are probably already familiar with this method from word processing programs.) Once you have highlighted the text, you can change it by choosing another font or style from one of two places:

■ The Character palette, shown in Figure 8-2, is best for advanced formatting.

Font family — Eurostile (T1) / Bold Ext... — Font Style
Font size — 54 pt / 7.34 pt — Leading (line spacing)
Kerning (character spacing) — 0 / 0 — Tracking (word spacing)
Scale vertical — 100% / 100% — Scale vertical
Baseline shift — 0 pt / Color: — Text color
Faux styles — T T TT Tr T¹ T₁ T T
Spell-check language — English: USA / Sharp — Anti-aliasing

FIGURE 8-2 The Character palette

■ The toolbar also has the basic formatting options, as shown in Figure 8-3.

FIGURE 8-3 The text options on the toolbar

When you choose the Text tool, the basic formatting options will automatically be shown in the toolbar. They will perform identically to the formatting options in the tool palette.

To launch the Character palette, press the toggle button on the toolbar, shown left.

Font Sizes

You can specify a font size or choose one from a list. To choose a size, click the Font Size text field and a list will appear with the most common sizes, in points. You can also type the size directly into the Font Size field in the palette. The beauty of typing directly into the field is that you can make the text any size that you wish, even sizes that aren't specified in the list.

Font Families

To select a new font, click in the font window of the
Character palette. You will see a list like the one
shown in Figure 8-4, which will contain all the
installed fonts that are available for use in Photoshop.
Choose the font you want from the list.

Font Styles

After you have chosen a font, you may want to apply
italics or boldface. These are called font *styles,* which
are simply variations of a font. The Font Style field
in Figure 8-2 displays a list of all the styles that are
available for your chosen font. Here are some of the
common styles:

- **Bold**
- **Italic**
- **Oblique**   Another name for Italic
- **Condensed**   Thin type style
- **Expanded**   Wide type style
- **Black**   Similar to bold
- **Heavy**   Very bold

Bold
Italic
Oblique - Another name for Italic
Condensed - thin type style
Expanded - Wide type style
Black - Similar to bold
Heavy- Very bold

FIGURE 8-4 The font menu

Faux Styles

Sometimes a style that you want does not appear in the list. This
is because you don't have that particular font installed, or it's
just not available. In either case, Photoshop will allow you to
"fake it." These styles are called Faux styles, and you can create

Regular

Bold

Italic

ALL CAPS

Small Caps

Superscript

S_{ubscript}

Underline

~~Strikethrough~~

them by clicking the little buttons (see Figure 8-2) on the Characters palette to apply a simulated style to the text.

- **Bold**   Thicker text
- **Italic**   Skewed text
- **All Caps**   Each character is displayed in capital letters
- **Small Caps**   Each letter is displayed a little smaller than the regular caps
- **Superscript**   Smaller text raised to the top of the text line, such as the squared sign in math: 2^2
- **Subscript**   The small text will appear at the bottom, such as the molecular structure in chemical notations: H_2O
- **Underline**   Appears along the baseline of the text
- **Strikethrough**   A line appears through the text itself

8

Color

What a cruel and ruthless world it would be if our favorite image editing program allowed us to produce text only in black. As luck would have it, Photoshop's color designers have included the ability to colorize text right into the Character palette and toolbar. Whenever you see a colored rectangle in a Photoshop tool, it's probably a link to a color picker; in the case of the Character palette, the word "*Color*" appears right next to this rectangle. The text color pickers work just like the others in Photoshop: click it, and a window will appear with lots of colors. Choose the color that takes your fancy and click OK.

To change the color of your text, click the Type tool and highlight the text you want to colorize. You can even highlight a character and make it a different color from the rest of the text to create a rainbow of text colors.

Using Advanced Character Formatting

You might want to tweak a bit more than the font, color, and size, and for that, you again use the Photoshop Character palette (none of the options we are about to discuss are available from the toolbar).

Figure 8-5 shows an example of the effect of each of these adjustments. These formatting options are applied just like the standard formatting options (unless specified otherwise).

- **Kerning** Adjusts the space between pairs of characters. To increase or reduce the kerning, insert the I-beam cursor between two characters and press the left or right arrow keys on your keyboard while holding down the ALT (OPTION on Mac) key, or you can enter a setting directly into the Kerning text field in the Character palette. Pay special attention to the spacing between capital and lowercase characters, as they can often use a little kerning.

FIGURE 8-5 Special formatting compared

- **Tracking** This is the overall space between characters in a word or series of words.

- **Leading** Adjusts the space between lines of text. The default setting is Auto, and this works for most cases. To change the leading, highlight the lines of text that you want to alter, and then enter a setting into the Leading text box in the Character palette. (Leading isn't shown in Figure 8-5 because it doesn't have an effect on single lines of text—it affects two or more lines only.)

- **Scale Horizontal** Allows you to stretch or compress the text horizontally. Use this feature sparingly, because text was designed to look best at the default proportions. If you are trying to fill space, you are much better off adjusting the tracking instead.

- **Scale Vertical** Same as Scale Horizontal, but works on the vertical instead. Similar warning goes here: consider leading first.

- **Baseline Shift** Allows you to move either entire words or individual characters up or down in proportion to the rest of the text. Select the character(s) you want to move and enter a setting into the text field. A positive setting will move the text up and a negative setting (prefaced by the minus sign) will move the text down.

Using Anti-Aliasing

Anti-aliasing refers to how smooth Photoshop will display the text. Without anti-aliasing, the text would appear a bit jagged. The anti-aliasing process blends the text pixels into the background, making a softer transition. There are five levels of anti-aliasing:

FIGURE 8-6 Examples of anti-aliasing

- None
- Sharp
- Crisp
- Strong
- Smooth

Figure 8-6 shows examples of how each level affects text. Notice that the effects are more evident on the smaller text. I use the Sharp setting, because it offers a small amount of font smoothing without getting blurry. Sharp was introduced for web use to accommodate the need for extremely sharp text at very small sizes.

 The sharper anti-aliasing settings look best at smaller sizes and the smoother settings look better at larger sizes.

Formatting Paragraph Text

You can define the formatting aspects of an area for multiple lines of text. The lines will break automatically and the text will wrap to fill the space you allocate. You can choose options for justification, indents, and paragraph spacing. Photoshop will now even hyphenate long words for more even-looking lines in the paragraph. Photoshop has come leaps and bounds in handling text and can really hold its own.

Creating Paragraph Text

Let's create a paragraph of text.

1. Choose the Text tool so you can define the text area.

2. Click and hold the mouse in the top left corner of the desired text area, and drag to the bottom right text area. Then release the mouse to create your text area. You will see a box with dashed borders, similar to the one shown in Figure 8-7.

3. From the Character palette, choose the font, size, and color you want. As you type, notice that the text wraps to the next line when it reaches the edge of the box. (If you don't like typing so much, you can cut and paste text from another source.) After you have entered several lines of text, it should look something like Figure 8-8.

4. Click the checkbox on the top right of the options bar to apply the text.

Adjusting the Text Box

You can resize your text box by clicking and dragging on any of the eight anchor points. The text will wrap automatically to fill the new size.

In Figure 8-8, our text area is horizontal, while the illustration of a piece of paper is angled on the screen. It would look so nice to have the text appear on the same angle as the paper. You can rotate the text box and all the text inside will rotate with it.

To rotate the text box, hover the mouse on one of the outside corners until you see a double-sided, curved arrow. When you see the arrow, click and drag. The text box will rotate with the arrow. The result is shown in Figure 8-9.

FIGURE 8-7 Creating the text area

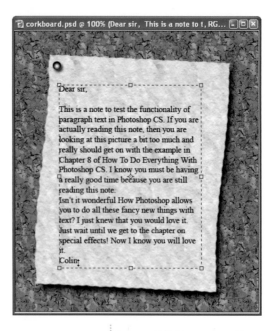

FIGURE 8-8 The text area with text added

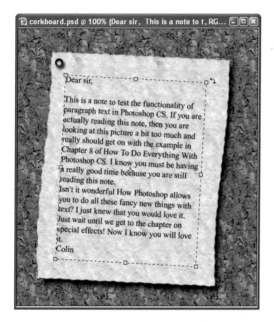

FIGURE 8-9 Rotating paragraph text

Click the checkmark on the toolbar or click any tool in the toolbox other than the Text tool to apply the text—in the same way we applied the basic text at the beginning of this chapter.

Formatting Paragraph Text

Do you remember how we formatted characters in the "Formatting Text" section? You can format the individual characters in the paragraph in the same way. Here, we'll use a few of the Paragraph palette's formatting tools, as shown in Figure 8-10.

FIGURE 8-10 The Paragraph palette

Indenting the First Lines of Paragraphs

Paragraphs are often indented on the first lines, which makes it easier to see where the paragraphs begin and causes the text to look better. Here's how this is done:

1. Choose the Text tool and highlight all the text by clicking and dragging through it. You are now ready to begin formatting the text.

Tip   *To select all the text in the box, click anywhere in the box and press* CTRL-A (CMD-A *on a Mac*).

2. Click the Paragraph tab to open the Paragraph palette, as shown in Figure 8-12.

3. 'Enter a figure into the Indent First Line text field. Indents are measured in points. For the text shown in Figure 8-11, I entered 25 points. See how the first lines of all the paragraphs are now indented?

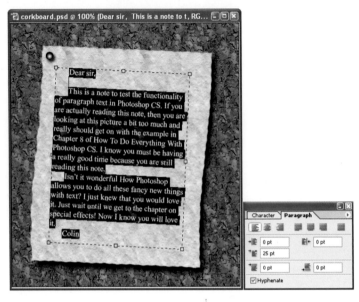

FIGURE 8-11 Indenting the first line of paragraphs

Adding Spacing Between Paragraphs

Let's add a bit of space between each of the paragraphs. Breathing space will separate the paragraphs of text and make the page look more balanced; as a result, it will be more inviting to read.

1. Highlight the text.

2. Open the Paragraph palette.

3. In the Space After Paragraph text field, enter a setting of **5** points, as shown in Figure 8-12.

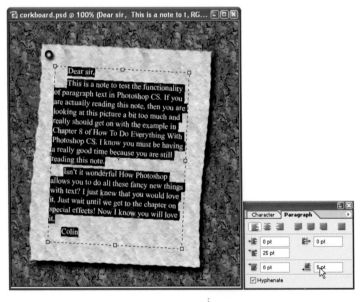

FIGURE 8-12 Spacing added between the paragraphs

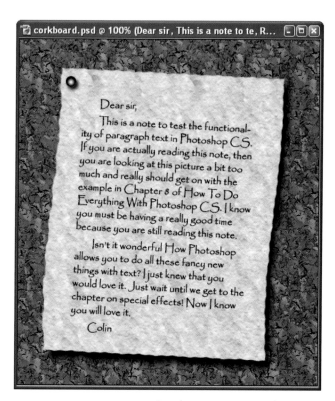

corkboard.psd @ 100% (Dear sir, This is a note to te, R...

Dear sir,

This is a note to test the functionality of paragraph text in Photoshop CS. If you are actually reading this note, then you are looking at this picture a bit too much and really should get on with the example in Chapter 8 of How To Do Everything With Photoshop CS. I know you must be having a really good time because you are still reading this note.

Isn't it wonderful How Photoshop allows you to do all these fancy new things with text? I just knew that you would love it. Just wait until we get to the chapter on special effects! Now I know you will love it.

Colin

FIGURE 8-13 The finished text with a little bit of fine-tuning

To wrap up the image, highlight the text again and choose a font that looks interesting and that suits the image with which you are working. In Figure 8-13, I used the font Papyrus because it has a nice feel to it and looks good on the paper. As a final touch, I also increased the leading a little bit because the lines looked too close together.

Spell Checking

Even the best of us are prone to a few typos every now and then. It can be frustrating to spend a lot of time designing a really nice piece with spectacular type effects and dazzling colors, only to be embarrassed by a nasty spelling error.

The good news is that Photoshop has its own built-in spell checker, and it's easy to use.

1. Highlight the text you want to check (if you want to check just a section). Otherwise, skip this step to check the entire document.

2. Choose Edit | Check Spelling.

3. The spell checker will do its stuff. After a little whizzing and whirring, if you're lucky, in a few moments a dialog box will pop up saying "Spell check complete," meaning that no spelling errors were found. You can click OK and go your merry way.

4. If you aren't so fortunate, you will see the Check Spelling dialog box shown in Figure 8-14. The suspect word will be displayed along with a list of suggested spellings.

5. If the word was spelled incorrectly, choose the correct word from the list or enter the correct spelling in the Change To text box. Then click Change. If more than one instance of the word is included in the document, click Change All.

6. If your word was spelled correctly and the spell checker's dictionary didn't recognize it, you can do one of two things:

FIGURE 8-14 Check Spelling dialog box

■ Click Add to add it to the dictionary. The next time you run the spell checker, it will remember the new word.

■ Click Ignore to ignore the instance of the word and continue running the spell check. You can also click Ignore All if more than one instance of the word appears.

7. Continue checking every word the spell checker identifies.

Setting Alignment

Now that we have all this fancy text in our document, let's learn about alignment.

Photoshop can check spelling in multiple languages. To check in a different language, change the language option in the Character palette before running the spell checker.

Figure 8-15 shows all the alignment options in the Paragraph palette. To apply these, highlight the text and choose one of the options by clicking its button.

■ **Left**   All the text is aligned to the left and the right edge is ragged.

■ **Centered**   All the text is centered.

Left aligned ──── Full justified
Centered ──── Justified last line right
Right aligned ──── Justified last line center
──── Justified last line left

FIGURE 8-15 The alignment options

- **Right**   Opposite of left; text is aligned to the right.

- **Full Justified**   The text is aligned left and right to form a box shape, and the last line is stretched to fit the box. (This option can leave some large gaps in the text.)

- **Justified Last Line Right**   Same as Full Justified, except the last line is aligned to the right; makes for less gaps.

- **Justified Last Line Centered**   Same as above, but the last line is centered.

- **Justified Last Line Left**   Justified with the last line left aligned. This is the most appropriate option for most justified text.

FIGURE 8-16 Examples of alignment

This is paragraph text that has been right aligned This is paragraph text that has been right aligned This is para-graph text that has been right aligned This is paragraph text that has been right aligned This is paragraph text that has been right aligned This is paragraph text that has been right aligned This is para-graph text that has been right aligned

This is paragraph text that has been center aligned This is paragraph text that has been center aligned This is para-graph text that has been center aligned This is para-graph text that has been center aligned This is para-graph text that has been center aligned This is para-graph text that has been center aligned

This is paragraph text that has been left aligned This is paragraph text that has been left aligned This is paragraph text that has been left aligned This is paragraph text that has been left aligned This is paragraph text that has been left aligned This is paragraph text that has been left aligned

This is paragraph text that has been Full Justified This is para-graph text that has been Full Justified This is paragraph text that has been Full Justified This is paragraph text that has been Full Justified This is paragraph text that has been Full Justified This is paragraph text that has been Full J u s t i f i e d

This is paragraph text that has been Justified Right This is paragraph text that has been Justified Right This is para-graph text that has been Justi-fied Right This is paragraph text that has been Justified Right This is paragraph text that has been Justified Right This is paragraph text that has been Justified Right This is paragraph text that has been Justified Right

This is paragraph text that has been Justified Centered This is paragraph text that has been Justified Centered This is para-graph text that has been Justi-fied Centered This is para-graph text that has been Justi-fied Centered This is para-graph text that has been Justi-fied Centered This is para-graph text that has been Justi-fied Centered

This is paragraph text that has been Justified Left This is para-graph text that has been Justi-fied Left This is paragraph text that has been Justified Left This is paragraph text that has been Justified Left This is paragraph text that has been Justified Left This is paragraph text that has been Justi-fied Left

Usually, the justified options look nice for wide columns of text to make them look formal and unified. The aligned paragraphs are better on narrower columns because they have more flexibility in line breaks and avoid the gaps between words. Single aligned text is also more casual in application.

Using Text Warp

If you are familiar with Word Art from Microsoft, you will already have an idea of the functionality of Text Warp. This is a fun and useful tool used to create interesting curves and waves that your text will follow. The best way to learn about this tool is to experiment. Let's walk through the basic functionality to learn how to use the tool. The Text Warp button (the T with the curve under it) on the toolbar is shown here.

Applying Text Warp

Whenever you want to apply text warp to your text, follow these steps:

1. Select the text you want to warp.

2. Click the warp text button from the toolbar.

3. You will see the Warp Text dialog box, shown in Figure 8-18. Click the Style drop-down menu.

4. Choose the style that is the closest to the shape you want. For this example, we'll choose Arc.

5. Adjust the Bend percentage to increase or reverse the effect.

6. Move the Horizontal and Vertical Distortion sliders to bend the text through space. Figure 8-17 shows some text in the shape of an arc, with a negative horizontal distortion applied. When you apply a negative amount in the distortion, the text appears to move away from you.

Figure 8-18 shows a positive amount on the distortion. Notice how it has the opposite effect and the text now appears to be coming toward you. We have also used the Flag shape for the style, which makes the text appear to "twist." Experiment with the different shapes and settings and you will get the hang of this tool really quickly.

You are bound to have a lot of fun with this tool. You can create some really funky text shapes with minimum effort. Hopefully, you can tear yourself away from all the fun soon, because we are about to look at what many consider the most exciting new feature of Photoshop CS, the Type On A Path tool.

FIGURE 8-17 Arc text with negative horizontal distortion

FIGURE 8-18 Flag text with positive horizontal distortion

Typing on a Path

You can align type on a path in Photoshop. Typing on a path is the ability to make your type follow the curvature of a path. In Chapter 7, we learned all about paths and how to create and manipulate them. We are about to learn how to make text flow with our paths. As we have also learned, two types of paths can be specified: open paths and closed paths. We will examine how to add text to both.

Typing on an Open Path

An open path is a path that has distinct start and finish points. It looks like a wave or a squiggle. These types of paths lend themselves very well as guides for text.

When you are drawing with the Pen tool, be sure that you select the path option, as shown here. This will ensure that a clean path is created.

Let's jump headfirst into creating our first type on a path effect:

1. Create a path with the Pen tool, as in Figure 8-19. (Refer to Chapter 7 for details on using the Pen tool.)

2. Choose the Type tool and select the formatting you want: font, color, size, and so on.

3. As you move your curser over the path, you will notice that it changes to an I-beam with a curve through it, as shown in Figure 8-20. This tells you that you are now in the "hot zone," and the Text tool is detecting the presence of a path. Move the curser to the approximate position where you want the text to begin.

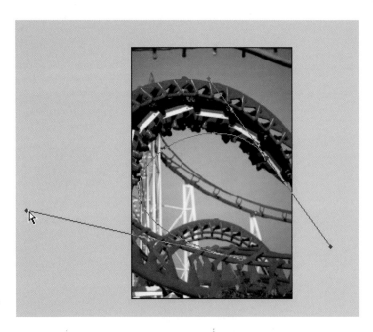

FIGURE 8-19 Using the Pen tool, create an open path.

4. Click where you want to begin typing. As you type, you will notice something very cool; the text follows all the contours of the path. Type in some words, as we did in Figure 8-21.

5. Click the checkmark on the toolbar or click another tool to apply the text.

Editing Type on an Open Path

You have learned how to create type on a path; you are now going to learn how to make changes to the text and to the path. You can format the text on a path by doing the following:

1. Before you can make formatting changes to the text, you must first select it. To select the text, choose the Type tool, and then click and drag through all the characters you want to format. The text should now be highlighted.

2. Make the formatting changes just like you would with normal text. Change the size, font, color, or any other attribute, including the tracking and kerning.

FIGURE 8-20 The cursor detecting a path

You can adjust the curve even with the text attached. The text will reflow to follow any changes you make on the curve. This is a great way to smooth out any little kinks in the way the text flows on the path.

If you want to reposition the text along the path, take these steps:

1. Choose the Path Selection tool from the tool palette.

2. Hover the tool near the end of the path until you see a small arrow. This arrow tells you that you are about to move the start/finish point of the text.

FIGURE 8-21 The text follows the path

3. Click and drag the type along the path, and release the mouse button when you are happy with the new position.

To get better results with text on a path, keep these tips in mind.

■   Adjust the tracking to get a nice flow. Generally, curved text should use wider than normal tracking because the insides of the curves bring the characters closer together than normal.

■   Adjust the individual kerning on certain characters to fine-tune the way they flow together.

■   Avoid sharp bends in the paths.

Figure 8-22 shows our effect with a few of these tweaks.

FIGURE 8-22 The finished text with some tweaks

Typing on a Closed Path

Typing on a closed path is similar to typing on an open path. The difference is that a closed path is a loop, so it has no definitive start or end points. An excellent example of this is a circle. You can use custom shapes with the Path Option tool chosen from the toolbar or create a closed path with the Pen tool.

Let's flow some text around a circle. This is a common use for text on a path for logo design, for example.

1. Choose the Circular Shape tool.

2. In the options bar, choose the Path option.

3. Draw a circle that is the same size and position as the object you want to flow the text around. Figure 8-23 shows an image with the circular path attached.

FIGURE 8-23 The circular path created on the image

 Tip   *When drawing with the Circular Shape tool, hold down the* SHIFT *key and the shape will be constrained to an even circle rather than an ellipse. Hold down the* SPACEBAR *while creating a shape to reposition the shape on the canvas while drawing.*

4. Click the mouse anywhere on the circular path; this will become your starting point to add text. Figure 8-24 shows the cursor ready for some text.

5. Begin typing your characters; you will notice that they flow nicely around the circle.

6. To adjust the font and size, format the text in exactly the same way you did in the previous section.

Figure 8-25 shows a sphere with the text wrapped around it.

 If your text is too large, some of the characters will not show when you create type on a path. To select all the text on the path (even text that doesn't appear on screen), click with the Text tool and press CTRL-A *(CMD-A on Mac); otherwise, all the text will not be selected. After you've selected all the text, reduce the size of the font to make it fit on the path.*

FIGURE 8-24 Ready to add some text

Typing on the Inside of the Path

While creating the type on the circle, you might have asked, "What if I want the text to go the other way, on the *inside* of the path?" You will be happy to know that this is easy to accomplish.

1. Choose the Text tool and hover the mouse at the beginning of the text area until you see the arrow appear.

2. Click and drag the mouse to the inside of the circle. The text will follow to the inside, as shown in Figure 8-26.

FIGURE 8-25 Text wrapped around the outside of a circle

FIGURE 8-26 Type on the
inside of the circle

3. You can also change the text back to the outside
   anytime by dragging it back to the outside of the circle
   or shape.

Filling a Shape with Type

We have looked at some neat features of the Type On A Path
tool. Now let's look at another feature of this unique tool. You
can fill shapes with text and, in effect, have the text flow in
the shape of the path. Figure 8-27 shows an advertisement I
designed to mock the wet weather in a gloomy city, and to ask
how to find the sunny weather of San Jose, California.

To fill a shape with type, follow these steps:

1. Create a path using the Custom Shape tool.

2. Set the path's options from the toolbar.

FIGURE 8-27 Type in a path

3. Hover the mouse cursor inside the shape. You should see an I-beam with what looks like brackets around it. This is the Type In A Path tool.

4. Click the mouse and begin to enter text (or paste it from another application). You will notice that the text will fill the inside area of the shape. The shape will act like a container for the text.

5. Click the checkmark or another tool to apply the effect. Text can be formatted just like all other text.

Chapter 9

Save Time with Automation

How to...

- Use tool presets
- Use actions
- Create your own actions
- Modify actions
- Load presets
- Create droplets
- Create a picture package
- Create a contact sheet
- Create a web gallery
- Produce a PDF presentation

Imagine that you must lay out and design a 50-page catalog. You need to extract images from a CD, resize them, and then insert them onto the pages. You also must insert a box, stock number, and heading on each page. In the midst of all this planning, you realize it's lunchtime. So you prepare one page, click a button, and let your computer keep working while you take a break. When you return, you see that all 50 pages are done. Science fiction? No, it's reality. Your lunch tasted great, and while you were eating, the graphics for your brochure was finished. After a little tweaking, it will be delivered to the client on time.

Productivity and automation are two of Photoshop's greatest strengths, and the information you'll learn in this chapter could make this book pay for itself many times over.

Creating and Using Tool Presets

You know the process by now: You choose a tool, select a color, select a size, apply, and do it all over again. The problem is, every time you need to go back to a setting, you must go through the entire process again. Not so with tool presets. You

Tool preset

A.

New Preset ⌐
Delete Preset ⌐

can choose all your settings, save them, and recall them for later use. Think of them as style sheets for all things Photoshop.

The tool presets work with all the tools in the tool palette, including the nested tools. The tool presets will remember all the options you set for any selected tool, including color, line width, font, style—and more.

Tool Presets Palette

B.

FIGURE 9-1 The Tool Preset Palette (A) and the palette showing tools for the Current Tool Only selected (B)

Figure 9-1 shows the Tool Presets palette, which can be accessed by choosing Window | Tool Presets. At the bottom of the palette, you'll notice a checkbox called Current Tool Only. When you check this box, only the options for the selected tool will appear on the palette. I keep this option turned on all the time; it is a great clutter reducer, as you can see in the palette on the right.

The Tool Presets palette can also be accessed by clicking the far left icon in the options bar. This icon is always the Tool Presets icon, no matter what tool is selected.

Creating Presets

Creating presets is a simple process:

1. From the tool box, choose the tool you want to use for a preset.

2. Choose all the settings for the tool as you normally would.

3. Choose Window | Tool Presets to open the Tool Presets palette and click the New Preset button.

4. In the New Tool Preset dialog box, enter a memorable name for the preset, as shown in the following illustration:

The new preset name will appear in the Tool Presets palette.

With a few tools, additional options are available via a checkbox located in the New Tool Preset dialog box. They're shown here:

Tool	Checkbox Option
Brush tool	Include Color
Gradient tool	Include Gradient
Pen tool	Include Color
Shape tool	Include Color

Using Presets

Using the presets you create is even simpler than creating them:

1. Choose a tool from the tool box.

2. Choose Window | Tool Presets, if the Preset Palette isn't already visible, and highlight the preset you want from the Tool Presets palette.

3. Use the tool with all the preset settings.

Working with Actions

The main automation tools in Photoshop are called *actions*. An action is the same as a macro, which is similar in concept to pressing the record button while you work. Actions record all your tasks—simple as that. The Actions palette, shown in Figure 9-2, records each click of the mouse. It will take note of all the settings and tools you used to achieve a particular task.

When you have finished the task, click the Stop button and the recording stops. Photoshop will remember all this information in an action file, a text file that's assigned an .atn extension. At

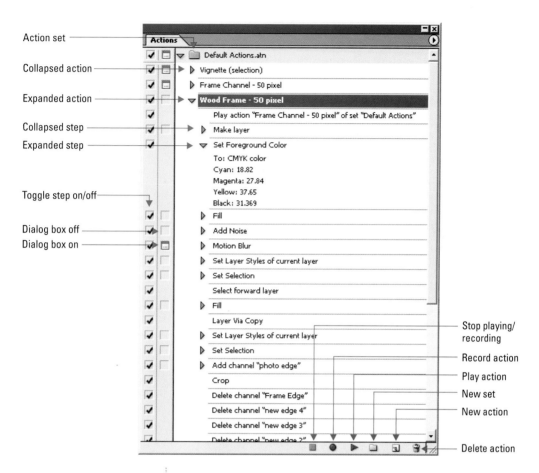

Action set

Collapsed action

Expanded action

Collapsed step

Expanded step

Toggle step on/off

Dialog box off

Dialog box on

Stop playing/
recording

Record action

Play action

New set

New action

Delete action

FIGURE 9-2 The Actions palette

any time, you can open another image, click Play, and Photoshop
will *run* the action. As the action runs, everything that you
recorded will take place on the current image. You can have
Photoshop take care of repetitive tasks automatically by using
actions.

Actions can be saved to a disk, shared with friends or
coworkers, and distributed to other users via the Internet. Sites
such as http://www.actionfx.com and http://www.actionxchange
.com have sprung up to accommodate the demand for these
actions to Photoshop users around the world.

All the functionality of actions are stored in the Actions
palette, which has two parts:

■   **The transport controls**   Where you record, stop,
play, create new, and delete actions. This set of controls

performs similarly to the controls on a tape recorder or VCR.

- **The Actions window**   Displays the following information:

  - **Action sets**   These collapsible folders contain groups of actions. Actions can be saved only as sets, or groups. Individual actions must be included in a set for the Save Action function to work.

  - **Actions**   Can be expanded to see the actual settings used in each step.

  - **A toggle step box**   Uncheck to skip certain steps of an action, if desired.

  - **A toggle box for dialogs**   Allows you to pause the action with an open dialog box so that you can make the adjustments manually. This is useful for effects such as sharpening and blurs.

Playing Actions

When you want to apply an action to an image, you call this *playing* or *running* an action (see Figure 9-3).

FIGURE 9-3 Image before action is run

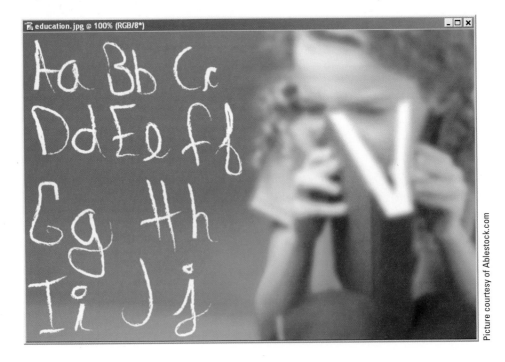

Picture courtesy of Ablestock.com

Here's how you run an action on an image:

1. If the Actions palette is not open, press F9 or choose Window | Actions to open it.

2. Choose an action from the Actions palette by clicking its name.

3. Click the Play button at the bottom of the palette.

4. Some preset actions display a dialog box containing information the creator of the action wants you to read. If this appears, read the message and then click OK.

5. Photoshop will run the action on its own.

6. The action will complete and you will see the result (see Figure 9-4).

FIGURE 9-4 Image after applying an action

Button Mode

You can also display the Actions palette by using *button mode*. In button mode, all the palette clutter is reduced, and you will see only a list of buttons labeled with the names of the actions, as shown in Figure 9-5. To run an action, you simply click its button. You cannot record actions in button mode.

 In button mode, you can assign keyboard shortcuts to run actions. This is a good time saver. We'll discuss how to do this in the next section.

Here's how to switch to button mode:

1. Open the Actions palette (see Figure 9-5).

2. Choose the top right arrow to open the flyout menu, and Choose Button Mode.

3. To switch back to normal mode, repeat steps 1 through 3.

Creating Your Own Actions

Although preset actions are available, as you'll soon discover, the real power of actions is that you can create your own. You may need to perform a unique task many times—such as reducing the size of a picture or adding a custom frame to a series of images. You can save a lot of time by performing this task once and saving it as an action.

Here's how to create an action:

1. Open the Actions palette and the image you want to work on.

2. Click the New Action icon (see Figure 9-6).

3. Choose a name and recording options, as shown here: This is where you can assign a keyboard shortcut to your action by choosing a function key and modifiers.

4. Click the Record icon.

5. Perform all the steps you want to include in the action.

6. Click the Stop icon.

Now your action is completed and ready for use.

FIGURE 9-5 The Actions palette in button mode

FIGURE 9-6 Creating a new action

Adding Pauses and Comments

Actions can record almost anything. However, you can't use actions to record manual work, such as painting, airbrushing, or other types of touch-up work.

To enable you to accomplish these tasks during an action, you can record some stops, or pauses, into your actions. These will pause the action, allow for you to perform the manual work, and then continue the action.

Here's how to add a pause while recording an action:

1. Begin recording the action.

2. When you come to a point at which you need to insert the stop, click the flyout menu and choose Insert Stop.

3. You will see the Record Stop dialog box, as shown in Figure 9-7.

4. Enter the message you want to display and click the Allow Continue checkbox so that the action can continue after the task has been performed.

5. Click OK and continue recording the action as usual.

FIGURE 9-7 Recording a stop in an action

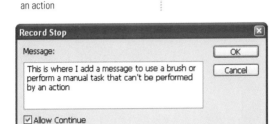

When the action is played back, your message will be displayed in a message box. You can then perform the task and click Continue. The action will continue playing until the end, although you can add as many stops as you wish into an action.

Using Modal Steps

Modal steps is a fancy name for making adjustments to dialog boxes as you are running actions. No two images are the same, and the settings that look great on one image may look less than ideal on another. For example, you may have created an action for scanning that sharpens and color corrects each image. You can cause the action to pause and wait for your settings each time a dialog box is used. This way, you can choose the best settings for your particular image.

To call up a dialog box during playback:

1. Click the toggle box to the left of the step for which you want to call up the dialog box (refer to Figure 9-2).

2. Play the action.

3. When the action reaches the marked step, the dialog box will open.

4. Make your adjustments to the settings, as shown in Figure 9-8.

5. Click OK in the dialog box.

6. The action will continue until the next pause or until the end.

Modifying Actions

After an action has been recorded, you can make modifications to it. You can add, delete, or modify steps.

To add a step:

1. In the Actions palette, click the action to expand it.

2. In the expanded action, click the point at which you want to add the step.

3. Click the Record icon.

4. Record the new step. When you're done, click the Stop icon.

To delete a step:

1. In the Actions palette, click the action to expand it.

2. Drag the step you want to delete to the Delete Action icon (which looks like a garbage can) at the bottom of the Actions palette.

To replace an action step:

1. Open an image.

2. Expand the Actions palette.

3. Double-click the step you want to modify or replace.

4. Make the changes.

5. Click OK.

FIGURE 9-8 Making manual adjustments during an action

Picture courtesy of Ablestock.com

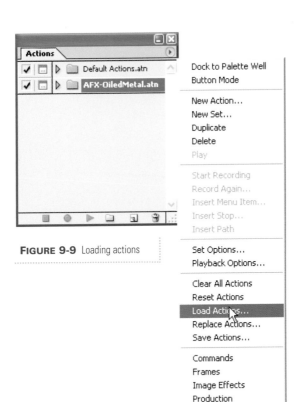

FIGURE 9-9 Loading actions

Loading and Saving Actions

Photoshop comes with quite a few actions already included. You can also purchase actions on CD, share them with friends, and download them from the Internet. Whichever method you use to obtain actions, they must be loaded into Photoshop before you can use them. You can always identify an action file, because it uses an .atn filename extension.

Loading New Actions

To load actions into Photoshop:

1. Open the Actions palette.

2. Click the flyout menu in the upper-right corner.

3. Choose Load Actions, as shown in Figure 9-9.

4. Navigate to the saved actions.

5. Click Load.

A quick way to add an action is to double-click its icon. It will be added to Photoshop and the Program will launch, if it's not already running.

In Photoshop, actions are cross platform—that is, they work on both Macs and PCs. Just make sure you add the .atn extension to the filename if you're moving an action from the Macintosh to a PC.

You can now play back the actions. Choose either the ones that ship with Photoshop or third-party actions, as shown in Figure 9-10, from actionfx.com.

FIGURE 9-10 A third-party action

Saving Actions

When you have invested some time creating all your new actions, you'll want to save them for later use.

To save your actions:

1. Open the Actions palette.

2. Choose an action set. As mentioned earlier in the chapter, individual actions cannot be saved; they must be part of a set. If you want to save an individual action, you must first create a set and then drag the action into the set.

3. In the flyout menu on the Actions palette, choose Save Actions.

4. Navigate to the location where you want to save the action, and then click Save.

Processing Multiple Images at Once

You can apply the same action to a group of images by using *batch processing*. The easiest way to do this is to create a new folder and copy the images to the folder that you want to process. Copying like this is a good idea, because if something goes wrong, your original images are still intact. The batch processing option will work on folders, too, so you can apply processing to all the files within the folder.

To run an action on several files at once:

1. Choose File | Automate | Batch.

2. Under Play, choose the set and action that you want to run.

3. Under Source, click Choose to select the folder of files to be affected. Four options are included in this area:

   - **Override Action "Open" Command**   If the action includes a step that tells it to open an image, check this box; otherwise, leave it unchecked.

   - **Include All Subfolders**   Any folders nested under the target folder will also be processed if you select this option.

   - **Suppress File Open Options Dialogs**   Checking this option will ignore any error or warning messages on the files. You can choose to check the warning manually. For a truly automated experience, check this box.

■ **Suppress Color Profile Warnings**   Choosing this option will display a warning if the color profiles are not matched. Check the box to prevent these warning dialog boxes from displaying, or monitor them manually and click OK on each one yourself.

4. Choose the destination folder where the files will be saved. You'll see two options here:

■ **Save And Close**   The files in the existing folder will be overwritten by the processed files.

■ **Folder**   The processed images will be placed in their own folder and the originals will remain intact. Options will become available for naming. Choose the desired options from the menus that appear, and enter a serial number; this number will represent the first image. All additional images will be named sequentially from the starting number you set.

5. Click OK.

You can also run all the batch actions from the File Browser.

Now go make some coffee. When you return, open the destination folder, and you'll see that all your files are done.

Applying an Action to a Folder of Images

Now let's walk through the process of applying an action to a folder of images. We'll change several images from color to grayscale and save the copies in a new folder.

FIGURE 9-11 Choosing the Play Options: (A) Choose an action; (B) Choose the Source Folder of Images; (C) Setting the playback options

1. Prepare a folder and place all the images that you would like to process into this folder. If you don't already have an action ready, record one now.

2. Choose File | Automate | Batch.

3. In the dialog box that appears, choose an action set and action from the Play options area, as shown in Figure 9-11A.

A.

Play

Set: Default Actions.atn

Action: Custom RGB to Grayscale

4. In the Source field, choose Folder.

5. Click Choose, and then select the folder from the pop-up menu, as shown in Figure 9-11B.

6. Choose the playback options to run the action without interruptions, as seen in Figure 9-11C.

7. In the Destination field of the dialog box, choose Folder.

8. Click the Choose button and the browser window will pop up.

9. Select a folder or create a new folder by clicking Make New Folder and naming it, as shown in Figure 9-12A.

10. If you create a new folder, name the new images. The default settings are fine for most cases, as shown in Figure 9-12B, or you can type in your own names.

11. Now, in the Errors field at the bottom of the dialog, choose an error option. You can choose one of two options:

   ■ **Stop For Errors**   If the file contains an error, the action will stop processing the rest of the folder.

B.

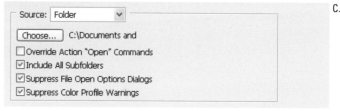

C.

FIGURE 9-12 Choosing a Folder for the Processed Image: (A) Create a new folder on your hard drive; (B) Setting the file's Save options

A.

B.

■ **Log Errors To File**   If you choose this option, the action will play until the end and any error messages will be saved in a file. Click the Save As button and choose a filename for the error log. The log will be saved as a text file.

12. At the upper-right of the dialog box, click OK, and the action will run.

13. If any steps are marked for your interaction, the action will pause for your input and then continue when you click OK. Otherwise, Photoshop will process all the images for you in one batch.

14. Open your destination folder and see all your images processed, as shown in Figure 9-13.

FIGURE 9-13 The processed images in a new folder

Using Droplets

A *droplet* is like an "action in a box." The droplet will appear as a small icon that you can add to your Desktop or in a folder.

When you drag and drop one or more files on the icon, Photoshop will launch and run the selected action on the file(s). This is a handy tool for people who must complete identical tasks on files on a regular basis.

Here is how you create a droplet:

1. Choose File | Automate | Create Droplet. You'll see the dialog box shown in Figure 9-14.

FIGURE 9-14 The Create Droplet dialog box

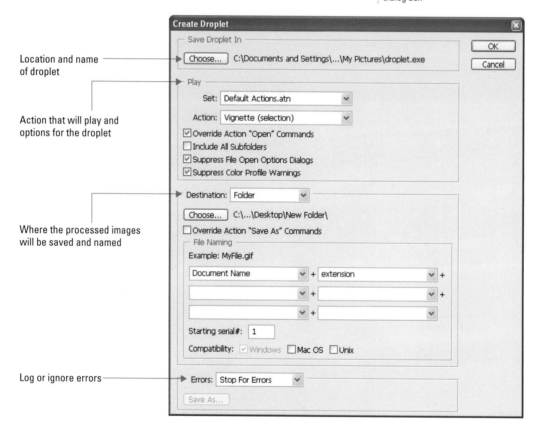

Location and name of droplet

Action that will play and options for the droplet

Where the processed images will be saved and named

Log or ignore errors

2. Click Choose. Type in a name for your droplet, and select the location where it will be stored.

3. In the Play options area, choose the Set and Action to play from the droplet. In this area, you can also choose Suppress Color Profile Warnings so that the action won't require your interactivity.

4. Choose a Destination folder for the processed files.

5. Choose an Errors option: Stop For Errors, or Log Errors To File. If you log the errors, they will be saved as a text file.

6. Click OK, and your droplet will be created.

Choose Suppress Color Profile Warnings so that the action won't require your interactivity.

When you go to the folder in which you created the droplet, you'll see an icon similar to that shown in Figure 9-15. To use the droplet, simply drag and drop your files onto the icon. You don't even need to open the files.

FIGURE 9-15 A droplet icon

droplet.exe

Creating a Picture Package

Do you remember when you received your high school photos? They came on a sheet with several different sizes for you to cut apart. In Photoshop, you can create a similar image grouping called a *picture package*. Photoshop can arrange your images onto sheets for you. You can then print the images and trim the photos. This enables you to cram many images on a sheet of paper, without having to do any math, and thus saving a lot of paper.

Here is how to create your own picture package:

1. Choose File | Automate | Picture Package. You'll see the Picture Package dialog box shown in Figure 9-16.

2. In the Source Images section, choose either File or Folder to process either a single image or a group of images.

3. In the document area, choose the Page Size you want.

4. Choose a Layout; you can choose from many preset options, or choose Custom to create your own layout.

5. Choose the Resolution.

6. Choose Flatten All Layers unless you need to retain layers for some reason.

7. For most instances of Photo printing, the mode should stay on RGB.

Choose either an image or a folder ──────

Locate the file ──────

Output size ──────

Choose a layout ──────

Choose a resolution ──────

Choose this option if you want to print text on an image ──────

FIGURE 9-16 Picture package options

8. In the Label area, choose whether or not you want to include labels to your pictures. If you want to add labels, type in the information here and select the formatting you want.

9. You'll see a preview in the layout window, as shown in Figure 9-16. If it all looks good, click OK, and Photoshop will process the images. You will see a lot going on. Grab a cup of tea and admire all the work that you don't have to do manually!

You can now print and trim the images. Send copies to your friends and family and show them what a Photoshop master you are!

Using Contact Sheet II

The *contact sheet* is widely used in the world of photography. When you order a set of prints, you sometimes have the option of also receiving a contact sheet, which shows all the photographs arranged into thumbnails so you can see a "thumbnail" of each photo on the same page.

Contact sheets are incredibly useful when saving files to a CD. Whether you're dealing with your artwork, pictures from a digital camera, or you're creating contact sheets and inserting them in the jewel cases, contact sheets offer a visual way to review the contents of a CD.

Photoshop can create multiple pages full of images, and it will produce as many pages as needed to index all the images in a chosen folder.

Here is how to create a contact sheet:

FIGURE 9-17 Contact Sheet II options dialog box

1. Choose File | Automate | Contact Sheet II. You'll see the Contact Sheet II dialog box shown in Figure 9-17.

2. In the Source Images section, choose the folder of images you want to include on the contact sheet.

3. In the Document area, select the document size and resolution.

4. For most purposes, the default setting on RGB mode and Flatten All Layers works best.

5. Choose Thumbnail options; Default should work for most needs, but you can change as many options here as you want.

6. The preview on the right shows you how many images and pages will be processed.

7. If you want to use the filenames as captions for the images, click the appropriate checkbox and choose formatting options.

8. Click OK when you're satisfied with your settings.

The images will be processed, and you will see a page similar to that shown in Figure 9-18. If you chose the option to do so, a filename will appear under each thumbnail. Print out this page and place it inside your jewel case along with the archived CD, or you can organize the pages into a little booklet or ring binder to help you locate images later.

Creating a Web Gallery

If you want to post a collection of images to an Internet site, you need to resize and optimize each image and then create thumbnails. Then you would create a web page for all the thumbnails, and then create a page for each of the images. Depending on the number of images you want to display, this process could take hours, or even days.

Using Web Gallery makes this job a snap. In just a few minutes, you can process dozens of images and build great looking web galleries.

FIGURE 9-18 The finished contact sheet

Here is how to take a folder of images and turn them into a web site:

1. Choose File | Automate | Web Photo Gallery. You will see the Web Photo Gallery dialog box, as shown in Figure 9-19.

2. In the Site area, choose the Style you want to use for the gallery. You can see how they will look in the preview.

3. In the Source Images area, choose the folder where your photos are located.

Choose a preset layout

Your e-mail address

The folder where the images are

Process subfolders

Where you want the web gallery located

Set the options

Preview

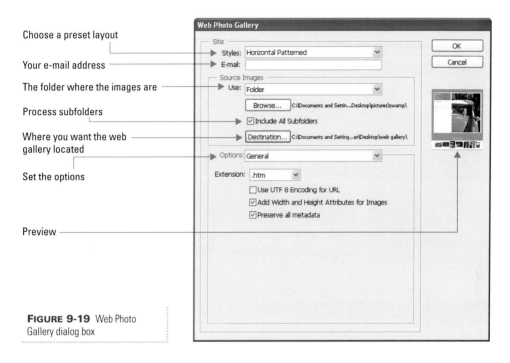

FIGURE 9-19 Web Photo Gallery dialog box

4. Check the Include All Subfolders box if you want to include images in subfolders of the folder you selected.

5. Click the Destination button to specify where on your hard drive (or elsewhere) you want the web page to be saved.

6. Set Options if you want to change any of the default settings.

7. Click OK when you're happy with your settings.

After a little processing time, you'll see the finished web page pop up in your browser, as shown in Figure 9-20. Click the thumbnails or arrows to browse all the images one by one.

If you go to the destination folder, you will see all the files that were created for the web gallery, as shown in Figure 9-21. To view them on the web, simply upload them to your web site.

To view the web gallery shown in Figure 9-21, point your web browser to http://www.photoshopcafe.com/la/.

FIGURE 9-20 The finished web page

FIGURE 9-21 The files in the web gallery

FIGURE 9-22 PDF Presentation
dialog box

Creating a PDF Presentation

Slide show anyone? With PDF presentations, you can create full-screen slide shows of your images, complete with transition effects.

Here's how to create a slide show presentation:

1. Choose File | Automate | PDF Presentation. You will see the PDF Presentation dialog box, as shown in Figure 9-22.

2. If you have images already open, click Add Open Files; otherwise, skip this step.

3. Click Browse to locate the images you want to add to the presentation.

4. Choose the files you want to add to the presentation by CTRL-clicking them (CMD-clicking on a Mac), as shown in Figure 9-23.

5. Click the Open button.

FIGURE 9-23 Adding images

6. Choose Presentation to indicate a self-running presentation.

7. In the Output Options section of the PDF Presentation dialog box, check the View PDF After Saving option to have the presentation run automatically when Photoshop has finished creating it.

8. In the Presentation Options section, choose a delay time between slides (see Figure 9-24). Click Advance Every… …Seconds and choose the number of seconds you want each slide to be displayed.

9. Choose Loop After Last Page to run a continuous presentation. Looped presentations start again from the top after the last slide is shown.

FIGURE 9-24 Choose delay time between slides.

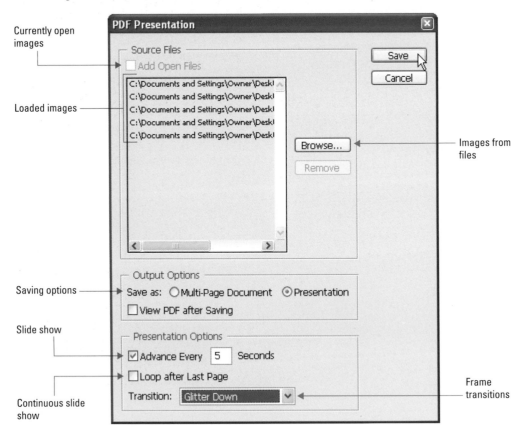

10. Choose a Transition effect for the images.

11. Click Save.

12. Choose the Output Options.

    a. Choose Multipage Document to output a typical PDF file.

    b. Choose Presentation to create a self-running slide show.

The presentation will take up the full screen and will automatically display all the images according to the transition effect that will display between images, as shown in Figure 9-25.

FIGURE 9-25 The PDF presentation showing a transition effect in progress

To advance the images backwards and forwards manually, click the left or right mouse button, respectively.

When you have finished the slide show or you want to stop the presentation, press the ESC key on your keyboard. A message will appear to inform you that special features have been created by Photoshop.

Part III The Fun Stuff

Chapter 10 Make Selections

How to...

- Understand selections
- Use selection tools
- Use the Marquee tool
- Feather selections
- Use Freeform Selection tools
- Select images with the Magic Wand tool
- Use the Color Range tool
- Refine the selection
- Transform selections
- Use Quick Mask
- Create a photographic edge with Quick Mask
- Remove matting

Making selections in Photoshop is similar to taking a pair of magic scissors to a photo and cutting out a particular piece you want to work with, even while the piece is still a part of the original photo. In Photoshop, you use selection tools to select only portions of an image that you want to work on. Other, nonselected, parts of the image are unaffected.

Understanding Selections

You can see a selection by what are known as the *marching ants*, the animated dashed lines that appear around the selected portion of an image. When you make a selection, only the selected area will be affected by any editing or adjustments you make to the image. For example, Figure 10-1 shows a selection surrounding an image of a cat. If we paint the cat selection with a paintbrush, only the selected portion of the image is affected, while the unselected portions are protected.

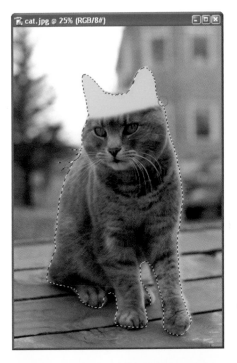

FIGURE 10-1 An image with a selection; only the selected area will be affected.

Have you ever seen anyone paint a car? The first thing they do is tear off huge chunks of masking tape and stick them on all the areas that they want to protect from the paint. Once all these areas are masked, the painter will spray paint over the car. When the masking tape is peeled off, the protected surfaces are free from the offending pigments.

When you make a selection using one of the selection tools in Photoshop, you are in effect protecting all the unselected portions of the image from "overspray." An example of this is shown in the image in Figure 10-2, where I selected the cat object and then made a radical color adjustment. Notice that only the selected area has been affected and the unselected areas are unaffected.

Feathered Selection

By default, all the selections have "hard" edges. If you need a softer edged selection, you can use feathering. You specify the amount of the feather in pixels, which set how soft the selection will be—a larger feather amount produces a softer selection. Figure 10-3 shows the difference between feathered and non-feathered edges.

You can apply feathering in two ways:

■ Choose a selection tool, and the options bar will allow you to enter a feather radius. This setting will apply to all future selections made with this tool. As a result, be sure that you set the feather amount before making a selection.

■ You can feather an existing selection by choosing Select | Feather and then entering a feather radius.

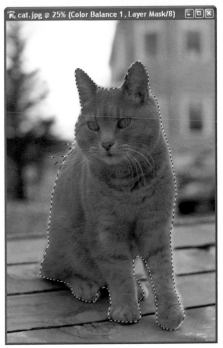

FIGURE 10-2 A selected area with a color adjustment applied

When setting a feather radius from the options bar, make sure you return the setting to 0 before making the next selection, or the feather will be applied to that selection also.

Using Selection Tools

Several selection tools are available within Photoshop. Each tool is designed for a specific selection task. In this section, you will learn how to use each tool and how to decide which tool is the best choice for your specific need.

Marquee Tools

The simplest and most commonly used of the selection tools are the Marquee tools, shown in Figure 10-4.

- **Rectangular** Creates a rectangular selection. Hold down the SHIFT key to constrain the selection to a perfect square.

- **Elliptical** Creates elliptical selections. Hold down the SHIFT key to constrain the selection to a perfect circle.

- **Single Row** Creates a single-pixel-high horizontal selection. To use this tool, click anywhere in the image area, and you will see a dashed horizontal line. Drag the mouse to the desired location.

- **Single Column** Creates a single pixel wide vertical selection. Used similarly to the Single Row tool.

After you select a tool, click and drag the mouse over the desired area to draw the selection.

Making Simple Selections

Execution of each of the Marquee tools is similar. Click and hold down the mouse button and drag over the image with the mouse to make the selection. All the pixels inside the dragged area will be selected. Figure 10-5 shows an elliptical selection in action.

FIGURE 10-3 An image showing the difference between a hard edge and one with a 25-pixel feather

■ [ ] Rectangular Marquee Tool	M
◯ Elliptical Marquee Tool	M
▱ Single Row Marquee Tool	
▯ Single Column Marquee Tool	

FIGURE 10-4 The Marquee tools

FIGURE 10-5 Drawing a selection with the elliptical marquee tool

FIGURE 10-6 Color applied to an inverted selection

Here are several tips to help you make accurate selections:

- To draw from the center, hold down the ALT key (OPTION key on a Mac) while dragging.

- To constrain the proportions, hold down the SHIFT key as you drag.

- To move a selection while drawing, hold down the SPACEBAR as you drag.

Inverting a Selection

You can also use selection tools to select an area, and then alter the entire image except for the selected area. This is called *inverting* the selection. The Inverse command swaps the selected and unselected areas. Choose Select | Inverse to swap the selected areas, or use the shortcut: SHIFT-CTRL-I (SHIFT-CMD-I on a Mac). Figure 10-6 shows a color adjustment applied to an inverted selection. In this case, the circle was the selected area.

Choosing Selection Options

By default, whenever you make a new selection, it will replace the existing selection. However, you can make more than one selection at a time using several options. Figure 10-7 shows the results of the various selection options, which are available from the options bar whenever you choose a selection tool.

- **New Selection** The default setting, which replaces the existing selection.

- **Add to Selection** Adds the new area to the previous selection.

- **Subtract from Selection** The new selection will be cut from the existing selection.

- **Intersect with Selection** The existing selection will be replaced by the overlapping area of the new selection.

FIGURE 10-7 Results of various selection options

By using one or more of these options, you can create some pretty complex selection shapes.

Freeform Selection Tools

So far, we have looked at selection tools that help you create selections based on predefined shapes. Another set of tools gives you much more freedom in your selections: the three Lasso tools. Figure 10-8 shows the tools in the tool palette.

FIGURE 10-8 The Lasso tools

Lasso Tool

The Lasso tool is at the top of the freeform selection tools. You can choose this tool and drag it around an image as you would a pencil on a piece of paper. Figure 10-9A shows a selection made with the Lasso tool.

When you have finished dragging the mouse around the selection, release the button and a closed selection will be created. All the options from the options bar are available with this tool, and with a bit of practice, you can create some very accurate selections. Figure 10-9B shows the selected portion of the image copied to a new layer. A radial blur was then applied to the background.

A.

B.

FIGURE 10-9 A selection created with the lasso tool (A) and an effect used with the selection (B)

Tips for Using the Freeform Selection Tools

You can use the various options from the options bar, but this can be a bit slow. Here are a couple of keyboard shortcuts to save some time:

- To add to the selection, press and hold the SHIFT key.
- To subtract from the selection, press and hold the ALT key (OPTION key on a Mac).

10

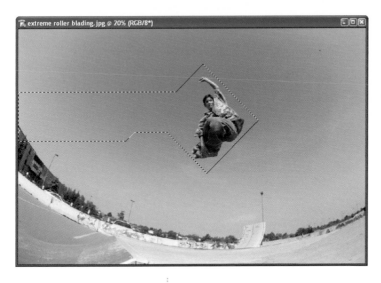

FIGURE 10-10 A selection made with the polygon lasso tool

Polygonal Lasso

The Polygonal Lasso tool differs from the Lasso tool in that it draws only straight lines and you cannot drag around your selection. Figure 10-10 shows an image with a selection created using this tool.

The Polygonal Lasso tool is a "clicking" tool; you cannot drag using this tool.

Here's how the tool works:

1. Click anywhere in the image.

2. As you move the mouse, you will notice that a line follows the curser, with one end attached to the click point.

3. Click again and the two points will be connected.

4. Repeat step 2 to click all the way around the image.

5. When you have finished making your selection, click the start point and the selection will be created.

 To constrain the angles to 45-degree increments, hold down the SHIFT *key.*

The Magnetic Lasso

This tool is designed to help you select objects in an image, in case you want to trace the outline of an image. The Magnetic Lasso tool detects the edge of an image and automatically adds temporary anchor points called *fastening points*. (See Chapter 8 for more information on anchor points.) The tool will detect changes in color and snap to the color's edges. Figure 10-11 shows the Magnetic Lasso tool in use.

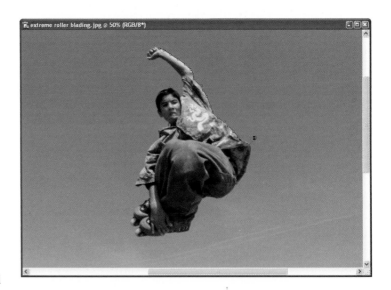

FIGURE 10-11 Drawing with the Magnetic Lasso tool

Here's how to use the Magnetic Lasso tool:

1. Choose the settings from the options bar:

    ■ **Width** Determines how far, in pixels, the tool will search for edges.

> **Edge Contrast**   This is the sensitivity setting. Use a higher number to ignore more subtle transitions.

> **Frequency**   How often fastening points are added. A higher number will add more fastening points.

FIGURE 10-12 A selection made with the Magnetic Lasso tool

2. Drag the mouse around the image. Watch as the tool begins to hug the edges and add fastening points.

3. You can force a fastening point by clicking the mouse. This is useful for areas of sharp transitions of shape or subtle changes in color.

4. Continue tracing all the way around the image until you click the start point.

5. When you click the start point, all the fastening points will disappear and a selection will be made like the one shown in Figure 10-12.

Even after a selection is complete, you can still use the options to further refine your selection.

Each time you click the DELETE key, the most recent fastening point will be deleted. You can press the DELETE key multiple times to delete multiple fastening points.

The Magic Wand

Imagine having a tool that could detect a certain color in an image and make selections based on the color. For example, suppose your image shows a pumpkin growing in a green field. You can use the Magic Wand tool to make a selection of just the orange pumpkin part of the image. This Magic Wand will not turn a pumpkin into a carriage, but it can turn a pumpkin into a selection.

This tool is useful for images with a large area of solid color, where the selected object is a different color from the background.

Using the tool is simple: just choose the desired settings, click the color you want to select, and the Magic Wand will do its work. The secret to success with this tool is in the settings:

- **Tolerance** This is the sensitivity setting. A low number will cause the Magic Wand to be very fussy and ignore subtle differences in color. A higher number will cause the tool to look for colors in the general range of the selected color. Experiment with this setting when making selections. The default setting is 32, which is a good starting point for most projects.

- **Anti-aliasing** Choose this option to create smoother edges on the selections.

- **Contiguous** Choose this option to limit the selection to adjacent areas of similar color. Deselect it to cause the tool to look at the entire image.

- **Use All Layers** By default, the Magic Wand tool will make selections based on the active layer only. By using all layers, it will look at the entire image.

FIGURE 10-13 An image with a selection by the Magic Wand tool

When you make a selection with the Magic Wand, some areas get missed in the selection because the color may have gradated to a hue outside of the chosen range—for example, see the bottom of the image in Figure 10-13. Here, the blue sky was chosen as the active color, but parts of the bottom portion weren't selected because of the other hues that appear there.

Use Magic Wand Hidden Settings

When using the Magic Wand tool, a hidden setting can affect the way the tool is used. If you click the Eyedropper tool, a Sample Size drop-down menu will appear in the options bar with three settings, which also affect the way the Magic Wand tool selects pixels:

- **Point Sample**   Sensitivity is at the pixel level. Samples the exact pixel that is directly under the cursor.
- **3 x 3 Average**   Takes the average reading for 3 pixels either direction.
- **5 x 5 Average**   Takes an average reading for 5 pixels either direction.

The Magic Wand is tied to the Eyedroppers tool's settings. If you are having a problem with your selections, try changing this tool's settings: switch to the Eyedropper tool, choose a different setting, and switch back to the Magic Wand tool.

Refining the Selection

You can try the following to refine the selection further:

- *Areas are missed.*   Press the SHIFT key and click in the missed area. This will cause the Magic Wand to add to the selection.
- *Subtle color differences are missed.* Choose Select | Similar.
- *You want the selection to fill more of the area.* Choose Select | Grow.
- *Too much of the image is selected.*   Lower the tolerance setting, and then, holding down the ALT key (OPTION on a Mac), click inside the area you want to remove from the selection.

Cleaning up the Edges

Once you have made the selection, you can remove the object from the current background and add it to another, as shown in Figure 10-14. Notice the subtle original background color that shows around the edges of the selection? You can remove those by choosing Layer | Matting | Defringe and entering a setting in pixels (see the end of this chapter for more on matting). This setting will determine how many pixels the filter will cut into the image to remove the hint of the original background.

10

Color Range

This tool is similar to the Magic Wand tool, but it offers more options and you have more control over the areas that are selected. When you choose the Color Range tool, a dialog box opens, where you can set options for finer control over your selection.

Choosing a Color

Figure 10-15 shows an image that we would like to select. It would take some time to trace all the outlines with the Lasso tools. It would also be difficult to select this image with the Magic Wand tool because of the various shapes and tones. You can see that the subject color is different from the background color. Because of this, the Color Range tool is the best choice for selecting this image.

Here's how to use this tool:

1. Open the image in Photoshop.

2. Choose Select | Color Range.

3. In the Color Range dialog box, shown in Figure 10-16, choose the Eyedropper tool and click anywhere inside the part of the image that you would like to select.

4. Increase the Fuzziness slider to refine the selection. The selected areas will be shown as white and the unselected will show as black. Getting the fuzziness just right is a balancing act and therefore will be different for each image. You will need to experiment. Figure 10-17 shows a good selection.

5. Click OK to apply the selection.

FIGURE 10-14 The object removed from its background and added to a new background

FIGURE 10-15 The original image—it could take a while to mask this image with the Lasso tools.

FIGURE 10-16 The Color Range dialog box

FIGURE 10-17 Adjusting the fuzziness

10

Refining the Selection

FIGURE 10-18 Grayscale preview allows you to see more details

You may refine the selection further by adding colors to the selected area:

1. For a larger and more precise preview, you can make a choice from the Selection Preview drop-down menu. In Figure 10-18, grayscale is selected for the preview. This will display a preview in the main image window.

2. Choose the Eyedropper tool with the plus sign next to it. This is the Add To Selection tool.

3. Click another color in the portion of the image you want to select. (Note that you will probably have to tweak the fuzziness whenever you add a color.)

4. Figure 10-19 shows a much stronger contrast between the selected

object and the background. This is the kind of selection that you want.

5. To apply the changes, click OK.

FIGURE 10-19 Adding colors with the selector increases the selection

Figure 10-20 shows the image with the ants marching around the selected objects.

As shown in Figure 10-20, you may find that a few stray pixels appear along with the selection; this is a good time to use the other selection tools, such as the Lasso and Marquee tools, to add to the selection and correct this. You can also use these tools to subtract from the selection to clean up any stray pixels in the background.

With experience, you will develop an eye for the type of images that lend themselves to the Color Range tool selection method.

FIGURE 10-20 The final selected image

Transforming Selections

When you make selections, you can adjust them beyond the ability of the selection tools alone. Let's look at the different ways that we can modify our selections.

Modifying Selections

Four options are available under the Select | Modify menu. The results of these options are shown in the images in Figure 10-21.

- **Border**   Creates a border from the selection. Enter a width in pixels.
- **Smooth**   Simplifies the selection.

- **Expand**   Increases the size of the selection.
- **Contract**   Decreases the size of the selection.

FIGURE 10-21
Modifying selections:
(A) Standard selection;
(B) Border;
(C) Smooth;
(D) Expand;
(E) Contract

Transform Selection

Another set of options is available to transform selections. These tools affect the shape of the selection. To activate these tools, choose Select | Transform Selection. You will see a bounding box and eight adjustment handles. To make modifications, drag the handles. Figure 10-22 shows these options in use.

10

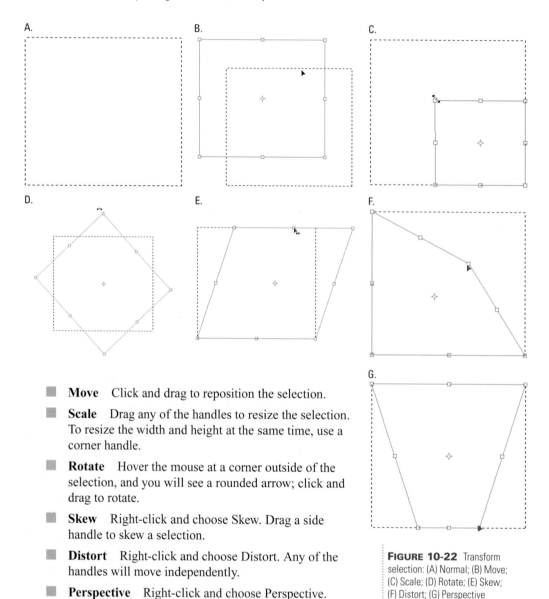

- **Move**   Click and drag to reposition the selection.
- **Scale**   Drag any of the handles to resize the selection. To resize the width and height at the same time, use a corner handle.
- **Rotate**   Hover the mouse at a corner outside of the selection, and you will see a rounded arrow; click and drag to rotate.
- **Skew**   Right-click and choose Skew. Drag a side handle to skew a selection.
- **Distort**   Right-click and choose Distort. Any of the handles will move independently.
- **Perspective**   Right-click and choose Perspective. When you adjust one corner, the opposite corner will adjust to match.

FIGURE 10-22   Transform selection: (A) Normal; (B) Move; (C) Scale; (D) Rotate; (E) Skew; (F) Distort; (G) Perspective

Press ENTER to apply the transformations, and the marching ants will reflect the changes.

Holding down the SHIFT *key will maintain the proportions of an image while transforming.*

Applying Quick Mask

FIGURE 10-23 Choosing the Quick Mask tool

Quick Mask is a unique tool; you can use it to create a temporary mask of a selection. You can then paint with all the painting tools and even use filters. It will look like a red brush turned down to 50 percent opacity. The magic happens when you switch off the Quick Mask tool. All the areas that were painted will become selections.

It works like this:

1. Click the Quick Mask tool on the toolbar, as shown in Figure 10-23 (or you can press the Q key).

2. Paint with the Brush tool wherever you choose.

3. Instead of the paint color, you will see a red mask appear, like that shown in Figure 10-24.

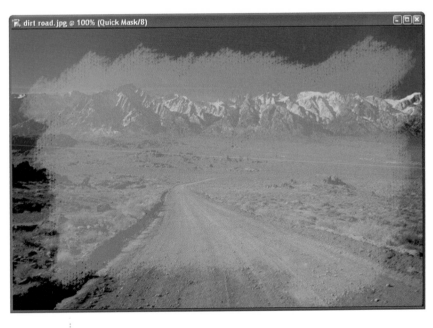

FIGURE 10-24 Painting in Quick Mask Mode

4. Use the Eraser tools to finesse your selection boundaries and also filters if you wish.

5. When you have finished painting, press the Q key again or switch back to normal mode from the toolbar.

6. You will see that all the painted areas are selected, as shown in Figure 10-25.

FIGURE 10-25 Returning to normal mode reveals the selection

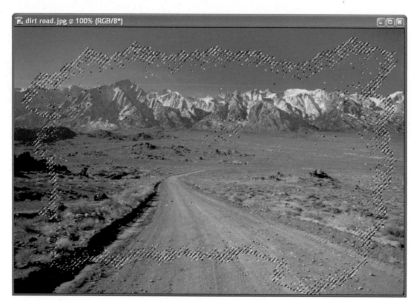

Creating a Photographic Edge with Quick Mask

One use for this type of selection would be to create a high-energy photo edge. Figure 10-26 shows how such an edge might look.

It's easy to reproduce this effect if you follow these steps:

1. Choose the Quick Mask tool.

2. Choose a Brush tool.

3. Paint the image area.

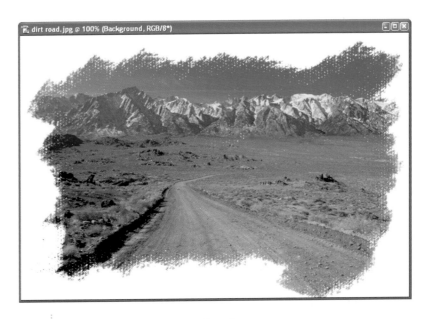

FIGURE 10-26 Picture edge from Quick Mask

4. Return to normal mode.

5. Copy the selection to a new layer by pressing CTRL-J (CMD-J on the Mac).

6. Fill the background with white.

Eliminating Matting

When you have finished removing objects from their backgrounds, you may notice some *halos*—also known as *matting*. Figure 10-27A shows an example of this problem before and Figure 10-27B shows after matting was removed. Notice the tiny white edges around the leftmost selection that give it an obvious cut-out look.

Photoshop has three tools to help you deal with this problem. These are found by choosing Layer | Matting:

- **Defringe** Enter a number in pixels. The chosen number of pixels will be deleted around the entire image. Use this option for a multi-colored halo.

■ **Remove Black Matte**   Removes a dark halo.

■ **Remove White Matte**   Removes a white halo, as shown in Figure 10-27.

FIGURE 10-27 Removing the matting from a cutout: (A) Image with a white edge halo; (B) After removing halo

A.

B.

Chapter 11

Make Images Pop with Special Effects

How to...

- Use filters
- Simulate movement
- Create a pencil sketch effect
- Create a pixelized effect
- Combine filters using the gallery
- Use the Liquify filter
- Change facial expressions
- Choose third-party plug-ins
- Use layer effects
- Use, create, and save styles

In this chapter, we get to play with all the cool toys. You have probably seen Photoshop images that use bevels, sheens, shadows, and other special effects. Perhaps it's this type of image that inspired you to learn how to use Photoshop. When it was first released in 1990, Photoshop was very primitive and had humble uses. Now just about all the major motion pictures incorporate the use of effects in Photoshop, including all the *Star Wars* movies.

In almost every recently made movie, Photoshop is probably used somewhere. If you see a great looking poster or magazine, Photoshop was probably used in creating it; in fact, Photoshop is everywhere, and almost everyone in the design and entertainment industries uses it. The reason is the program's flexibility and the way that Photoshop can manipulate images with the use of native and third-party filters. Layer styles add another dimension to images; it's amazing how easy it is to transform a dull image into something interesting with just a click or two.

Filters

You use filters in Photoshop to modify images—to change the texture, shape, form, or color of images. Filters can sharpen or blur an image, or they can be used for complex manipulation, such as lighting effects and distortion. You can filter images beyond recognition or just make subtle changes.

Figure 11-1 shows an image that was created with nothing but filters. I started with a blank canvas and added a Lens Flare and Radial Blur filter. The layer was duplicated and rotated, and the same effect was applied several times.

Two types of filters can be used in Photoshop. The first group, I call *production filters,* are used to enhance your images (such as sharpening a photo), and what I call *creative filters* produce special effects that can mimic reality or mock it (such as blurring or distorting a photo).

FIGURE 11-1 "Microscopic" image created with filters

FIGURE 11-2 The Filter menu

The Filter Menu

You access the filters in Photoshop by choosing them from the Filter menu, shown in Figure 11-2.

From the menu, 13 main groups of filters are available; each of these groups contains several filters. The main groups are listed here:

- **Artistic** (Creative) These filters mimic traditional art such as watercolor and pastel work.

- **Blur** (Production/Creative) These filters blur pixels in various ways.

- **Brush Strokes** (Creative) These filters give the images brushed appearances.

- **Distort** (Production/Creative) These filters allow you to bend and warp images.

- **Noise** (Production/Creative) These filters either introduce or reduce film grain.

- **Pixelate** (Creative) These filters introduce uniform patterns that give the image a pixelized look.

- **Render** (Creative) These filters introduce new objects or create a 3D effect.

11

- **Sharpen** (Production) These filters sharpen the edges of pixels and sharpens the image.
- **Sketch** (Creative) These filters work from the current foreground and background color swatch.
- **Stylize** (Creative) These filters allow for special effects mainly dealing with the edges of images.
- **Texture** (Creative) These filters add various real-world textures to images.
- **Video** (Production) These filters are used for video production work.
- **Other** (Production/Creative) These filters are used to perform assorted tasks.

Figure 11-3 shows a gallery of images.

A. Blurs and wave filters

FIGURE 11-3 Examples of filter use

B. Major use of Difference Clouds

D. Fibers, motion blur, and displacement

E. Blurs and polar coordinates

Many of the filters in Photoshop will not work in CMYK mode, so it's advisable that you work in RGB mode if you need to do extensive filter work.

Using Filters

Because Photoshop comes with so many filters, we won't be able to walk through the use of each one. We'll cover a few of the important ones in this section. As for the others, you'll find that once you begin to use the filters, a little experimentation will go a long way. Spend some time playing around with the filters, and you'll soon begin to find out what each one does. Try combining two or more filters to achieve interesting results. For a good resource on filters and special effects, check out the *Photoshop Most Wanted* series of books (by Colin Smith and Al Ward, Friends of Ed publishing, 2002). You'll also find a number of free tutorials at http://www.photoshopcafe.com.

In this section, we walk through a few easy-to-produce special effects using some of the filters that ship with Photoshop.

C. Brush filters and blurs

F. Background uses noise and lighting effects

Using Radial Blur to Zoom into an Image

This effect is great for adding movement and excitement to an image. The zooming effect is similar to a photographer snapping a picture while zooming into an image. This effect is difficult to achieve with a camera, but it's easy to do with Photoshop.

1. Begin with an image in RGB mode, as shown in Figure 11-4.

2. Choose Filter | Blur | Radial Blur.

3. In the Radial Blur dialog box, choose the Zoom Blur Method, and set the Amount slider to a small amount, such as 16, as shown in Figure 11-5.

4. Click OK.

11

FIGURE 11-4   The original image

FIGURE 11-5   Radial blur added

You should now see something like the image shown in Figure 11-6. If the effect is too intense, try again with a lower Amount setting.

 The Good Quality setting works well and is much faster to render than the Best setting.

Using Motion Blur to Simulate Movement

This effect will add the streaks that you see in an image behind an object that appears to be moving with speed. This is a great effect to use with sports photos, because it adds some extra action to the image.

FIGURE 11-6   The result

1. Begin with a new image in RGB mode.

2. Duplicate the background layer

3. Extract the image from the background on the new layer (see Chapter 10).

4. The Layers palette should now look something like that shown in Figure 11-7.

5. Hide the top layer.

6. Choose the bottom layer.

FIGURE 11-7 Original photo with a copy of the subject on a new layer

FIGURE 11-8 Adding Motion Blur (A), and the effect (B)

A.

B.

7. Choose Filter | Blur | Motion Blur.

8. In the Motion Blur dialog box, choose the Angle and Distance, as shown in the left image in Figure 11-8. The effect of your choice is shown in the image at the right.

9. Show the top layer again.

10. Position the top layer near the beginning of the motion trail, as shown in Figure 11-9.

FIGURE 11-9 Final result

If you want to blur only the subject and not the background, duplicate the extracted layer (step 2), and then blur the duplicated layer instead of the background.

Adding a Pencil Sketch Effect

This effect is so popular that I wish I had a dollar for every time someone has asked me to explain it. Using the effect, you can make a photograph look just like a pencil sketch. This is easy, and the result is stunning.

Photo courtesy of Hemera Images

1. We start with a photograph in RGB mode, as shown in Figure 11-10.

2. Choose Filter | Sketch | Find Edges.

FIGURE 11-10 Original photograph

3. The image will change to colored line art like that shown in Figure 11-11. You can stop here or continue working on the image.

FIGURE 11-11 Result of choosing Find Edges

4. To remove all the color, choose Image | Adjustments | Desaturate.

5. Choose Image | Adjust | Levels, and adjust the grayscale midtones to get the balance you want.

6. Figure 11-12 shows the final image. I used the History brush on the face, with Before Levels state selected to soften up the face. (See Chapter 3 for more about the History brush.)

Adding a Pixelized Effect

In a digital age where everything is nice and perfect, sometimes you might want to add some imperfections to an image. We have learned how to avoid pixelization in this book, but at times you may want to break the rules for the sake of special effects. We are going to take an image and pixelize it; this will add a "digitized" feel to the image.

FIGURE 11-12 The image converted to grayscale and levels

1. We begin with an interesting image in RGB mode, as shown in Figure 11-13.

FIGURE 11-13 Original image

FIGURE 11-15 The final image (notice that the hand and light bulb are not pixelized)

2. Choose Filter | Pixelize | Mosaic.

3. In the Mosaic dialog box, choose a setting that will show the pixels at the size you want. You can use the plus (+) and minus (–) buttons in the thumbnail preview to zoom in or out of the image. Figure 11-14 shows the Cell Size set at 24.

FIGURE 11-14
Cell Size setting in the Mosaic dialog

4. The image will now appear pixelized. To make the effect look as though it is pixelized on purpose—and not just a bad scan—use the History brush to remove the effect from the foreground objects. This gives the image a pixelized depth-of-field effect, as shown in Figure 11-15.

Combining Filters Using the Filter Gallery

Now let's use a filter for art lovers. You can create the illusion of a hand painting or a pastel image from any photograph. Here, we'll use the Filter Gallery to combine filters in tandem without damaging your original image. When you start applying a lot of filters, you can quickly lose image integrity if you are not careful.

Figure 11-16 shows an image that we are going to turn into an art effect.

11

1. Choose Filter | Dry Brush. The Filter Gallery will open.

2. Choose the settings shown in Figure 11-17A.

3. Click the New icon at the bottom of the rightmost window.

4. In the box shown at the top center of the Filter Gallery settings area (which shows Dry Brush in Figure 11-17), click the down arrow and choose Smudge Stick.

5. Adjust the settings so that they're similar to those shown in Figure 11-17B.

6. You can add as many filter layers as you wish to build up your effect.

7. Click OK when you're done.

Photo courtesy of Hemera Images

FIGURE 11-16 Original image

FIGURE 11-17 (A) Dry Brush filter; (B) Smudge Stick filter combined

A.

B.

FIGURE 11-18 Final "hand painted" image

Your image will now look like it was painted by hand, as shown in Figure 11-18.

The Liquify Filter

Perhaps the most fun tool in Photoshop is the Liquify filter, and no chapter on special effects would be complete without discussing this tool. Liquify allows you to mold your image like putty so that you can change facial expressions and do some downright weird things to your images. Figure 11-19 shows the Liquify interface.

Along the left side of the Liquify window are all the tools available with the filter. The area at the right of the window shows tool options and masking tools, which are used in combination with selection tools or masks in the original image and with the Freeze tool in Liquify. The image preview appears in the center of the window.

Changing Facial Expressions with the Liquify Tool

We can easily change the expression on our subject's face by using the Liquify tool. For instance, we could turn the corners of his mouth up to express happiness or down for sadness. In this case, we'll give the boy an angry/sulky look. We'll exaggerate the effects to create a caricature. (For realism, you can use more subtle movements.)

1. Open the image in Photoshop.

2. Choose Filter | Liquify.

3. Choose the Push tool, as shown in Figure 11-19.

4. Push the boy's forehead down with a large brush size, as shown in Figure 11-20.

5. Push the ends of the eyes upward to enhance the emotion.

Using the Freeze Tool

When you use the tools in the Liquify window, all the pixels around the brush will be affected. If you want to protect portions of the image, you can apply the Freeze tool. This will protect and "freeze" portions of the image so that they aren't distorted with the rest of the image.

1. Choose the Freeze tool from the tools on the left of the Liquify window.

2. Paint around the boy's chin to preserve the shape of his face, as shown in in Figure 11-21A.

Photo courtesy of Hemera Images

FIGURE 11-19 Original image inside the Liquify window

FIGURE 11-20 The Push tool in action

A.

B.

FIGURE 11-21 Adding a Freeze mask (A) and transforming with the frozen region protected (B)

FIGURE 11-22 The altered image

3. Use the Push tool to alter the mouth, as shown in the right image in Figure 11-21B.

4. Make any other final adjustments until you are happy with the effect.

5. Click OK.

The boy now looks very upset in Figure 11-22.

Using the Bloat and Pucker Tools

In this tutorial, we'll turn the picture of the boy into an *anime*-type caricature. We will mainly use the Bloat and Pucker tools in Liquefy. The Bloat tool causes everything to "swell up" and the Pucker tool has the opposite effect.

1. Open an image in Photoshop.

2. Choose Filter | Liquify.

3. Choose the Bloat tool, as shown in Figure 11-23A.

4. Click one of his eyes, and hold down the mouse button as it grows, as shown in Figure 11-23B.

5. Use the Bloat tool to increase the size of the other eye. (You may need to bloat from the colored part of the eye and move the tool around in a slow circle to achieve the desired result.)

6. Choose the Pucker tool, as shown in Figure 11-24A.

7. Apply the pucker to the nose, mouth, and cheeks for an *anime* effect, as shown in Figure 11-24B. Click and hold the mouse button for a dramatic effect, or click and drag for a more subtle effect.

8. Click OK to apply the transformation.

A.

B.

FIGURE 11-23 Using the Bloat tool (A) to enlarge an eye (B)

Using a Noise Filter to Soften the Image

For a more cartoonlike effect, we will need to simplify the detail in the image. You can use the Median filter at a very low setting to remove noise and moiré patterns from the image.

A.

1. Choose Filter | Noise | Median.

2. In the Median dialog box, use a low Radius setting, such as 4 pixels, as shown in Figure 11-25.

The image will now have a softer appearance.

B.

FIGURE 11-24 Choosing the Pucker tool (A) and applying the pucker tool (B)

FIGURE 11-25 Adding the low filter setting

FIGURE 11-26 The finished image: a human *anime*

For the final image, I did a little brushwork on the eyes to get more of the *anime* effect. I also adjusted the tones using curves (see Chapter 12) to get a slight poster-like effect. Figure 11-26 shows the final image.

Third-Party Plug-ins

One of the reasons for the success of Photoshop is the way it is built: The core part of Photoshop controls all the functionality and file handling, and extensibility is handled by plug-ins, which are available from other software makers. Each plug-in filter is built on its own and is used with Photoshop via a little file called an 8-bit filter (.8bf). To add a new filter, you simply drop it into the Filters directory of Photoshop and it's ready for use.

Several companies make plug-in filters that you can purchase to extend the functionality of Photoshop. Some of the most popular are listed here:

- **Alien skin Software (http://www.alienskin.com)** Eyecandy, Xenofex, Image Doctor, Splat!
- **Extensis (http://www.extensis.com)** Mask Pro, pxl Smart Scale, Phototools, PhotoFrame
- **Auto-FX (http://www.autofx.com)** DreamSuite, Mystical Lighting, Mystical tint-Tone-Color, Photographic/Edges, Auto Eye
- **Corel (http://www.corel.com)** KPT "Kais Power Tools" Series (the original Photoshop Plug-ins developed by Kai Kruse), Knockout
- **Andromeda (http://www.andromeda.com)** Scatterlight Lenses, Red Eye Pro, Cutline Filters, Etchtone Filter
- **The Plugin Site (http://www.thepluginsite.com)** Check out this site for more resources.

Layer Effects

Layer effects can be used to add dimension and special effects to your layers with one simple click. These effects can be easily applied and customized. You are not limited to a single effect, because all the various effects can be mixed and matched to achieve a huge array of effects. Once you have achieved an effect, it can be saved to a library and recalled in a single click as a layer style. Even a beginner can achieve stunning results using layer effects.

 Layer effects will not work on backgrounds or flattened images. You must start with an active layer to apply the effect. See Chapters 4 and 5 for more on Layers.

Let's apply a layer effect:

1. Choose a layer by clicking it in the Layers palette.

2. Click the little *f* at the bottom of the Layers palette.

3. Choose an effect from the drop-down menu, as shown in Figure 11-27A.

4. In the Layer Style dialog box, make adjustments, as shown in Figure 11-27B.

5. Click OK to apply the effect.

FIGURE 11-27 Adding a layer effect: (A) Applying a layer effect; (B) Layer styles dialog box

Using Different Effects

You can add more than one effect to an image via the Layer Style dialog box. Here's how:

1. In the Styles column at the left of Figure 11-27, check the box next to the name of the effect that you want to use.

2. Make adjustments to the effect.

3. Click the name and the options will change to the chosen effect.

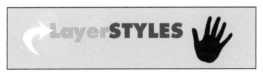

Here is a quick rundown of what each effect does. The illustrations show the original image for a visual example of the layer effects.

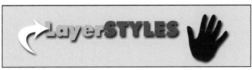

■ **Drop Shadow**   Adds a soft shadow under the layer that makes the layer appear to "float" in the air.

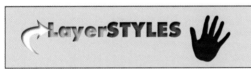

■ **Inner Shadow**   Adds a soft shadow that makes the layer appear cut into the page.

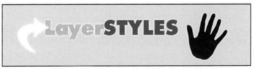

■ **Outer Glow**   Adds a soft glow around the layer.

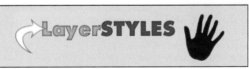

■ **Inner Glow**   Adds a glow on the inside of the layer.

■ **Bevel and Emboss**   Adds a 3D look to layers.

■ **Satin**   Applies a sheen to the surface of the layer.

11

- **Color Overlay** Changes the color of a layer object to a solid color of your choice.

- **Gradient Overlay** Same as Color Overlay except a gradient is used.

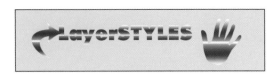

- **Pattern Overlay** Applies a pattern texture to your layer.

- **Stroke** Adds a colored outline to your layer.

Copying Effects to Layers

After you have created an effect on a layer, you can easily copy the exact settings to another layer or another document. Two simple methods can be used for duplicating effects to other layers. Here's the first one:

1. Position your mouse pointer over the word *Effects* on the Layers palette.

2. Drag the mouse to the layer to which you want to apply the effect, as shown in Figure 11-28.

3. Release the mouse and the effect will be duplicated to the other layer.

Here's a second method to duplicate effects onto other layers. This method works best on multiple layers at once. It's a great method to use when you're experimenting with web buttons and other items that you need to create over and over again:

1. Link all the layers to which you want to add the layer effects.

2. In the Layers palette, right-click the word *Effects* on the layer with the effect you want to copy.

3. From the context menu, choose Copy Layer Style.

FIGURE 11-28 Copying a layer effect to another layer

4. Right-click again.

5. From the context menu, choose Paste Layer Style To Linked. The effect will now be replicated to all the linked layers.

Managing Layer Effects

When you use two or more effects at once, you'll see a list of effects under the layers in the Layers palette. To turn off individual effects, click the eye icon to the left of the effect name in the palette, and that effect will be toggled off; only the visible effects will show in the layer effect. To show the individual effect again, click the eye icon again.

Layer Styles

When you use two or more effects together, it is called a *layer style*. Layer styles can be saved for later use, which is nice, because it means you will not have to re-create each effect every time you want to use it. You save the styles in a library called the Styles palette (Figure 11-29), which comes with a collection of *presets*. You can download extra sets from the Photoshop CD or from the Web, or you can purchase collections from third parties.

FIGURE 11-29 Applying a layer style

The premade effects can be applied to your layers in a single click. This can be done in one of two ways:

- Highlight the layer and click a style from the Styles palette.
- Drag and drop a style from the Styles palette onto the layer.

Creating Styles

When it comes to creating styles, there is no substitute for experimentation, because the possibilities are endless. To give you a head start, let's look at the components that make up a beveled gold layer style that we'll create.

11

1. Create a new Layer.

2. Choose a Gradient Layer effect from the menu.

3. In the dialog box that opens, create a new golden gradient (see Figure 11-30A). Make sure you change the Angle setting.

FIGURE 11-30 Creating a gold layer style

A. Choosing a colored gradient

4. Click Bevel, and use similar settings to those shown in Figure 11-30B. Pay attention to the Gloss Contour.

B. Adding the bevel for the depth

5. Apply a Bevel contour, as shown in Figure 11-30C.

C. Adding a bevel contour for shape

6. Choose Satin, set the color to white and the blend mode to lighten, as shown in Figure 11-30D.

D. Adding a satin sheen

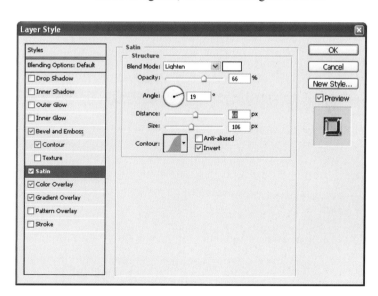

11

7. Click on Drop Shadow, change the Softness, Distance, and Opacity like we did in Figure 11-30E.

E. Adding a drop shadow

8. Figure 11-30F shows the layer style applied to some different layers.

F. The end result

Saving Styles

Now that you know how to create and use layer styles, you might like to know how to add them to the library and save them for future use.

1. Open the Styles palette.

2. Click the word *Effects* in the Layers palette.

FIGURE 11-31 Saving a Layer Style (A) and (B)

3. Drag the style from the Layers palette into the Styles palette, as shown in Figure 11-31A.

4. Release the mouse, and the New Style dialog box will open, as shown in Figure 11-31B.

5. Enter a name in the dialog box, and then click OK. The style is added to the library.

Saving the Styles to Disk or to the Internet

You can also save the styles to disk and upload them to the Internet or put them in a safe place for later use:

1. Click the arrow in the upper-right corner of the Styles palette.

2. Choose Save Styles from the menu.

3. Choose a location to which you want to save.

4. Click OK, and the styles are now saved.

 To load styles, repeat these steps, except choose Load Styles in step 2.

Part IV The Real World

Chapter 12

Enhance Your Photographs

How to...

- Fix less than perfect photos
- Make tonal adjustments
- Understand the histogram
- Use brightness/contrast
- Make shadow/highlight corrections
- Use curves and variations
- Set color balance and change hue saturation
- Adjust color with curves
- Automatically crop and straighten photos
- Use the Healing brush and Patch tool
- Use the Clone stamp
- Remove red eye

Whether you have scanned pictures, pulled them off CDs, or imported them from a digital camera, most of the following principles will apply to all photos you work with in Photoshop. We'll look at ways to get the best out of every photograph and them move on to ways to manipulate photos and create works of art.

You don't always get the exact shot you want when you're shooting with a camera. Sometimes the image is too dark or blurry, or perhaps unwanted objects are included in the picture. Even if the picture is perfectly shot, you may still need to make changes to the subject—perhaps your beautiful model had a battle with acne the night before the shoot and you want to perform a cosmetic touch-up. No matter what your needs, you'll probably find the answer in the pages of this chapter.

In this chapter, we'll repair some of the most common problems often encountered in photography: brightness and color adjustments, sharpening issues, cropping to contain the essence of an image, and correcting damage to photographs.

Tonal Adjustments

A color image has two parts: the grayscale tones that give the image its definition and detail, and the information that makes the image appear in color. *Tone* refers to the grayscale information in an image. It's probably easiest to think of the image tone as a black-and-white photo. Generally, if a photo is too dark or too bright, the problem is in the tonal area of the image, and no amount of color correction can fix the problem. In Photoshop, you can fix tonal problems without too much difficulty using the tonal correction tools.

The Histogram

The histogram in Photoshop provides a visual cue to the tonal properties of an image. This histogram is important because it lets you see at a glance how the tones are spread over the image, and it alerts you to any potential problems in the image tone. The histogram shows a graph of the tonal range and dispersion of an image—it shows you where the pixels are concentrated and how dark or light they are.

Histograms are located in two places: in the Levels dialog box shown in Figure 12-1, and in the new Histogram palette, shown in Figure 12-2. Figure 12-1 shows an image with its corresponding input and output levels in the Levels dialog box.

Colin Smith

FIGURE 12-1 A histogram and its parent image

12

To open the palette shown in Figure 12-2, choose Window | Histogram.

In the Histogram palette, the "mountainous" region represents the pixels in your image. The histogram displays the tones left to right, with black on the left and white on the right. All the tones in between represent shades of gray in an image, from dark to light.

FIGURE 12-2 The Histogram palette

The more the graph peaks at a certain point, the more pixels are located in that tone of gray. As you can see in Figure 12-2, a lot of pixels range in the very light region, and the next most concentrated area is in the dark gray region. The valleys in the histogram, indicate less pixel concentration in the image. No information appears at the far left and right in the histogram. This means that no pixels are present for those particular shades.

You should be aware of the following settings on the histogram:

- **Channel**   Allows you either to view the color image (default) or view a separate histogram for each composite color channel. This is useful for identifying problem areas in your image.

- **Layer**   Allows you to view a histogram on a multi-layered image. Choose between viewing a histogram for the entire image or for each layer.

- **Refresh**   If you see a little triangle under this button, click it to see the latest version of the image. Photoshop uses a technology called *screen cache* (which stores some information to memory) to speed up the display. The result is that sometimes the histogram is not up-to-the-minute. It takes only a second to update the view, and the added performance is worth the extra effort.

- **Options**   This drop-down menu contains several advanced viewing options for the histogram:

  - **Compact**   Displays the histogram in a small palette; this is handy because it stays out of your way while you work.

FIGURE 12-3 The Histogram palette in All Channels View with Statistics and Channel In Color turned on

- **Expanded**   Shows a larger view so that you can view more detail. (Figure 12-2 shows the expanded view.)

- **All Channels View**   Opens a histogram for each channel; this allows you to compare the various channels' histograms at once. It's informative, but it uses a lot of screen space. Figure 12-3 shows the histogram in All Channels View.

- **Statistics**   Displays information about the image. You can click and drag your mouse inside the histogram to get readings on the selected portion of the histogram.

- **Channel In Color**   Displays the channels' histogram in their respective colors, as shown in Figure 12-3.

Four tools are used in Photoshop to change the tone of images. We'll start with the simplest and quickest and work our way up to the more complex tools.

Brightness/Contrast Tool

The Brightness/Contrast tool is simple and quick to use. However, when using the tool, you have no control over the finer aspects of tonal correction, so if you lighten an image using this tool, everything is lightened across the entire image—it works similar to the brightness/contrast controls on your monitor.

Figure 12-4 shows an image in desperate need of help. This image is very dark and lacking in punch. We'll use the Brightness/Contrast tool to improve the image.

1. Image | Adjust | Brightness/Contrast. You will see the Brightness/Contrast dialog box with two slider controls as shown in Figure 12-5:

   - **Brightness**   Controls the lightness or darkness of the image

   - **Contrast**   Controls the intensity of the shadows

2. Move the Brightness slider up until you are happy with how light the image appears.

3. When you lighten an entire image, the shadows are also

FIGURE 12-4 The original image

lightened; this causes a loss of contrast and makes the image appear washed out. Enter the second control: The Contrast slider (Figure 12-6) compensates for the loss of contrast by allowing us to bring it back. Slide the Contrast slider up until you are happy with the way the image appears.

As you can see, you can get some pretty decent results without breaking too much of a sweat.

Shadow/Highlight Correction Tool

The next tool is Photoshop's latest tone correction tool that was added especially for photographers. The Shadow/Highlight Correction tool performs in a similar way to the Brightness/Contrast tool, but it gives us much more control over details. This tool allows you to selectively lighten shadows in overly dark images and darken highlights in overly bright images. The advantage of this tool is that you can choose the range of shadows and highlights to be effected. The disadvantage is that it's a bit more tricky to use than the Brightness/Contrast tool.

Figure 12-7 shows a photograph that I took on a rainy night with no flash. I avoided flash because it would reflect on the metal and ruin the image. Because flash wasn't used, the image is a bit dark. When I shot this image, I knew I could bring it home to Photoshop and make it as bright as I wanted.

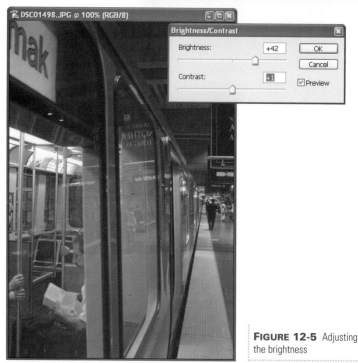

FIGURE 12-5 Adjusting the brightness

FIGURE 12-6 Adjusting the contrast

FIGURE 12-7 Original image

1. Choose Image | Adjust | Shadow/Highlights.

2. In the Shadow/Highlight dialog box, select the Show More Options checkbox at the bottom of the dialog if it not already selected. You will now see the entire dialog box.

3. Let's first make adjustments using the Shadows and Highlights sliders. Each offers three settings:

   ■ **Amount** Controls the intensity of the effect.

   ■ **Tonal Width** Adjusts how far into the midtones you want to affect with the adjustment. With the Shadows slider all the way to the left, you adjust the very darkest shadows; as you move the slider to the right, you affect more of the lighter shadows and midtones. The same is true for the Highlights slider.

   ■ **Radius** Affects how the adjustment will interact with the neighboring pixels. Adjusting this setting will allow you to target your area of interest. Experiment for the best setting.

4. Slide the Shadows and Highlights sliders until you are happy with the results.

5. Adjust the Color Correction slider a little; this controls the color saturation of the changed pixels only. Choose a smaller amount to tone the colors back to a realistic level.

6. Slide the Midtone Contrast slider higher to strengthen the image (see Figure 12-8).

See the difference this tool makes to the picture? It transformed a photo taken at night without a flash into an image that looks as if it were taken in daylight. This tool is especially useful for images with strong backlight.

12

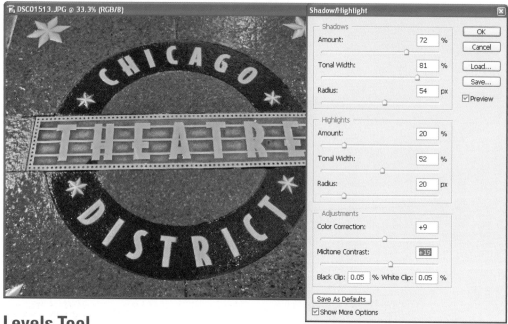

FIGURE 12-8 Final adjustments

Levels Tool

The Levels tool is deceptively easy to use; the Levels dialog box contains a histogram with sliders, as shown in Figure 12-9. You can slide any of the histogram's three triangles to alter the tonal qualities of the image. The left slider (black) controls the shadows, the middle (gray) slider controls the midtones, and the right (white) slider controls the highlights.

The histogram sliders control shadows on the left and transitions to white on the right. When you move a slider to the left, it will darken the range of the image. When you move a slider to the right, it will brighten the affected range.

FIGURE 12-9 The Levels dialog box

Fixing Highlights

One of the most common problems in photos is a lack of light, which causes the image to appear too dark. This can be adjusted while shooting by using a slower shutter speed, thus letting in more light. Of course, if you are now working on an image in Photoshop, it's a bit late to wind back the clock and change your shutter speed. Fortunately, the Levels tool comes to the rescue.

The image in Figure 12-10 looks dull and lacking in brightness. Choose Image | Adjust | Levels, and you will see that the histogram doesn't show any information on the right end. This means that all the pixels are concentrated in the midtones and shadows portions of the image. The lack of histogram peaks on the right means that no highlights are present in the image.

By sliding the Highlight slider (white triangle in Figure 12-9) to the left and causing it to touch the area where the histogram information begins, we have brightened up the image (see Figure 12-11).

FIGURE 12-10 Dull image lacking in highlights

FIGURE 12-11 Brightening up the image

Fixing Shadows

Another common problem with images is a lack of contrast. All the pixel information is concentrated in the midtones and highlights. This results in a faded appearance that lacks visual punch. Figure 12-12 shows a washed-out image. If you look at the histogram, you can see that information in the shadow area (the leftmost area) is lacking.

This is easy to fix. Drag the Shadow slider (black triangle in Figure 12-9) toward the right, and notice the contrast change in the image as the shadows are darkened, as shown in Figure 12-13. We moved the slider a little to the right, close to the Midtone area. In this case, we also increased the highlights a little by moving the Highlights slider to the left.

Colin Smith

Fixig Midtones

At times, the shadows and highlights in an image are correct, but the image still doesn't look its best. The problem, in the case of Figure 12-14, is in the midtones. The shadows are nice and dark and the highlights are nice and bright, but the midtones are dark and don't show much detail.

FIGURE 12-13 Darkening the shadows

Slide the Midtone slider (gray triangle) to the left. As you move the slider, you will see the image midtones brighten up. If you slide to the right, the midtones will get darker.

In Figure 12-15, we have moved the slider to the right and the midtones are much improved. Notice that details, such as the curtain, are now showing; these details were lost in the shadows before we made the adjustments.

Auto Levels

In the Levels dialog box, click the Auto button, and the brightest point in the image will be set to white and the darkest point will be shifted to black. All the tones in between will compensate automatically. This setting works well for some images and not so well for others. It is usually best to set the levels manually so that you can control the results. If you are in a real rush, however, you could try the Auto setting—if the result is not what you want, you can simply undo the change and make the adjustments manually.

You can also access the auto controls by choosing Image | Adjustments, and then choosing Auto Levels or Auto Contract.

FIGURE 12-14 Midtones are too dark

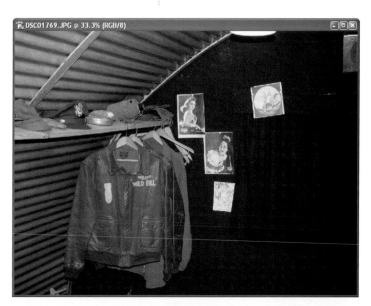

Curves Tool

Curves are the most advanced way to correct image tones in Photoshop. They allow you the most precise control—and also the most potential for messing up your image if you don't know what you're doing. The price that comes with the precision is the price of learning.

Figure 12-16 shows the Curves dialog box.

FIGURE 12-15 Lightening the midtones

The following three areas are of most concern:

- **Input** The horizontal gradient runs from dark to light (left to right). The gradient represents the shades in the existing image. The input reflects the shades before any changes are made; think of the horizontal gradient as the base of the histogram.

- **Output** The vertical gradient shows the output or the tone after changes are made. This runs from dark to light (bottom to top).

- **Curve** This is where you will work. You can click and drag on this line to alter the way the tones are mapped on an image.

FIGURE 12-16 The Curves dialog box

In Figure 12-16, you will notice that the curve is in its default state—bottom left to top right, diagonally. Choose a point on the input and follow it up to the curve (the green line in the figure). See where it intersects with the curve? Follow it to the left and you will see the new output shade as displayed in the Output gradient bar. Follow any point in the default curve and you will see that all the shades are equal, Input to Output.

In Figure 12-17, we have dragged the curve upward; this has resulted in brightening the image. Follow the green line, and you can see how much lighter the output is from the input. That change will be made to the image.

FIGURE 12-17 Lightening an image with curves

Use Curves

Let's use the Curves dialog box to manipulate an image:

1. Open an image.

2. Choose Image | Adjust | Curves.

3. Click anywhere on the curve to add an adjustment point.

4. Drag the point with your mouse to adjust the curve.

5. Move the point up or down vertically to lighten or darken the selected tone.

6. Move the point left or right to select a different tone to adjust.

7. To remove an adjustment point, drag it out of the window.

You can add up to 16 adjustment points per curve.

FIGURE 12-18 Faded image with little contrast

Colin Smith

Increase Contrast in an Image with Curves

An image lacking good dark shadows and strong highlights is lacking contrast. This gives a picture a faded appearance. Figure 12-18 is a perfect example of an image that is lacking in contrast.

Let's use curves to fix the image. What we are about to do is called the classic "S" curve. This curve will increase contrast in an image.

1. Choose Image | Adjust | Curves.

2. Click the curve about a quarter of the way from the left. This is the shadow/midtone region.

3. Drag the curve point down and notice that the shadows in the image get darker, as shown in Figure 12-19.

FIGURE 12-19 Darkening the shadows

4. Now we will increase the highlights. Click about three quarters of the way along the curve.

5. Drag up, as shown in Figure 12-20. The highlights have now brightened. The overall result is an image with more contrast.

Targeting a Specific Tone with Curves

The best thing about curves is that they give you the ability to target a particular object in an image and bring out its details. When you begin to experiment, you will be surprised at how much detail you can squeeze out of an image. Areas that look totally black or white could in fact be harboring valuable image details.

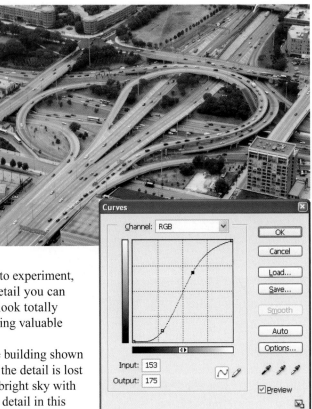

FIGURE 12-20 Increasing the highlights

The decoration on the front of the building shown in Figure 12-21 looks interesting, but the detail is lost because the camera has balanced the bright sky with the dark windows. Let's bring out the detail in this image using the targeted method. This method doesn't really target objects as much as it targets particular tones in an image. We can then darken or lighten the tones to achieve the best results.

1. Open the Curves dialog box—choose Image | Adjust | Curves.

2. You will notice that the cursor turns to an eyedropper tool when it is inside the picture. Hold down the mouse button, and you will see a circle on the curve, as shown in Figure 12-21.

3. This circle shows you where the tone area is set on the curve. Move the point until it is on a tone area that you want to adjust.

4. CTRL-click (CMD-click on the Mac) to add a point to the curve.

5. Drag the point down to darken or up to brighten the image, as shown in Figure 12-22.

FIGURE 12-21 Indicating the tone on the curve

Notice how much detail is now showing in the image as compared to the original.

FIGURE 12-22 Brightening a targeted tone in the image

12

Color Correction

Without light, it would be impossible to take pictures. Different types of lights have different effects on our images. In general, light can be classified as two types: cool and warm. An example of cool light is moonlight, which is typically bluish. A warm light example is a light bulb, or incandescent light, and it gives off a warm, yellowish hue.

About the most accurate light you can get is natural sunlight on a slightly overcast day. Most of the time, when you shoot photos under artificially lit conditions, you will experience color shift—that is, the appearance of color in your photograph is affected by the spectrum of light available in the artificial light. So while a color may appear a particular hue in natural light, under a florescent or incandescent light. the hue may appear a little different. The most common color shifts are toward yellow or green. We will examine several tools and methods you can use for correcting color shifts.

Variations Tool

Variations is a simple to use color correction tool. It lets you view several versions of the image side by side. The Variations dialog box shows your original image in the center, surrounded by versions that use different color tints. Simply click the thumbnail that you prefer and the image will take on the new color tint. This is a great way to correct the color in an image.

Figure 12-23 shows an image with a green color shift; we will correct this using the Variations tool.

To open the Variations palette, choose Image | Adjust | Variations.

At the top of the Variations palette, you will see two thumbnails:

FIGURE 12-23 Image with a greenish tint

Colin Smith

- ■ **Original (Input)**   Displays the open image before correction.

- ■ **Current pick (Output)**   Displays the result of the correction. This window will always display the last used setting. To reset, click the Original thumbnail.

Next to the thumbnails at the top are two sets of controls:

■ **Range** Allows you to target the Shadows, Highlights, Midtones, or Saturation.

■ **Sensitivity** Sliding to the left (Finer) makes the change more subtly, and sliding to the right (Coarse) will make it more drastic. I recommend using a finer setting and applying it several times.

The Show Clipping checkbox (see Figure 12-24) will highlight colors that cannot be reproduced. In the rightmost column of the filter window, you will see thumbnails with options to lighten or darken the current image.

Your current image appears in the center of the window, with six different color possibilities surrounding it. These thumbnails are arranged in a ring around the current pick and

FIGURE 12-24 The Variations filter

are opposites on either side, as shown in Figure 12-24. Choose the tone that best fixes your image color, and click the thumbnail to update the Current Pick.

Let's correct our image.

1. Choose Image | Adjust | Variations.

2. Click the Original thumbnail at the top to reset the options.

3. Choose the Midtones radio button option, since our green color shift is in the midranges.

4. Lower the sensitivity slider (under the radio buttons) one notch, and notice that variations update to reflect the new sensitivity setting.

5. Since our shift is to green, click the opposite, which is More Magenta.

6. Lower the sensitivity and keep choosing options until you are happy with the view shown in the Current Pick.

7. Click OK when you're done.

Figure 12-25 shows the corrected image. Notice that the green color shift has now gone and the colors are looking more true to life.

Color Balance

Another tool used for color correction is the Color Balance tool, which consists of three sliders. The Color Balance tool produces a result similar to the Variations tool, but it is a bit more hands on.

Figure 12-26 shows an image with a significant warm color shift toward the yellow/reds.

FIGURE 12-25 The corrected image

1. Choose Image | Adjust | Color Balance.

2. In the Color Balance dialog box Tone Balance area, choose Shadows, Highlights, or Midtones. We'll choose Midtones.

3. Move the color sliders in the opposite directions to the color shift to compensate, as shown in Figure 12-27.

4. Repeat for the highlights and shadows.

5. Click OK.

After the image is corrected, some oversaturation in the skin tones is still visible, but the overall image is looking better.

FIGURE 12-26 Uncorrected image is too warm

Note *This method is easy to use, but it lacks the ability to target a specific tone.*

FIGURE 12-27 Balancing the color

Hue/Saturation Tool

Another tool for color correction is the Hue/Saturation tool, which gives you control over three areas of the image:

- **Hue**   The actual color.
- **Saturation**   The quantity of the color.
- **Brightness/Lightness/Darkness**   Shifts everything across the board. I don't recommend using this control for correcting image brightness; the Levels or Curves tools are much better for correcting lightness and darkness.

Figure 12-28 shows an image that is too yellow. The solution may not be adding blue to the image to compensate, because the old picture will lose its historic feel. Instead, we can just reduce the yellow a bit.

Sometimes all that is required to color correct an image is to reduce the *saturation*, the amount of color applied to an image. Oversaturated images have too much of a particular color or colors and appear unreal. The opposite end of the spectrum would be zero saturation—that would be grayscale with no color at all.

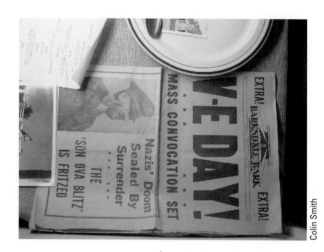

FIGURE 12-28 Image before, with an oversaturation of yellow

1. Choose Image | Adjust | Hue/Saturation. You will see the Hue/Saturation dialog box shown in Figure 12-29.

2. Slide the Saturation slider to the left until the image looks more natural.

A quick way to correct color is to choose Image | Adjust | Auto Color. This is a hit-or-miss approach, however, and is generally not the best solution.

See the difference made just by reducing the saturation (Figure 12-29)? It's always a good thing to be creative when correcting images. This image still has a bit of a yellow cast, but it still works for the old antique effect that we want.

FIGURE 12-29 Adjusting color with the Hue/Saturation tool

FIGURE 12-30 Image with a yellow color cast

Adjusting Color with Curves

The most accurate, and tricky, way to correct the color on images is by using curves. See the section "Curves Tool" earlier in this chapter for an understanding of how curves work.

Figure 12-30 shows an image that has a warm color cast because of the lighting. The difficult part of this image is removing the color cast without affecting the blue glow too much, since we want to keep that color.

Using the Curves tool, you are not just limited to correcting the tones of grayscale. You can go into each color channel and adjust it individually.

1. Choose Image | Adjust | Curves.

2. In the Curves dialog box, drag the mouse over the area with the most color cast, and you will see the circle on the curve indicating the range.

3. CTRL-SHIFT-click (CMD-SHIFT-click on the Mac) to add the adjustment point to each of the channels. (Note that the point will not show in the RGB composite channel.)

4. Click the Channel to open the drop-down list, and choose each channel one at a time to see the adjustment point on each channel. You'll see where that tone is in each color.

5. Make adjustments to each of the color channels.

6. You will notice that if the color shows high on a color curve, it should be darkened to neutralize it, as shown in Figure 12-31A in the Red channel. (Drag the point down.)

7. If the point is around the middle of the curve, it is already neutral and won't require any adjustment normally, as shown in the Green channel in Figure 12-31B.

8. If the point shows low on the curve, as in the Blue channel in Figure 12-31C, it should be brightened to neutralize the color. (Drag the point up.)

12

A.

B.

FIGURE 12-31 Making adjustments to the channels
(A) Red channel
(B) Green channel
(C) Blue channel

C.

Figure 12-32 shows the image after making the correction with the Curves tool. Curves are the most accurate way in Photoshop to color correct images.

Sharpening

Many images tend to look a little blurry. At least a bit of sharpening couldn't hurt them. When you scan or resize an image, a little sharpening is usually in order, to enhance things a bit.

Unsharp Mask

The best sharpening tool in Photoshop has the least likely name—the Unsharp Mask. The Unsharp Mask detects the image's edges and then enhances them by adding a tiny white halo. This may sound strange, but it is effective, and

FIGURE 12-32 The corrected image

when sharpening is performed correctly, the viewer's eye will not notice the halo. Instead, the eye will notice the more predominant edges, which created the illusion of a sharper image.

The Unsharp Mask filter has three settings, all demonstrated in Figure 12-33. The final image in the figure shows a properly sharpened image. Notice that the effect is subtle; it just enhances the image and doesn't change it dramatically.

A.

B.

- **Amount** The strength of the halo. If you turn up this setting, the edges become very predominant; if you turn it down, the effect is less pronounced.

- **Radius** The size of the halo. As you turn up this setting, the white actually turns into a glow; a lower setting will create a more subtle effect.

- **Threshold** Adjusts the sensitivity of the edge detection. Turning this up will soften the effect and cause only the most predominant edges to be detected. A 0 setting will cause the filter to work full strength on the entire image.

12

C.

D.

FIGURE 12-33 Unsharp Mask
(A) The amount turned up
(B) Increasing the radius
(C) Increasing the threshold
(D) Properly sharpened image

Using Unsharp Mask

Figure 12-34 shows an image in which the color balance and the tonal balance are good. A little bit of sharpening could further enhance the image.

1. Choose Filter | Sharpen | Unsharp Mask.

2. In the Unsharp Mask dialog box, click Preview so that you can see the result on the main image.

3. Adjust the Amount and Radius sliders until you get a good balance. Turn the Preview on and off for a comparison of the effect before and after.

FIGURE 12-34 Image before sharpening

4. Set the Threshold slider to an acceptable level, affecting only the detail that you choose.

5. Click OK.

Figure 12-35 shows the sharpened image and the settings in the Unsharp Mask dialog box. These are pretty average settings to use on people.

FIGURE 12-35 Image after Unsharp Mask

Cropping

Cropping is another word for *trimming*. When we crop an image in Photoshop, it is the equivalent of taking out a pair of digital scissors and trimming away the portions of the image we want to discard. You may want to crop an image for several reasons.

- **Remove unwanted subjects**   Perhaps you love the photo of yourself but you don't want your ex to appear in the image. Or you may have shot an image on the beach, but the porta-loo on the edge of your photo ruins the shot. Whatever the subject, it can be cropped away.

- **Emphasize a particular area**   You can change the focus of an image by cropping the image into the subject tightly and discarding all the distracting scenery.

- **Enhance the image creatively**   You can turn a boring photo into a work of art by using some creative cropping.

- **Adjust proportions**   You may have set proportions within which the image needs to fit, such as within a layout, and you will need to trim some pixels off one or more of the edges.

Whatever your reason for cropping your image, Photoshop comes equipped with a powerful cropping tool that will help you out.

FIGURE 12-36 The Crop tool in action

Cropping an Image

Many times, you will have an image that has a lot of boring scenery that adds nothing to the image. We'll use the Crop tool to make a more interesting composition.

1. Choose the Crop tool from the tool palette.

2. Click and drag inside the image, as you would with the Rectangular Marquee tool.

3. Click and drag any of the eight resizing handles to change the size of the marquee. You can see the handles in Figure 12-36.

4. Click inside the selected window and drag to reposition the cropped area.

5. To apply the crop, double-click your mouse inside the cropped area. It is now a much more interesting composition and draws the viewer's attention to the subject matter.

You can set a couple of settings in the options bar:

- **Shield**   Shows the area that is to be cropped away. You can change the color and opacity of this shield. It provides a visual guide to the cropping.

- **Delete or Hide**   Available only if you are working on a layer. It gives you the option to crop the image and discard the pixels, or if you use the Hide option, the canvas size will be reduced without deleting any pixels. You may reposition this layer later if you wish.

Straightening Photos

The Crop tool can do more than just trim an image. You can also use it to straighten crooked images while you are cropping them. This comes in handy, for example, when you scan an image that wasn't quite straight on the scanner, or when you took a photo and the camera was aimed crooked. Here's how to fix a crooked picture.

1. Choose the Crop tool from the tool palette.

2. Click and drag the rectangular marquee, as in the previous exercise.

3. If you hover your mouse outside of the cropped area over one of the corners, it will change into a curved, double-sided arrow.

4. Click and drag to rotate the crop selection to compensate for the crooked picture, remembering that the cropped image will fit the selected area, as shown in Figure 12-37.

FIGURE 12-37 Rotating the cropped area

DSC01759.JPG @ 40% (RGB/8)

Colin Smith

FIGURE 12-38 Straightened picture

Colin Smith

FIGURE 12-39 Original image with barreling

5. Double-click inside the crop area to apply the crop. The image will now be straight, as shown in Figure 12-38.

Correcting Perspective

Because of the curved shape of a camera lens, a phenomena called *barreling* can occur, in which the edges of the image roll off. In the case of a tall building, this may be acceptable because of the *perspective*—as something is located further away, it appears smaller. Perspective allows us to judge size and distance. In the case of Figure 12-39, the perspective is exaggerated by the curvature of the lens and it is undesirable.

When you click and drag with the Crop tool, you will notice a Perspective checkbox in the options bar. Clicking this option allows you to change the perspective of an image. The perspective works in the same way as the rotated crop. The cropped area will be rectangular and the entire image will be distorted to fit.

1. Click and drag with the Crop tool.

2. Drag the crop area until it covers the entire area that you want to keep in the image.

3. Click the Perspective checkbox to turn it on.

4. In the image, click and drag the top right corner a little toward the center of the picture. Drag it until the rightmost line is at the same angle as the desired straight line in the image. (I have used the windows in the buildings as a guide, as shown in Figure 12-40.)

12

5. Then drag the top left corner in until the side is aligned with the desired straight edge of the picture.

6. Apply the crop by double-clicking inside the image area.

Figure 12-41 shows the corrected image. Notice how much better the picture looks— it doesn't look like the sky is falling in.

FIGURE 12-40 Adjusting the perspective

FIGURE 12-41 Corrected image

Automatically Crop and Straighten Photos

When scanning images, you can save a lot of time by placing several images on the scanner platen at the same time and scanning them at once. The drawback, however, is that you have to separate the images. This can be very time-consuming and cumbersome. A brand new feature in Photoshop CS automates the entire process. This new feature, aptly named Crop and Straighten Photos, does exactly what it says.

After you open the composite image, to break images apart, choose File | Automate | Crop And Straighten Photos. That's all you have to do; sit back and Photoshop will do the rest.

When Photoshop has finished, it will have created a new document for each of the images in the composite. Each will be perfectly cropped, and even if an image was askew in the scan, it will be shown straightened out.

Repairing Images

Photoshop has long been the standard software used to "repair" damaged photos. Photoshop can "fix" anything from tears and scratches to creases and stains. Two tools stand out as almost magical in their application: the Healing brush and the Patch tool. These tools are unparalleled in any other application and almost too easy to use.

Healing Brush

The Healing brush is as simple to use as a standard paint brush. The brush is so intelligent that it samples the image where you are painting and compares it to another portion of the image that you choose. The Healing brush then simulates the texture and blends the brush stroke into the image seamlessly. The result is that you can effortlessly brush away all manner of damage in the image. It even works on wrinkles!

Figure 12-42 shows an image with heavy damage from scratches and chipping—a perfect target for the Healing brush. This image can be found on your Photoshop Install directory under *samples*. The nice people at Adobe have given you an image to use for practice.

1. Choose the Healing brush from the tool palette.

2. Choose a brush size appropriate for the image. It's a good idea to use a smaller brush for small areas, but you can change the brush size while you're working.

3. Hold down the OPTION key and click in an undamaged portion of the image, close to where you want to make repairs. You have now taken a sample.

4. Click and drag the mouse to paint over the damaged portion of the image. You will see the cross hairs in the sampled region.

5. When you release the mouse button, you will see the brush stroke "morph" into the image, effectively brushing away the damage.

FIGURE 12-42 A perfect target for the Healing brush

12

6. Continue repairing the image in the same manner, remembering to resample as often as possible; this is the key to good healing.

Figure 12-43 shows the image mostly repaired except for the top left region. I have left this alone on purpose to experiment with a more heavy-duty tool, the Patch tool.

Patch Tool

The Patch tool is designed to sample a large area of texture and blend it into larger damaged areas. This tool works just like the Healing brush, but on a larger scale.

1. Choose the Patch tool from the tool palette.

2. Choose the Destination radio button from the tool options.

3. Draw a selection around a good, clean portion of uniform texture. (This portion of the tool works just like the Lasso tool.)

4. Release the mouse and you will see a selection.

5. Click and drag the selection on top of a damaged section of the image.

6. Release the mouse and the selected texture miraculously blends into the texture, eliminating all damage.

The selection is reusable; you can click and drag it again. The Patch tool has made short work of the damaged picture. Combined with the Healing brush, the image in Figure 12-44 is as good as it was on the day it was taken.

Clone Stamp

When it comes to having fun with photos in Photoshop, it's pretty hard to beat the Clone Stamp tool, which allows you to sample a part of the image and then paint with the actual sampled pixels on another portion of the image. This is great for removing objects from pictures or duplicating objects.

FIGURE 12-43 The image after using the Healing brush

FIGURE 12-44 Restored image

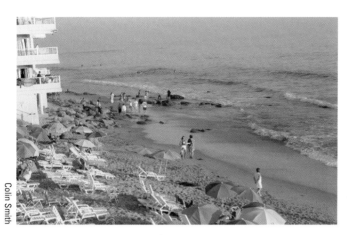

Colin Smith

FIGURE 12-45 The original image with the building

In the picture of Laguna Beach, California, in Figure 12-45, the ocean and beach look very inviting, but someone built a house right on the beach. This may be very nice for the people living in the house, but for everyone else, it is an eyesore. Hiring a bulldozer to tear it down would be a bit drastic; instead, we can remove it from the picture using the Clone Stamp tool.

1. Choose the Clone Stamp tool from the tool palette.

2. To sample a portion of the image, hold down the ALT key (OPTION on Mac) and click. You will see a target, as shown in Figure 12-46A; this is the area from which we will copy the pixels.

3. Click and drag through the unwanted portion of the image, as shown in Figure 12-46B. The cross hairs show the area to be cloned, and the circle shows the size of the brush. The brush will duplicate the pixels from the sampled region.

FIGURE 12-46 The Clone Stamp tool in operation
(A) Sampling
(B) Area to be cloned
(C) Painting with the clone stamp

4. Drag the Clone Stamp tool through the top of the house, replacing it with ocean and sky, as shown in Figure 12-46C. Resample as often as needed to make the image look real.

12

A.

B.

C.

5. Switch to a smaller brush size for the beach and rocks, because you will need more precision.

6. Watch for obvious duplicated regions, as indicated in Figure 12-47.

7. In Figure12-48, we have used a smaller brush and sampled sand from different parts of the image to avoid any obvious duplication of objects. We left the duplicated people in the image just for fun.

We have just performed magic by making an entire house disappear through the power of the Clone Stamp tool.

FIGURE 12-47 Duplicated regions

FIGURE 12-48 The house removed

Removing Red Eye

Red eye occurs when the camera flash is too close to the lens of the camera and it reflects in the eyes of a person when you are taking his or her picture. This is a common problem with flash photography and causes a demonic red glow to the pupils of the subject's eyes. Figure 12-49 shows an image with some pretty bad red eye.

This is very easy to fix using the Replace Color brush. The brush will paint with the foreground color. But instead of painting with a solid color, it will use the color information only and preserve the luminance of the image. In plain terms, that means that none of the highlight and shadow detail will change—only the color hue.

FIGURE 12-49 Red eye

FIGURE 12-50 Removing the red eye

1. Choose the Replace Color brush from the toolbar.
2. In the tool options, choose the following:
   - Mode: Color
   - Sampling: Continuous
   - Limits: Find Edges
3. Zoom in to the image so that you can see the subject's eyes up close.
4. Choose a dark gray/black for the foreground color.
5. Paint inside the pupil, as shown in Figure 12-50. The red will be replaced by the dark gray.

Repeat for the other eye, and voila, a quick fix.

Colin Smith

FIGURE 12-51 The original picture with a dull sky

Replacing the Sky

It's difficult to get a picture of a nice, blue sky unless you are using a polarizing filter on your camera lens. Even then, if you are in the big city, chances are that the sky will be gray. You are about to learn three ways to add a blue sky to your picture. Figure 12-51 shows a picture with an overcast sky. It's time for the sun to come out.

Using the Magic Wand tool, make a selection of the sky area. (See Chapter 10 for more on selections.)

1. Set the foreground color to blue, R=80, G=120, B=234.
2. Set the background color to white.
3. Choose the Gradient tool.
4. Choose Foreground To Background and Linear.

We are now set up to create the sky.

Method 1: Clear Sky

1. Click the New Layer icon in the Layers palette. This will create a new layer with the selection still active.

2. Drag the Gradient tool from the top of the image to the bottom.

3. Your sky now fades from white to blue, as shown in Figure 12-52—a typical cloudless day.

Method 2: Cloudy Day

1. Select the sky area.

2. Create a new layer.

3. Select white for your foreground color and a light blue for the background.

4. Choose Filter | Render | Clouds. Your image will now show a cloudy sky. If the clouds look too fake, add a bit of a blur to them.

Method 3: The Ultimate

This is the most realistic of the three methods. (Actually, it's a combination of the first two.)

1. Create a sky using Method 1.

2. Create a new layer, and then create the cloudy sky using Method 2.

3. Make sure that the cloudy layer is on top.

4. Change the blending mode to lighten.

5. To lessen the effect of the clouds, lower the opacity of the top layer. Our new sky is shown in Figure 12-53.

FIGURE 12-52 A cloudless sky

FIGURE 12-53 The best sky of all

Chapter 13 Take It to the Web

How to…

- Use ImageReady
- Choose the best workflow
- Slice images
- Add links to slices
- Optimize images
- Use web-safe colors
- Create image maps
- Create rollovers
- Export as a web page
- Make images transparent
- Animate images
- Export as a Flash file

It seems everyone has a web page these days, and now that you are using Photoshop, there's no reason for you not to have a nice one, too. When it comes to building web sites, Photoshop is one of the best graphics programs to use. Several features are unique to web work, and we explore these in this chapter to start you on your journey. If you are already building web sites, you'll notice some features in Photoshop that will help you work more efficiently—such as a secret weapon called ImageReady, an application that's bundled with Photoshop. ImageReady and Photoshop work seamlessly together to help you produce artwork that can be sliced, optimized, and served on the World Wide Web.

Originally, the ImageReady product was released as a separate product for processing web graphics. Since Photoshop version 5.5, ImageReady comes bundled with Photoshop. The two programs have become tightly integrated. ImageReady offers features specifically for web work, such as image slicing and optimizing. One big difference you will notice with

ImageReady is that when you use the Selection tool on an object in the image window, that object's layer will become activated automatically, so you don't have to hunt through the Layers palette to find a layer. This *object-based interface* is new in ImageReady CS.

For a complete walkthrough of a site's construction, check out From Photoshop To Dreamweaver *(by Smith and Waters, 2003) published by Friends Of Ed.*

FIGURE 13-1 Launching ImageReady

To launch ImageReady, click the bottom button on the toolbar, as shown in Figure 13-1.

The ImageReady interface is shown in Figure 13-2.

FIGURE 13-2 The ImageReady interface

The Workflow

When you're preparing images for loading on the Web, the most efficient workflow will go something like this:

1. Create the page in Photoshop.

2. Launch ImageReady.

3. Slice the image.

4. Add any special features, such as rollovers or image maps.

5. Optimize the image.

6. Export the page as an HTML page.

 See the appropriate sections in this chapter for details and instructions.

Your graphics are exported all ready for porting to the Web with all layers and slices intact. We'll follow this workflow when working with ImageReady in this chapter.

 When you create a web page, bear in mind that not everyone will be using the same screen resolution that you use, so plan accordingly. The lowest screen resolution commonly used is 800×600 pixels, so a page that is 775×550 pixels would work well. You need to allow some extra pixels to accommodate the toolbars and scrollbar in the web browser.

Slicing Images

Slicing is a crafty technique commonly used by web designers. When you slice an image, you cut a large graphic into several smaller images that will be joined together seamlessly. This works in a similar way to a jigsaw puzzle, except you don't see any seams. You may want to slice an image for several reasons:

- You want to make a slice clickable, allowing the visitor to move to another part of the web page.

- You want to optimize each slice differently.

- You want to add special features, such as rollovers and animations, to the slices.

- You want to use slices to help your web page load faster.

You can do your slicing in either Photoshop or ImageReady. Usually, you produce your graphic in Photoshop and then launch ImageReady without closing the document. The ImageReady interface will load inside Photoshop. You can also slice from within Photoshop, but ImageReady has more robust features, such as allowing you to add a link to your slices.

ImageReady will construct an HTML page complete with an invisible table, with a cell for each slice. The images will be placed inside each cell so that they are all flush with one another. When the visitor views your web page, they will not see separate images; instead, they will see one image and the seams will be invisible.

User Slices

Let's walk through the process of slicing an image that will be used as an interface. You need to plan ahead a bit before you begin slicing. Consider the following:

- Any button interfaces should take preference, because you want each button to be a single slice so that you can assign the click action to each button.

- Try to separate important areas of detail versus nonessential portions of the image. This will allow you to optimize with a higher quality setting for essential portions of the image and a higher compression/lower quality for nonessential portions.

- When you create slices, keep the number of slices to a minimum. If you create too many slices, they can cause the page to load slower because the computer will have to process all the data.

- You may choose to use guides to help you slice the images. You can choose a snap-to guide to help define the slice placement. (See Chapter 1 for more on using guides.)

Let's begin slicing an image. We'll use an image that visitors to our web site can click to move from one page to another.

1. Choose the Slice tool from the toolbar.

2. Position your mouse pointer at one of the corners of your desired slice, as shown in Figure 13-3A.

3. Click and drag the mouse to define the slice in the same way that you would draw with the Marquee tool.

4. Release the mouse button and a numbered slice will appear, as shown in Figure 13-3B.

5. Photoshop automatically slices the rest of the image to accommodate your slice.

13

To hide the numbered slice, press CTRL-H (CMD-H *on the Mac).*

A.

B.

FIGURE 13-3 Using the Slice tool (A) and the finished slice (B)

Whenever you create a slice, ImageReady assigns it a number. This helps you track the slices later on. When you export the page, each slice will become a separate image, labeled with the number by default. For example, an image named webpage.jpg that's been sliced three times will become webpage-01.jpg, webpage-02.jpg, and webpage-03.jpg. Figure 13-4 shows the interface with all the slices in place (left) and with the image hidden (right) so that you can get a good look at the slices.

A.

B.

FIGURE 13-4 The image with the slices (A), and just the slices (B)

You will notice that some of the slices's boundaries have a solid line and some have a dotted line. The solid lines are the slices that you have created yourself. The dotted lines are auto slices added by Photoshop. Whenever you modify one of your user slices (those you have created yourself), the auto slices will automatically adjust to make your slices work, such as filling in the missing pieces of a jigsaw puzzle.

Modifying Slices

After you have created all your slices, you can modify them at a later time. The Slice Select tool is next to the Slice tool on the toolbar. Using the Slice Select tool, click inside any slice to make it active; you will see a bounding box around the selected slice. To adjust a slice, click and drag the bounding box.

You can also click and drag inside a slice's boundaries. The auto slices will adapt to fit your slice's new shape and/or position.

Converting an Auto Slice to a User Slice

If you click an auto slice, you'll notice that you cannot make modifications to it, as no bounding box or selection handles appear. If you want to make changes to an auto slice, you will need to convert it. In ImageReady vernacular, this is called *promoting* a slice. Here's how it's done.

1. Choose the Slice Select tool.

2. Click an auto slice to make it active.

3. Right-click (CONTROL-click on the Mac), and THEN Choose Promote To User Slice. You will see the bounding box, with selection handles indicating that the slice is now a user slice.

Combining Slices

When you are slicing an image, it's a good idea to cut down on any "stray" slices. For example, the selected slices in Figure 13-8 are disjointed, and a single strip would be much more efficient. The good news is that we can combine slices.

1. Select the first slice with the Slice Select tool.

2. Hold down the SHIFT key as you click each slice that you want to add to the selection. Figure 13-5 shows multiple slices selected.

3. Choose Slices | Combine Slices. The individual slices will be merged into one slice, as shown in Figure 13-6.

Splitting a Slice

You might want to divide a slice into segments—perhaps you need to insert a new image into a slice. You can use two methods for dividing a slice into segments: the first method uses the Divide Slice tool, and the second method involves resizing a slice and using auto slice.

FIGURE 13-5 Selecting multiple slices

The first method is great for dividing complex and precise slices:

1. Choose the Slice Select tool.

2. Select a slice to divide.

3. Choose Slice | Divide Slice.

4. In the Divide Slice dialog box shown in Figure 13-7, enter settings for the split.

5. Choose the Preview checkbox to see a live preview.

6. After you are satisfied with your changes, click OK, and your slice will be divided into multiple slices.

FIGURE 13-6 Combining the slices

The second method for splitting slices is not so scientific— it involves resizing an existing slice and allowing the auto slice feature to add the new slice.

FIGURE 13-7 Divide Slice
dialog box

1. Choose the Slice Select tool.

2. Select a slice to divide.

3. If you selected an auto slice, choose Promote To User Slice.

4. In the new user slice, click one of the bounding box handles.

5. Hold down the mouse and drag the handle of the slice to resize the slice. As you resize the slice, a new auto slice will be created.

6. To apply the changes, release the mouse button.

Hiding the Slices

You can toggle the view of slices on and off using the Show Slice Toggle button on the toolbar, as shown in the illustration. Although the slices are still there, they are hidden from view. To show them again, just click the same button.

Adding Links to Slices

FIGURE 13-8 The Slice palette

You can turn any slice into a button, and you can assign web links to buttons on the image. When the user clicks this button, he or she will be taken to a new page or a new web site. You add links to slices in the Slice palette, shown in Figure 13-8, which offers access to several useful features:

- **Name**   Type in a name for the slice.

- **URL**   Type in the web link, technically known as the uniform resource locator (URL), that you want to jump to when the slice is clicked.

- **Target**   Tell the browser how to open the window with the new link—used mainly when a page is inside a Frame Set.

- **Alt**   Type in the text that will appear on the page when the image is loading. The text will also show as a tool technically known as thetip if a user hovers the mouse over the button.

Here's how to assign a link to a slice:

1. Choose the Slice Select tool.

2. Click the slice that you want to become the button.

3. Open the Slice palette.

4. Type the link into the URL field. You can type in one of two types of links:

- **Relative**   Links to a page on an existing site, such as tutorials.htm.

- **Absolute**   Links to a page on a different web site or to the full path on the existing site—for example, http://www.osborne.com or http://www.photoshopcafe.com/tutorials.htm.

When you export the page to the web, these links will be assigned to the slices.

 For more information on assigning links to images on your web page, see the section entitled "Setting Image Maps" later in this chapter.

Optimizing

When dealing with web pages, you want to make the file sizes as small as possible to accommodate modem speeds and the time it takes to transfer images. For example, you might want to adjust your images and web page content to accommodate the slowest modem speed found on most dial-up modems these days—56 Kb (kilobytes).

You can shrink file sizes dramatically by using *compression* on the images. This compression process is called *optimizing* an image. When you compress an image, you will lose some quality—this is called *lossy* compression and is the most common type in use today. The trick to compressing an image is to balance the image quality with the image size. As you increase compression, the quality decreases; as you increase quality, the file size will also increase. A correctly optimized image will find the happy medium of quality and file size; finding this happy medium is a balancing act. Fortunately,

ImageReady has some features that will help you find the right balance.

The two most common image compression formats are JPEG and GIF.

JPEG: Joint Photographic Experts Group

JPEG or JPG (Pronounced "*jay-peg*") is the preferred compression format for photos and images on the Web that contain a lot of *gradients*, or color progression. This format compresses images by discarding pixel detail and simplifying the image. The more you compress images using this format, the more the image quality will deteriorate. Even so, you can actually compress an image quite a bit before it is noticeable to the naked eye. It is not uncommon to reduce a file size to a tenth of its original size and barely notice any difference as far as appearance.

Figure 13-9 shows an image that has been compressed using JPEG. At the highest compression, the image can look pretty bad. If you take into account the fact that the original image is 350K in size, even the minimum compression still cuts the file size down a lot, and it doesn't change the image's appearance too much.

A.

B.

C.

FIGURE 13-9 JPEG compression applied to an image: (A) minimum compression, 74K; (B) medium compression, 32K; (C) maximum compression, 10K

13

GIF: Graphical Interchange Format

GIF compresses images by breaking down the image into lines and then scanning the lines for repeating information. When it finds repeated information, it discards the repeating pixels. GIFs allow you to reduce the number of colors used in an image. As you reduce the colors, you'll get more "matches" and thus a smaller file size. GIFs work best for images that contain areas of flat information and for images with repeating patterns. GIFs also produce the sharpest results for text. A GIF can contain a maximum of 256 colors and a minimum of 2 colors. GIF is currently the only format that supports animation. It also supports transparency, in which you cut out an image and place it on a background that shows through.

Figure 13-10 shows an image that has gone through several GIF compression formats.

FIGURE 13-10 GIF compression: (A) 256 colors, 58K; (B) 64 colors, 37K; (C) 8 colors, 11K; (D) 2 colors, 2K

PNG: Portable Network Graphic

This file format will reduce the file size without any loss of quality to the images—PNG is a *lossless* compression. It also supports 256 levels of transparency; GIF supports only one level. The drawback to PNGs are that the files are larger in size compared to JPG, and older browsers don't support this format without special plug-ins. I suggest using this format only if you need complex transparency effects or you are exporting to another program such as Flash.

Optimizing in ImageReady

Let's take a look at how to optimize an image in ImageReady. You will notice four tabs at the top of the ImageReady image window; each tab represents a particular view:

- **Original**   The is the default view.
- **Optimized**   Perform your design work and slicing, and preview your image optimization (see Figure 13-11).
- **2-Up**
- **4-Up**

FIGURE 13-11 Optimized view

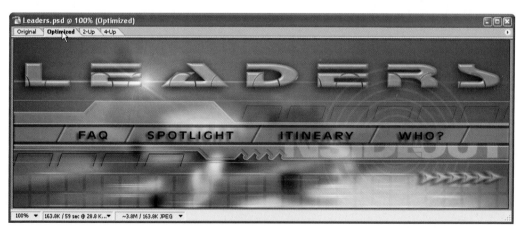

First, let's optimize an image using JPG compression:

1. Open your Image in ImageReady.

2. Choose the Optimized view.

3. Open the Optimize palette, shown in Figure 13-12A.

4. In the Format drop-down box, choose JPEG.

5. In the Quality drop-down box. make make adjustments to the slider.

A.

B.

FIGURE 13-12 Setting JPEG compression (A) Optimize palette; (B) Setting compression

6. Now slide the Amount slider, shown in Figure 13-12B. Slide to the left for lower quality and smaller file size; the most common settings used for web images are in the 30–50 range.

7. Check the image preview for visual quality and the statistics in the status bar at the bottom of the image window for file size, as shown in Figure 13-13.

FIGURE 13-13 Stats on the optimized image

8. Choose File | Save Optimized to save the optimized image.

Optimized file size

Original file size

Download time of image

Optimized file size

If you are working with slices, you can select each slice and optimize each individually using the same basic method.

You will see a "blur" option, adding a small amount of blur will help get the file size down even more.

Viewing Statistics

You can change the type of statistics shown for your images at any time by clicking the arrow to the right of the file size information along the status bar at the bottom of the Optimize window, as shown in Figure 13-14. Simply choose a setting to

FIGURE 13-14 Changing the statistical information on the status bar

Original/Optimized File Sizes
Optimized Information
Image Dimensions
Watermark Strength
Undo/Redo Status

Original in Bytes
Optimized in Bytes
Optimized Savings

Output Settings

Size/Download Time (9600 bps Modem)
Size/Download Time (14.4 Kbps Modem)
✓ Size/Download Time (28.8 Kbps Modem)
Size/Download Time (56.6 Kbps Modem/ISDN)
Size/Download Time (128 Kbps Dual ISDN)
Size/Download Time (256 Kbps Cable/DSL)
Size/Download Time (384 Kbps Cable/DSL)
Size/Download Time (512 Kbps Cable/DSL)
Size/Download Time (768 Kbps Cable/DSL)
Size/Download Time (1 Mbps Cable)
Size/Download Time (1.5 Mbps Cable/T1)
Size/Download Time (2 Mbps)

FIGURE 13-14 Changing the statistical information on the status bar

display it in the status bar. You can choose from the following settings:

- **Original/Optimized File Sizes**
- **Optimized Information**   Settings and format used.
- **Image Dimensions**
- **Watermark Strength**
- **Undo/Redo Status**
- **Original In Bytes**
- **Optimized In Bytes**
- **Optimized Savings**
- **Output Savings**
- **Size/Download Times**

Optimizing Views

While optimizing an image, you may find it useful to compare the optimized image to the original. This gives you a visual cue as to whether the optimization looks OK, and it helps you to decide how much quality loss is acceptable. You can choose either the 2-Up or 4-Up tab to compare various settings simultaneously, as shown in Figure 13-15. To save your favorite view, simply click it and then choose File | Save Optimized.

13

FIGURE 13-15 Different optimized views: (A) a 2-Up view; (B) a 4-Up view

A.

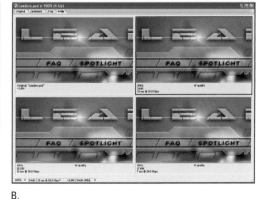

B.

Optimizing GIFs

The process for optimizing GIFs is a little different from that for JPGs. You'll remember that optimizing GIFs means reducing the amount of color in an image. Figure 13-16 shows an image with the highest quality GIF, at 256 colors.

Let's reduce the file size using the GIF format:

FIGURE 13-16 A GIF image with 256 colors

1. Open the Image in ImageReady.

2. Choose the Optimized view.

3. Open the Optimize palette.

4. In the Optimize palette's Format drop-down box, choose GIF.

5. Choose one of the following Reduction formats to build the color table:

   ▪ **Perceptual**   Gives preference to colors that are predominant to the human eye

   ▪ **Selective**   The default selection, which produces the most accurate color table

- **Adaptive**   Uses the most common color in the images

- **Restrictive Web**   Uses the 216 web-safe colors. (See the section "Web-Safe Colors" later in the chapter.)

6. From the Colors drop-down list, choose the number of colors. We chose 128 in Figure 13-17.

FIGURE 13-17 The same image reduced to 128 colors; the difference is hardly noticeable

Dithering   In the Optimize palette, you can set the dithering options to smoothen out the transition between colors. Because we are reducing colors, the transitions can be very abrupt, especially in gradients. Dithering applies patterns to the transitions, simulating more colors and smoothing the transitions.

Reducing Colors Manually in the GIF Format   If you click the icon to the right of the Colors field on the Optimize tab, the Color Table will open, showing all the colors present in the image. You can choose to adjust the colors manually by using some of the options in the Color Table.

About Web-Safe Colors

Because every computer and web browser displays colors differently, the W3C World Wide Web Consortium decided that a standard for 8-bit images (images of 256 colors) needed to be created. The web-safe palette was invented to solve some of these color issues. The palette consists of 216 colors that are deemed common for most web browsers on most computer operating systems. If your browser uses the web-safe palette and you view an image on a computer with 256 colors, no dithering will appear in the solid colors of the image, and the colors will be clean, sharp, and relatively accurate.

Select the color by clicking on the color's box in the Color Table, as shown in Figure 13-18. Hold down the CTRL key (CMD on the Mac) to select multiple colors.

After you select a color, you can use the delete color button to remove the colors from the palette, thus removing them from the image and reducing its file size.

FIGURE 13-18 Choosing a color from the Color Table

Selected color

Transparency

Snap to web safe color

Lock color

New color

Delete color

- ▉ **Transparency** Turns selected colors into transparent areas.
- ▉ **Snap to Web-Safe Color** Shifts the selected color to the nearest web-safe color. A diamond shape inside a color box indicates that it is a web-safe color.
- ▉ **Lock Color** Prevents the color from shifting—indicated by a small square on the bottom right of a color box.
- ▉ **New Color**
- ▉ **Delete Color** Deletes the selected color.

Setting Image Maps

Image maps, also known as "hot spots," allow you to assign web links to portions of images. When the user clicks in the defined image map area, another web page opens. Image maps will appear invisible to the user until the mouse rolls over a hot spot.

The mouse pointer will change to a hand, which indicates that something will happen if the mouse button is clicked. Image maps are simple to create in ImageReady and can be used when you want to define an odd-shaped clickable region or you don't want to use slices. Image maps and slices can also be used together on the same web page or image.

Let's create an image map:

FIGURE 13-19 Choosing the image map tool

1. From the toolbar, choose one of the Image Map tool shapes, as shown in Figure 13-19.

2. Click and drag to create the image map area on your page. The image map is placed on the page wherever you let go of the mouse button.

3. You may add as many image maps as you want to a page.

4. Open the Image Map palette.

5. Type the URL into the URL field, as shown in Figure 13-20.

FIGURE 13-20 Setting the link

6. Choose an Image Map tool shape to set the next image map area.

7. Repeat step 2–5.

8. To test your new image map, click the Preview In Browser button on the toolbar.

9. The image will open in a web browser. Roll your mouse over the image map areas. The mouse pointer should change to a hand when it hovers over the "hot" regions.

13

Creating Rollovers

Rollovers are used on web pages, video games, and DVD menus; when the mouse moves over a button or portion of the image, the image changes—for example, the image may glow or appear depressed. It's common to use this technique with buttons on interactive web sites or other media.

What actually happens behind the scenes to create this illusion is this: You create a slice that is set as a rollover. When the slice detects mouse activity, it swaps the sliced image for another image, which creates the illusion of the image changing. When the mouse moves out of the rollover region, the slice will switch back to the original image.

To create a rollover, you need two things:

- A slice with the original image (in its normal state).

- An "activated" image (in its rolled-over state) of exactly the same size as the slice. ImageReady takes all the hard work out of creating rollovers; you don't have to try to reproduce a small image at exactly the same size as the slice. Instead, you can simply create an effect on a layer and cause Image Ready to show or hide the layers when the mouse passes over them. ImageReady creates all the HTML and JavaScript code for you. Layer styles can also be used to create rollover effects, by showing or hiding the layer styles when the mouse hovers over them.

Preparing the Rollover Images

Before we can apply a rollover effect to a web page or interface, we first need to prepare all the graphics. Figure 13-21 shows the interface that we will use for this example. We'll make the buttons glow as the mouse rolls over them, to tempt the user to click the buttons.

FIGURE 13-21 The image without rollovers (normal state)

1. Create a new layer for each button and create the effect of the buttons glowing in that layer—for the "rollover" state. The glows will be activated as the user rolls the mouse over each button. Figure 13-22 shows our interface with all the rollover states applied. (Chapter 11 told you how to create glows.)

FIGURE 13-22 The image with rollovers active (over state)

2. Turn off all the rollover layers. The image should now look as it did in Figure 13-21 in the normal state, but with all the glowing buttons hidden. Figure 13-23 shows the hidden layers in the Layers palette.

3. Slice the image using the method discussed in the section "Slicing" earlier in this chapter. Create a slice for each button and then optimize each slice.

Creating the Rollover Effect

Now that the images are prepared, we can use the tools in ImageReady to create the rollover effect. You don't have to know a single thing about the code to create and enjoy this effect, because ImageReady will create all the JavaScript coded needed to make this effect work.

1. Using the Slice Select tool, choose one of the buttons.

2. Open the Web Content palette. You'll see your slice highlighted in the palette, as shown in Figure 13-24.

FIGURE 13-23 Hiding the rollovers in the Layers palette

3. Right-click (CONTROL-click on the Mac) the layer thumbnail in the Web Content palette and choose New Rollover State. You'll see a new thumbnail appear, called Rollover.

4. Now open the Layers palette and show the rollover layer for the glow on the selected button, as shown in Figure 13-25.

5. The effect will be reflected in the Web Content palette, as shown in Figure 13-26.

6. Set the link in the Slice palette, as shown in Figure 13-27.

7. Click the Preview In Browser button on the toolbar.

8. The image will appear in your web browser.

9. Roll the mouse over the button to test it.

10. The button should now glow, as shown in Figure 13-28.

Whatever is visible in the Over state thumbnail in the Web Content palette will appear when the mouse rolls over the slice.

FIGURE 13-24 The highlighted slice in the Web Content palette

FIGURE 13-25 Showing the layer

FIGURE 13-26 Setting the rollover images

FIGURE 13-27 Setting the link

FIGURE 13-27 Setting the link

FIGURE 13-28 The image in the browser

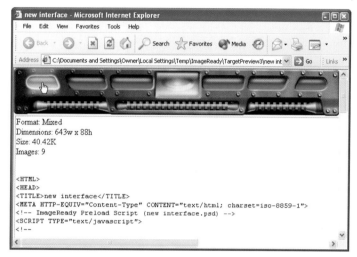

Exporting a Web Page

As you can see, we have followed a workflow to complete our project. First, we created a web page in Photoshop, then we sliced it, we optimized the slices, and then we created image maps and rollovers and set the links. After you have tested the page in a browser and you are happy that everything works as you have planned, you are ready to create the final piece to post on the Web. ImageReady will create two parts:

- All the optimized slices will be turned into images and placed in a folder.

- The HTML page will be generated for you. This page will include all the tables, HTML code, and JavaScript to make everything work.

Let's get started:

1. Choose File | Save Optimized.

2. In the Save Optimized dialog box, choose a location on your hard drive to save the web site and create a new folder. Then click OK. All the files will be saved to the chosen folder.

13

3. Open the folder, and you will see all the parts of the web page, as shown in Figure 13-29.

interface_01.jpg   interface_01-over.jpg   interface_02.jpg   interface_03.jpg

interface_04.jpg   interface_05.jpg   interface_06.jpg   interface_07.jpg

Double-click the HTML file to launch the site in your browser, and you'll see the working web page.

FIGURE 13-29 All the files on the web page

4. Now transfer all the files to the Internet to have a fully functional web page.

Note *Contact your web host or ISP for information about uploading files. Most web sites use FTP (File Transfer Protocol). Your web hosting company should have all the information you need to upload the files and make them live on the Internet.*

Using Transparent GIFs

A transparent GIF is an image that appears as a cut out shape with a transparent background. You use a transparent GIF to create the illusion of a nonrectangular transparent shape that allows the background to show through in the transparent areas.

First, you need to create an image on a transparent background. We will crop the image as tightly as possible; even though the transparent pixels are invisible, they still take up file space. To crop as tightly as possible quickly, choose Image | Trim from the Photoshop main menu. You'll see the Trim dialog box shown in Figure 13-30.

FIGURE 13-30 The Trim dialog box

To isolate an image from the background, place the image on a new layer and delete the background. Then you'll have a cropped image with a transparent background, as shown in Figure 13-31.

FIGURE 13-31 Transparent image

 For more on extracting images, see Chapter 11.

You can prepare the image in one of two ways:

- Open ImageReady and use the Optimize palette, which is best if you need to use advanced features such as rollovers, image maps, animation, and HTML pages
- Use the Save For Web feature in Photoshop, which is best for images only

For this example, we'll use the Save for Web feature in Photoshop. Choose Image | Save For Web, and in the Save For Web window shown in Figure 13-32, choose GIF from the Preset area at the right (or choose PNG 8, which works exactly the same as a GIF). You should recognize the controls in this window, because they are exactly the same as ImageReady, but they are presented in one palette instead of several palettes.

13

FIGURE 13-32 The Save For Web window

Matting

In the Presets area of the Save For Web window, you'll see a drop-down box next to an option called Matte. A *matte* is used to create a smooth edge around a transparent image. When the transparency is made, it can produce a rough edge around the image. A matte adds a thin border (called a halo) around all the edges in the chosen color. When the image is placed on a background of the same color, a very smooth edge will result.

Here's how to create a matte:

1. In the Save For Web palette Preset area (Photoshop), or on the Optimize palette under Transparency (ImageReady), click the arrow to open the Matte drop-down list.

2. Choose Other.

3. You will see the Color Picker. Click the Only Web Colors checkbox.

4. Choose the color that you want to use for your web page background, as shown in Figure 13-33, and then click OK.

5. A thin halo will appear around your image. Click Save in the Save For Web window (Photoshop), or click Export Your Image from ImageReady.

FIGURE 13-33 Choosing a color

You can see the difference that matting makes. Figure 13-34 shows the image placed on a web page, with a matte on the left and without on the right. Notice how much smoother the matted edges look.

FIGURE 13-34 The transparent GIF with a matte (left) and without (right)

Using Animated GIFs

Animated GIFs are a series of images grouped together into one image. Each image in an animated GIF is called a *frame* and is displayed as part of a sequence of images, just like in traditional animation. When you quickly play the frames, it gives the illusion of movement. ImageReady is a great program to use for creating animations.

In this example, we will create an animated web banner.

1. Create a new file. Choose Web Banner for the preset size. (This preset is only in ImageReady.)

2. Type in some text on a new layer, as shown in Figure 13-35.

3. Drag the text, as shown in Figure 13-36, all the way to the left until it is just off the screen. The beginning of the text is the starting point of the banner animation.

4. Open the Animation palette.

5. We now want to duplicate the frame. Click the Duplicate Frame button, as shown in Figure 13-37.

6. With the new frame still selected, drag the text until it is centered on the stage (Figure 13-38). This text phrase will mark the end point of the animation.

FIGURE 13-35 Text on a new layer

FIGURE 13-36 Dragging the text off the screen

FIGURE 13-37 Duplicating a frame

Tweening

To create smoother animations, we can add more frames between the start and finish points of the movement. Rather than make all the frames ourselves, ImageReady has a feature called *tweening* that will automatically create all the in-between frames to smoothen our animation.

1. In the Animation palette, click the arrow at the far right and choose Tweening.

2. In the Tween dialog box, set the Tween With option to Previous Frame, and type **5** in the Frames To Add text box, as shown in Figure 13-39, click OK.

3. Click the Play button and you will see that the animation runs smoothly. However it is mving a bit rapid you can see that each frame shows for 0 seconds in the time indicators at the bottom of each frame, as shown in Figure 13-40. This is a bit too fast, so we will fix it in the next section.

FIGURE 13-39 Setting the Tween options

13

FIGURE 13-40 Testing the animation

Setting a Delay

The animation is now working. However, with the default settings, it happens so fast that it's hard to read what the banner says. The solution is to set the delay. We can tell ImageReady how long to pause on each frame. We can either set a number of frames at once or we can set the frames individually. Let's set multiple frames at once.

FIGURE 13-41 All the frames selected

1. Select the last frame in the animation.

2. Scroll to the first frame, and hold down the SHIFT key while you click Frame 1.

3. All the frames will now be highlighted, as shown in Figure 13-41.

4. Click on the characters "0 Sec" and choose a delay time. We chose 0.2 seconds in Figure 13-42.

5. Click any frame to unselect all the frames.

6. Select the last frame.

7. Set the delay to 5 seconds. This will keep the text visible for 5 seconds before looping back to the beginning of the animation.

FIGURE 13-42 Setting delay time

Creating a Fading Animation

So far, we have created an animation that moves from left to right, pauses for 5 seconds and then jumps back to the start. It would be much smoother if the text faded out before restarting. We can easily create a fading effect with the Animation palette.

1. In the Animation palette, duplicate the last frame.

2. Hide the text layer on the final frame, as shown in Figure 13-43.

FIGURE 13-43 Hiding the text on the final frame

3. We now need to create the fade effect between the last two frames. Choose the Tween option from the pop-up menu at the top right of the Animation palette.

4. Set the tween to add 5 frames with the previous frame (see Figure 13-44).

5. Set the delay time for the new frames to 0.1 seconds.

6. Test the animation by clicking the Play button. The text should now fade out smoothly at the end of the animation.

7. Set the looping options in the bottom left corner of the animation window. Choose any setting from Once to Forever for the playback.

FIGURE 13-44 Adding new Tweened frames

Saving Animations

Now we need to save our animation so that it can be used on a web page. Before you save an animation, make sure you optimize the file size, as we did earlier in this chapter under "Optimizing."

Saving as a GIF

GIF is the traditional web format for animations. Animated GIFs will work on any web page and in any web browser without the need for any plug-ins. GIFs work the best for raster graphics.

1. Choose File | Save Optimized.

2. Navigate to the location at which you want to save the file.

3. Click Save.

4. Add the image to your web page by using an HTML editor or by hand.

13

Exporting as a Flash File

SWF (ShockWave Flash) is the format for Macromedia Flash animations. These animations are the best for vector formats. If you are working with vector shapes and text in ImageReady, these will be preserved when you export your animation as a SWF. This will result in a very small file size. The web browser will have to be equipped with the Flash Player plug-in for the SWF file to work. At the time of this writing, more than 80 percent of web browsers in use are Flash equipped.

1. Create the animation.

2. Choose File | Export | Macromedia Flash SWF.

3. In the Macromedia Flash Export dialog box, shown in Figure 13-45, use the settings shown in the figure. These work best for most cases.

4. Make sure that you choose the Generate HTML checkbox.

5. Choose a location in which to save the file.

6. Save the file.

7. Open the HTML page in a browser to watch the Flash animation. Our banner's file size was only 2K! This is compared to 11K for the GIF animation.

FIGURE 13-45 The Export dialog box

Chapter 14 Print Your Masterpiece

How to...

- Print in Photoshop
- Set the printing options
- Use the page setup
- Change the output size of the image
- Set visible printing options
- Print proofs for a professional print job
- Create printer's marks
- Set color management for predictable results
- Use color calibration

After you've spent hours working in Photoshop, the time will come when you'll need to print your masterpiece. At the least, a friend or client may ask you for a printout, or perhaps you just want to print out a single copy so you can pin it to your wall. On a grander scale, you may want to print a proof to look at before you rush it off to the printers to mass produce 100,000 copies. In this chapter, we look at what you need to know to get a good print from Photoshop for all your printing purposes. We look into the dark realms of outputting for a printing press, and we touch on some color management issues as well.

Printing in Photoshop

If you want to simplify things, choose File | Print and walk away. The problem with this method, however, is that you may see a dialog box containing a message something like, "Clipping will occur, proceed anyway?" If you are prone to panic attacks, reading such a message without knowing what is happening might not be good for you.

Another reason why you need to understand the printing features in Photoshop is because of what I call the "Cell Phone Principle." I admit that I love gadgets, but I hate to read manuals. I bought a fancy new cell phone because I liked all the buttons and the nice, big LCD display. It plays cute music and shows little animations on the screen. I had used this phone for a while when a friend purchased the same brand of phone. One day he said to me, "I love the way you can do this on the phone," and proceeded to show me some clever new features. I didn't even realize that my phone had these features, because I never took the time to read the manual.

That's how it is with the Print options in Photoshop. If you just choose Print and walk away, you miss all the exciting features. (By the way, when Photoshop says that an image will "clip," it means that the image is too big for the piece of paper you want to print onto.) You can click OK and hope for the best, or use some of the following information to make the most of this feature.

FIGURE 14-1 Image ready to be printed

Printing Options

Figure 14-1 shows the front panel for a CD. After spending some time experimenting with a design, you'll need to print it out to see how it looks on paper. For some reason, things always look a little different after they are printed.

When you are ready to print, choose File | Print With Preview. You'll see the Print dialog box, offering quite a few options. You'll also see a preview window that gives you an idea of what, exactly, will be printed (see Figure 14-2).

14

FIGURE 14-2 Print
dialog box with print
preview

Setting Up the Page

You may want your image to print at the actual
size, or you may want to change the size of the
image to match the size of the paper. Let's set
the options for the paper size.

FIGURE 14-3 Page Setup
dialog box

1. Click the Page Setup button. You'll
   see the Page Setup dialog box shown
   in Figure 14-3.

2. Choose the paper size from the
   drop-down Size list.

3. Choose the Orientation of the
   paper—either Portrait (tall) or
   Landscape (wide).

4. Click Printer to select the printer
   if more than one is connected to
   your computer.

5. Click OK to close the dialog.

Back in the Print dialog box, check your
settings and the preview to make sure everything is as you want

it, and then click the Print button. Or, read on to make other adjustments.

For printing to an inkjet printer, your resolution should be set to a minimum of 150ppi (pixels per inch). For a photo printer, it should be set to 200ppi.

You may also be a bit confused with the term ppi and dpi (dots per inch). They are basically the same thing when it comes to units of measure. Pixels refer to the pixels on screen and dots refers to printed dots. A printer does not use pixels, but tiny dots to make up the image. If you fit 300 dots into an inch space, the resolution of the printer is 300dpi. More about resolution in Chapter 2.

Changing the Output Size of the Image

One of the Print With Preview option's best features is that it lets you control how large the image will print. Here's an example using this feature.

1. In the Print dialog box, click the Show Bounding Box option in the Scaled Print Size area.

2. Click a corner point in the preview and drag to make the preview larger or smaller, as shown in Figure 14-4. Or, you can enter a percentage setting in the Scale field.

FIGURE 14-4 Scaling the preview

You can also change the position of the image in the window. This will cause it to print on a position of the paper that you choose.

3. Uncheck the Center Image checkbox in the Position area.

4. Either drag the image to a new position on the preview page or enter the coordinates into the Top and Left position fields (see Figure 14-5).

5. Recheck the Center Image checkbox to center the image again if you change your mind.

FIGURE 14-5 Changing the image position

If you don't want to mess with settings, you can let Photoshop do the work for you. You can force the image to print at the largest possible size for the paper and printer you are using. The image will be printed as large as possible without any of the edges being cut off the page.

 Most printers cannot print all the way to the edge of the page; a small margin is needed for the printer to feed the paper. The top and bottom page margins are generally larger than the side margins.

Media is a fancy word for paper. Sometimes, people may use transparent sheets for overhead projectors of clear plastic sheets, so media is an all encompassing word for "whatever you put in the printer."

To let Photoshop do all the thinking for you, choose the Scale To Fit Media checkbox.

Whenever you are ready to print the image, click Print.

Choosing Visible Printing Options

If you don't want your image to be printed on a plain background—perhaps you want to make a greeting card or you just want to display your proof with a nice background—you can change the background color. Here's how:

1. In the bottom half of the Print dialog box, click the Background button.

2. You will see a color picker. Choose the color you want to appear on the background.

FIGURE 14-6 Colored background

3. Click OK.

The color is displayed behind the image in the preview, as shown in Figure 14-6. You can also set a border around the image by clicking the Border button and choosing a border thickness. This feature is especially useful if you are printing an image with a white background on white paper and you want to show where the image ends.

14

Printing Proofs for a Professional Print Job

Remember that before you print on a professional press, you must have your image set at 300ppi for a good quality print. You'll also need to convert it to CMYK mode—choose Image | Mode | CMYK. This makes the image ready to be printed on a printing press. Let's look at the print options.

 The next couple of options are meant to prepare proofs for a professional printing press. You won't need to be concerned with this set of options if you are printing on an inkjet or laser printer for your own use.

Setting Bleeds

You know that desktop printers cannot print all the way to the edge of the page. But with some professionally printed jobs, you may want your image to print all the way to the edge of the paper, as you often see in posters, postcards, CD inserts, and brochures. What you need to do is set up something called a "bleed."

When you're printing a bleed in Photoshop, you take a larger piece of paper than your target size. You then create the image slightly larger than what is needed, and trim it to the exact size you want. The excess will be trimmed away on the edges and guarantee that your image prints all the way to the edges.

 Never place any important design information all the way to the edge of the page, because it may get trimmed off in a bleed.

Photoshop can create a bleed for you.

1. In the Print dialog box, select Show More Options if it's not already checked.

2. Choose the Output option in the drop-down menu at the top of this area.

3. Click the Bleed button. A bleed dialog box will open, as shown in Figure 14-7.

FIGURE 14-7 Setting a bleed

4. Set the Width in inches or whatever measure you choose. The standard for most bleed purposes is .125 inches.

5. Click OK.

Adding Printer's Marks

Printer's marks are added to a printed sheet to help the printer accurately align and crop the image (see Figure 14-8). The following checkboxes should be selected in the lower section of the Print dialog box to set up printer's marks:

FIGURE 14-8 The printed document showing crop marks and registration marks

frozen-journey.jpg

- **Registration Marks** These marks are needed for a *color separation*. The professional printer will break the image into four separate files, one for each ink color. The registration marks, which look like circles with crossbars in the middle, show the printer where to align the separations.

- **Corner Crop Marks and Center Crop Marks** These marks show the printer where to trim the image. The crop marks are a trimming guide to help the printer cut the image to size.

- **Description**

- **Labels**   Prints information for the printer's reference, such as file names and other information.

14

 If you are making a final print, it's a good idea to set the image scaling to 100 percent.

Color Management for Predictable Results

One thing's for sure: just about every computer displays colors differently. Monitors, printers, and scanners all play a part in how the colors are displayed. To try to bring a standard to the print and design industry, *color management* was invented. It sets a standard for measuring color and attempts to bring some consistency across the board—to keep printers and designers happy. ICC, the International Color Consortium, is a group whose goal is to set color standards in the color world.

Calibrating Color

When you buy a piece of computer equipment, check its documentation for information about its ICC profile. Some printers, monitors, and scanners come with calibration software. If this is the case, follow the directions and calibrate your hardware. During calibration, you match the ICC color with your device's colors to produce consistent and predictable results.

The calibration process can range from simple to complex. For example, a less expensive monitor may come with software or perhaps even a color strip that you hold against the monitor and match the colors by eye. The Kodak Colorific devices are inexpensive color calibration devices. On the other end of the scale are electronic devices that you hold against your screen that take measurements; these are called Colormetric devices. These can cost several hundreds to thousands of dollars.

Using the Color Settings in Photoshop

Photoshop allows you to set up your color management and allows you to assign color "profiles" to your images. These color profiles help you produce consistent colors even when using different systems.

- First, we will look at the color settings in Photoshop.
- Choose Edit | Color Settings.
- You will now see the dialog box as shown in Figure 14-9.

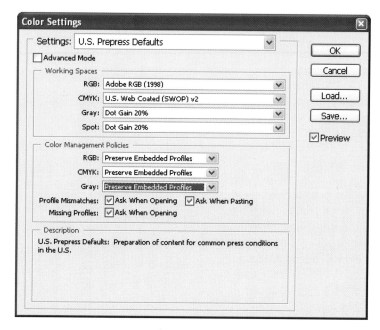

FIGURE 14-9 Color Settings dialog box

Let's start with the Settings drop-down menu. Here, you can choose regional settings—for example, U.S. Prepress Defaults sets up your colors to match most prepress requirements for printers in the United States.

- If you are using Photoshop for printing to a commercial printing press, choose the prepress region that is closest to your country.

- For general work and printing to an inkjet printer, choose a General Purpose default; for example, in North America, you'd choose North American General Purpose Defaults.

- If you are creating mainly online graphics, choose Web Graphics Defaults.

You can customize these settings further. In the Working Spaces area, change the RGB settings for your specific purpose; these are the three that probably concern you:

- **Adobe RGB**   Best choice for print work

- **Monitor RGB**   Best choice if you want your web images to look consistent with Photoshop

- **sRGB**   Best choice if you are putting your images on the Web and want consistent color with other types of monitors

Whenever you create a Photoshop document, the profiles you have created will be embedded in the document. If you try to open a document with a different color profile embedded, Photoshop will give you the choice of using the embedded

14

profile or replacing it with your working profile (the settings you have just made). The best choice generally is to keep the embedded profile of the image, because that way it will maintain the appearance the original designer intended.

You can turn on and off the profile mismatches in the Color Settings dialog box. If accurate color is not important to you, you can turn off these warnings so that they don't bug you whenever you open a document. If accurate color is important, turn on these options.

When you are saving a document, it will give you the option to include the color profile. It's a good idea to use this option if you are using color management. To use it, just click the checkbox. If you don't want to add a color profile, uncheck the box.

You have just finished your crash course on printing and color management. If you want to get serious about color management, entire books are devoted to the subject.

Behind the Scenes

A GALLERY WITH TECHNIQUES FROM THE PROS

Some of the most gifted and recognized digital artists working with Photoshop have submitted examples of their art to include in this gallery. Each piece of art is accompanied by step-by-step tutorials that show you how to create at least one aspect of the composition, offering a behind-the-scenes look at how professional artists use Photoshop in their work. Here you get a glimpse of the range of techniques that can be applied using the tools you learned about in this book. More than likely, most readers will not have reached the level at which these artists have arrived. The purpose of including such stunning art is not to intimidate you, but rather to give you something to aspire to. Enjoy!

Texture

Oliver Ottner

Vienna native Oliver Ottner is the owner of advertising agency iService, which works with clients such as Estée Lauder and Clinique. His popular web site, at http://www.effectlab.com, displays some of his work, such as the *Naturemorphosis* series, as well as his Photoshop tutorials.

Ottner approached creating this piece, entitled *Naturemorphosis XII*, by playing with different techniques and discovering what works through trial and error. He says that while there is "no major trick to teach" in creating such a piece, he can teach you to understand how to use the best paths and techniques as a good starting point from which you can explore various methods that work for you. In each of his pieces, he uses a different blending mode in combination with various opacity settings for the layers. (Refer to Chapter 5 for more on blending modes and layers.)

Naturemorphosis XII

1

To prepare the image, Oliver opened a photo of a face in a .psd file with a texture on its own layer.

2

He reduced the opacity of the texture layer so the face beneath shows. Oliver used his favorite Photoshop selection tool (Chapter 10) to delete all unwanted Texture areas.

He used the Rubber Stamp tool for the final touch-ups, zooming into the image and moving it around, deleting with various brush sizes until it fit perfectly.

3

Next, he activated the texture layer by clicking it and cycled slowly through the layer blending modes. (In most cases, one blending mode will look best, letting the face shine through but at the same time showing enough texture.) Oliver decided "soft light" was a good start, because it allows the wood structure to show through but the highlights and shadows of the face are still visible.

4

Oliver wanted the cracks in the image to look realistic. To accomplish this, he first duplicated the texture layer. Next, he cycled through the blend modes again. The blend mode Multiply brings back what he lost before.

5

Since the image now looked much too dark, he chose Image | Adjustments | Curves (explained in Chapter 12) to make the layer lighter. Notice how the cracks keep their highlights and shadows, the colors are realistic, and the face behind shows its depth again.

6

Oliver wanted to correct the light to make the image look real and to give the piece more drama. To accomplish this, he made a copy of the face layer, and then he chose Image | Adjustments | Desaturate to turn the layer to grayscale. Next, he loaded the selection of the texture layer, and then he inverted the selection by choosing Select | Inverse.

7

Then, to ensure that the grayscale face layer was still active, he pressed delete to leave just the texture area. He brought up the curves again to darken the grayscale and set its blending mode to Overlay (after again cycling through the modes to see what could fit best). Note the good contrast and dramatic lighting. Oliver then reduced the opacity of this layer to 60 percent so the effect wasn't overly dramatic.

8

Oliver finished the piece by touching up the shadows. First, he created a new layer above the grayscale layer and set its blend mode to Multiply. He chose a medium-size, soft-edged brush and selected black as the foreground color; then he painted where he wanted to add or darken shadows.

Hair

Malachi Maloney

Arizona-native Malachi Maloney first tapped into his artistic talent as a boy, when he began drawing monsters as a way of coping with his nightmares. As an adult, he frequently applies his training in traditional media to a subject far less frightening than monsters: pin-up models, created using Photoshop. Malachi has developed a reputation as one of the most impressive pin-up artists to come along in decades, working with Playboy Playmates, Penthouse Pets, Perfect 10 models, and various sci-fi and fantasy cover models, among others.

To accommodate this demonstration, Malachi quickly made a mannequin head on which to paint the hair.

Next, he sketched in the hair—just enough to give him a rough idea of the type of hair style he wants her to have. For sketching, he used a 2-pixel airbrush set to multiply at an opacity of 70 percent and a hardness of +50. Next, he set the layer style to multiply and duplicated the layer. Finally, he merged the two sketch layers together and lowered its opacity to around 50 percent.

Army Brat

Malachi is constantly experimenting with techniques to improve his work. His method for painting hair, shown in this tutorial, is the result of a couple of years' worth of experimentation. Even after investing this much time to get the process right, he claims it's possible he won't use it forever, since he might discover a better method as he continues to play with processes and learn. For this technique, Malachi suggests you use a graphics tablet and that you paint at a high resolution—the higher the better. For this example, he painted at 2x2 inches at a resolution of 300ppi.

3 He created a new layer under the sketch layer, which he named "Hair." He started blocking in the shape of the hair with a paintbrush at an opacity of 100 percent. After he got the shape he wanted, he cleaned up the edges with a hard eraser at 100 percent opacity and a fine tipped smudge tool at an opacity of around 90–95 percent.

4 He locked the layer transparency so he could paint on just the part that's blocked in without affecting the rest of the layer's surface. Then, to establish the lighting, he used a soft airbrush at an opacity of 3–7 percent to paint in the basic shadows and highlights, making sure to vary the colors every so often for a realistic effect.

To form the basic shapes, he first used a soft smudge tool set to an opacity of around 65–70 percent to form the shapes and clumps of hair. Then he went in with a High Opacity Blur tool to soften everything, including the edges.

To prepare to paint the individual hairs, Malachi used a soft low opacity airbrush and lightly erased around edges and at the tips of the hair to make them slightly transparent, which makes the hair look lighter and more natural. Malachi painted the individual

hairs by first creating another layer above the main hair layer. With a 2-pixel paintbrush, set to an opacity of 90 percent and a hardness of +50, his brush options all set to Stylus except for color, he started to paint in the individual strands of hair.

Again, he repeated the process described above over the entire surface of the hair.

Malachi painted in some loose strands of hair on two layers: one above the main hair layer and one below it. After they were painted, he merged them to the main hair layer and used a Low Opacity Blur tool to soften areas of the hair and a little bit of Low Opacity Sponge tool to increase the saturation in certain areas.

Next he added a shadow. First he made another layer beneath the hair layer. Then, he CTRL-clicked the hair layer to select its shape and filled it with a dark color on the layer below. Malachi usually chooses a dark color that corresponds with the color of the skin/surface on which he's casting a shadow.

Next, Malachi locked the transparency of the layer on which he painted the strands. Using a large, soft airbrush set to an opacity of 10 percent, he painted in the appropriate colors and highlights. After the strands had been colored, he unlocked the layer's transparency and went over the strands with a Soft Blur tool set to around 15–20 percent. Next, he used a soft, low opacity eraser to make the tips of the strands slightly transparent. After the strands of hair were painted, he lowered the layer's opacity to 85–90 percent and merged it with the main hair layer, as shown here.

The same process was repeated over the area a few times to build volume.

After the shadow was done, he moved it and distorted it using free-transform to get it into a position that corresponded with the light source. After a little light blurring, and a little light erasing, it was done.

Depth

Philip H. Williams

Philip Williams began his professional career as a commissioned portrait painter after graduating from a coordinated program between the Pennsylvania Academy of Fine Art and the Graduate School of Fine Arts at the University of Pennsylvania. In the early 90s, when desktop computers began to show promise as creative tools for the visual arts, Phil migrated toward web site design and illustration. Today, he spends most of his time on commissioned illustration work and his personal artwork, all of which is created digitally.

Phil started by laying out a rough composition.

He then constructed some of the foreground buildings, as shown here. Phil approached his "epic" pictures almost like an engineer approaches the design of a complex object: he started with an overall concept and then built the elements and stuck them together. Photoshop, with all its adjustment capabilities, is the perfect tool for working this way.

Cityscape

Phil had the movie *Blade Runner* in mind when he designed the building in the foreground of *Cityscape*. The other large buildings are his own creations, while most of the small buildings are based on existing buildings in New York City.

3

To help with the perspective of the image, Phil created grids on a new layer using the Line tool. The Free Transform and Perspective Transform tools were used to shape the grids. After the larger objects were built, Phil started to add some detail in the foreground.

4

5

Phil roughed in the background and the sky. Here you can see how Phil achieved depth by placing objects in the foreground and background and by using the Brush tool to airbrush at different thickness settings.

Phil added more detail to the foreground and background and began to rough in the mid sections of the image.

8

9

To bring all the foreground and background together, Phil created a bridge to "bridge the gap," so to speak.

Phil added lighting and touched up the color, to finish off the image.

6

Details were then added to the mid section.

7

Phil brightened the image up a bit to create a "golden city."

10

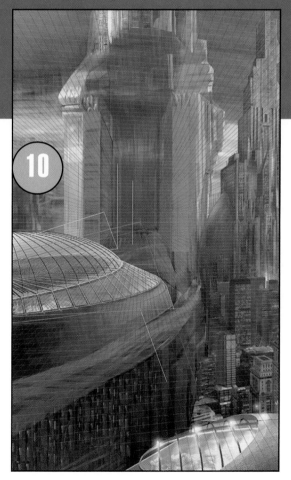

Here is a close up of the grid system that Phil developed to help keep everything in perspective. Lines and grids can be stored in a layer set to make it easy to turn them on and off as needed.

Shadows

Bert Monroy

Bert Monroy was born and raised in New York City, where he spent 20 years in the advertising industry as an art director and creative director for various agencies, including his own. He now lives in Berkeley, California. Bert embraced the computer as an artistic medium early on, with the introduction of the Macintosh 128 in 1984; he is considered one of the pioneers of digital art. He has written numerous articles and books, including co-authoring the award-winning *The Official Adobe Photoshop Handbook* (Bantam Books, 1991), the first book written on Photoshop.

In addition to writing and lecturing, Bert continues to serve his installed base of clients, which includes Apple Computer, Adobe Systems, Pioneer Electronics, Fujitsu, SONY, AT&T, Chevron, and American Express. Since May 2001, Bert has shared Photoshop tips and techniques as a regular guest on the TechTV channel show "The Screen Savers."

In *Shadowplay*, Bert uses shadow to achieve realism. The cast shadows, so-called because they are produced by light cast on an object, have been distorted and wrapped around different objects. In the tutorial that follows, I applied the technique Bert used in *Shadowplay* for creating cast shadows to a simple object, a flower.

Shadowplay

1 To start, I created an image in its own layer using the Custom Shape tool.

2 I duplicated the layer and hid the original so I could see what I was doing. Then, using Free Transform, I chose Skew and distorted the layer in the direction I wanted the shadow to fall.

3 To soften the shadow a bit, I chose Filter | Blur | Gaussian Blur.

4 As shadows get further away from the object casting them, they soften. To achieve this effect in my image, I needed to create a softer shadow. First, I duplicated the shadow layer, and then I hid the original shadow layer.

5 I chose Filter | Blur | Gaussian blur and used a setting of around 8 pixels to produce a very soft edge.

6 I then lowered the opacity to around 10–15 percent.

7 Next, I blended the two shadow layers together to get a gradual softening of the shadow. First, I made the original Shadow layer show again, and then I blended between the two shadow layers. Finally, I created a layer mask on the top shadow layer.

8 To smooth the blended shadow, I used the Gradient tool, chose Linear, Foreground to Background, and reset the colors to the default by pressing the d key on the keyboard. With the layer mask still selected, I dragged the gradient from the top to the bottom of the shadow area.

Imported Images

Jens Karlsson

Born in Sweden, Jens Karlsson now resides in Beverly Hills, California, where he works as a Senior Designer at DNA Studio. After discovering a love for photography, Jens studied media communications, graduating with a degree from Hyerisland School of New Media Design, Scandinavia's most prominent school in this field. In addition to founding two design companies and working for various design firms in New York and Los Angeles, Jens manages his personal web project, Chapter3.net. Chapter3 is a ubiquitous name in the online design scene as a result of Jens's success in both his noncommercial and professional work, as well as his dedication to making the digital tool accepted in the art world.

The foreground environment in *Pegasus* was modeled in 3ds max and imported into Photoshop. You can import 3D images created by other artists into Photoshop if you don't know how to use 3D programs yourself—see Chapter 2.

Before Jens modeled the foreground environment, he planned where the sky in the background would be really bright. Knowing where the main light source was going to be placed in the image, he set up the lights in his environment to cast shadows that would match the surroundings once composited in Photoshop.

Pegasus

Jens began with a 3D render and opened it in Photoshop.

This render was created in 3ds max with an alpha channel. It's useful to use alpha rendering in the 3D application so that you can separate the 3D object from its background. Jens chose the Channels palette and CTRL-clicked (CMD-click on the Mac) the channel thumbnail to turn on the selection. He returned to the Layers palette and copied the selected object to a new layer. The effect for the sky was also a 3D render. Jens brought it into Photoshop and sized it on a new layer.

Jens used the Hue/Saturation adjustments to add some color. He chose the Colorize option.

4

Jens duplicated the cloud render, added 10px of Gaussian blur to the duplicate, and erased some parts of the duplicated layer to add texture. He duplicated the original cloud render layer once again and set the New Layers Blending mode to Multiply, and then scaled it down to cover some parts of the underlying layers to achieve the contrast-rich explosion.

5

Next, Jens brought in some more 3D renders for the particles in the sky, used layer masks or the Eraser tool to softly blend them into the background and remove the harsh edges.

6

He duplicated one of the objects, filled it with white, and added a radial blur to begin the process of creating the light rays.

7

Jens duplicated the light rays, resized and added a blur, and added some color with Hue/Saturation and experimented with the blending modes. He continued to build up the image by adding objects, duplicating, and blurring. He continuously experimented with the blending modes to produced a nice result. Also, he added dodging and burning to the layers using the Dodge and Burn tools to build up the shadow, highlights, and texture.

Details

Colin Smith

When I produce a photo-realistic illustration, I take great care in creating the details. That's what gives an image the touch of realism. You must be patient and avoid the temptation to skip details, or your images will never look truly photo-realistic. Here I'll show you how I created the texture of the wound strings in the guitar image.

First I prepared a pattern to use as the texture. I created a new document, only 2 pixels by 4 pixels in size.

I magnified it to 1600%, made a selection over half of the document, and then filled it in with black.

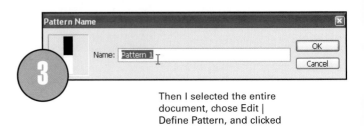

Then I selected the entire document, chose Edit | Define Pattern, and clicked OK to save the pattern. I then closed the document.

Guitar

Fill

Contents

Use: Pattern

Custom Pattern:

Blending

Mode: Normal

Opacity: 100 %

☐ Preserve Transparency

OK

Cancel

5

I created a new layer above the string, chose Edit | Fill and selected a pattern from the custom patterns.

Layers | Paths | Channels

Overlay | Opacity: 56%

Lock: ☐ ✎ ✛ 🔒 | Fill: 100%

👁 ✎ | Layer 2

Layer 1

Background 🔒

6

I changed the blending mode to Overlay and reduced the opacity to 56%.

4

I created the basic guitar string on a new layer using a rectangle and a gradient, then selected the string.

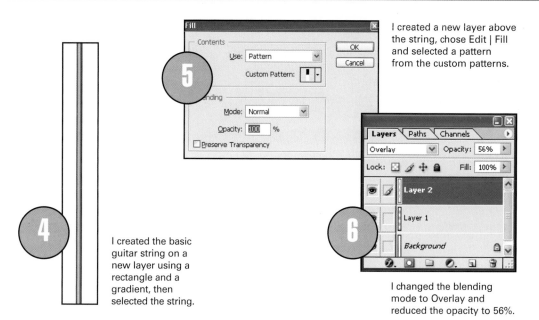

7

The result is a textured string.

Artists

Jens Karlsson

jens@chapter3.net

www.chapter3.net

Malachi Maloney

malachi@liquidwerx.com

www.liquidwerx.com

Bert Monroy

bert@bertmonroy.com

www.bertmonroy.com

Oliver Ottner

info@naturemorphosis.com

www.effectlab.com

www.naturemorphosis.com

www.iservice.at

Colin Smith

colin@photoshopcafe.com

www.photoshopcafe.com

www.pixeloverload.com

Philip H. Williams

phil@eyewoo.com

www.eyewoo.com

Index

INTERNATIONAL CONTACT INFORMATION

AUSTRALIA
McGraw-Hill Book Company
Australia Pty. Ltd.
TEL +61-2-9900-1800
FAX +61-2-9878-8881
http://www.mcgraw-hill.com.au
books-it_sydney@mcgraw-hill.com

CANADA
McGraw-Hill Ryerson Ltd.
TEL +905-430-5000
FAX +905-430-5020
http://www.mcgraw-hill.ca

GREECE, MIDDLE EAST, & AFRICA
(Excluding South Africa)
McGraw-Hill Hellas
TEL +30-210-6560-990
TEL +30-210-6560-993
TEL +30-210-6560-994
FAX +30-210-6545-525

MEXICO (Also serving Latin America)
McGraw-Hill Interamericana Editores
S.A. de C.V.
TEL +525-1500-5108
FAX +525-117-1589
http://www.mcgraw-hill.com.mx
carlos_ruiz@mcgraw-hill.com

SINGAPORE (Serving Asia)
McGraw-Hill Book Company
TEL +65-6863-1580
FAX +65-6862-3354
http://www.mcgraw-hill.com.sg
mghasia@mcgraw-hill.com

SOUTH AFRICA
McGraw-Hill South Africa
TEL +27-11-622-7512
FAX +27-11-622-9045
robyn_swanepoel@mcgraw-hill.com

SPAIN
McGraw-Hill/
Interamericana de España, S.A.U.
TEL +34-91-180-3000
FAX +34-91-372-8513
http://www.mcgraw-hill.es
professional@mcgraw-hill.es

UNITED KINGDOM, NORTHERN,
EASTERN, & CENTRAL EUROPE
McGraw-Hill Education Europe
TEL +44-1-628-502500
FAX +44-1-628-770224
http://www.mcgraw-hill.co.uk
emea_queries@mcgraw-hill.com

ALL OTHER INQUIRIES Contact:
McGraw-Hill/Osborne
TEL +1-510-420-7700
FAX +1-510-420-7703
http://www.osborne.com
omg_international@mcgraw-hill.com